EYEWITNESS NEWSMAN

EYEWITNESS NEWSMAN

Albert T. Primo

Library of Congress Control Number: 2008901813
ISBN: Hardcover   978-1-4363-2559-2
                 Softcover   978-1-4363-2558-5

To order additional copies of this book, contact:
Primonews@AOL.com
1-203-637-0044

www.EyewitnessNewsman.com
P.O. Box 116
Old Greenwich, CT 06870
1-203-637-0044

DEDICATION

This book is dedicated to the memory of my son, Albert Christian Gregg Primo, who passed away March 31, 2007, three days before his forty-fourth birthday. It is also dedicated to Rosina Primo, my wife and inspiration for forty-seven years; our two daughters, Juliet and Valeri; and Grand Daughters Livia and Eden Primo Lack. Their enduring support has made my life complete.

Acknowledgments

Special tribute is made to Randy Tatano whose editorial support for *Eyewitness Newsman* enabled me to finally publish this book after twenty years of writing.

Byron Graziano, who's devotion to Eyewitness News, researched and found many of the photographs used to illustrate this personal history.

Ricardo Jaque who created and designed the website, *www.eyewitnessnewsman. com.*

Introduction

by James Brady

In the turbulent year of 1968, Martin Luther King Jr. and Bobby Kennedy were assassinated, the Democratic Convention in Chicago descended into chaos and riot, Nixon was elected to a first term, and a hotshot young television news director named Al Primo packed his bags in Philly and departed for New York's WABC-TV, ambitious to compete in the biggest of all big leagues, armed with the exotic notion of launching something he called *Eyewitness News.*

The country hasn't quite shaken off or forgotten any of these momentous events. And television news straight across the country has never been the same. More than a hundred markets have taken the *Eyewitness News* name to label their own featured local newscasts and others are using Primo's concept under different names for their own formats.

The big media guru at the time, communications theorist Marshall McLuhan, so influential and recognizable that Woody Allen put his character into a movie, declared that Primo's concept of *Eyewitness News* was "a revolutionary event in telecommunications." New York's *Daily News,* then an irresistibly lively tabloid and the largest circulation daily in the country, described Primo as the guy "who almost single-handedly changed the face of broadcast journalism."

And just what the hell was the gimmick? Was *Eyewitness News* just a marketable logo? Or was it a lot more than that, a shift in tectonic plates, something frighteningly original, an egghead's innovative dream, or merely a transparently simplistic slogan?

It was really very simple. In Primo's words, "*Eyewitness News* was the first newscast to put reporters on the set, replacing the solo male anchor as 'the Voice of God.'"

And who was this subversive iconoclast? And who was he to dare take away our beloved and credible local anchorman? What impudence!

Albert T. Primo took his undergraduate BA degree from the University of Pittsburgh and as a kid was hired by KDKA-TV. At KYW-TV, Philadelphia in 1965, he came up with his inspired idea, which allowed reporters on the set to report their own stories directly to the audience instead of feeding information for the anchor to intone in varying degrees of authoritative baritone.

That was just for openers. Primo turned his news team into a "melting pot" that reflected the racial, ethnic, and gender makeup of the audience and beyond that, of the local community. His newscast rejected the image of female broadcasters as mere "weather bunnies" and gave women meatier roles. *Eyewitness News*, he claims, was the first newscast to incorporate the use of graphics, music, and "teases" to hype stories that were "coming up."

All this now seems so self-evident and commonsensical you marvel that no one ever did it before Al came along. But they didn't—and he did!

And what was the WABC-TV evening news show that Primo took over? "It was situated in the old St. Nicholas Arena at 77 West Sixty-sixth Street (a small-time professional boxing venue that had known better days and apparently once been a stable) and you could smell the horses. Roger Grimsby was there then (the tough, skeptical anchor who had fought in Korea and would eventually be teamed by Al with Bill Beutel in a twin anchor role) and Rona Barrett was doing gossip, Howard Cosell doing sports, with Jimmy Breslin dropping by from time to time. "I kept Grimsby and got rid of everyone else except for Howard, dear Howard. I remember Rona went to Chairman Leonard Goldenson of ABC to complain, but they heard her out and let her leave."

Primo then went to work restaffing the station's newsroom with the kind of talent he wanted. He hired quirky Tom Snyder; Geraldo Rivera, a merchant seaman turned lawyer; ex-Yankee pitcher/writer Jim Bouton; and Rose Ann Scamardella, who would inspire the *Saturday Night Live* character "Roseanne Roseannadanna." The tough New York audience lapped it up, the ratings soared, WABC-TV management rubbed its hands, and even the network suits were impressed. The brilliant but prickly Geraldo, in and out of trouble with the brass, was given an investigative news series of his own; Snyder went on to network fame and riches. Newer talent was recruited to succeed new talents that have gone on to better things. Al and Rivera did an expose of the shocking conditions at Willowbrook, a local institution for the retarded, and Al was awarded the prestigious Peabody Award as executive producer. Geraldo blossomed and job offers flooded in. Everyone wanted to work for Al, by now nicknamed, and admiringly so, El Primo. And the ABC network beckoned.

By 1972, Primo was the youngest corporate VP ABC ever appointed and two years later joined ABC News as executive producer of The Reasoner Report. And his personal media reach was broadening. Al bought a local newspaper in Greenwich, Connecticut; a radio station in Waterbury; and became a limited partner in Cablevision, at that time a groundbreaking move into something exotic called cable TV. He began consulting with stations around America that wanted to improve their local news coverage, vetted and auditioned the reels of on-air talent, collecting big fees all the way.

The ABC network gave him a late evening hour to play with, mounting a not terribly serious challenge to Johnny Carson and his *Tonight Show*. New York's glamorous former mayor John V. Lindsay was roped in to host and I was hired to do interviews in Europe. Off we went, Primo and I, joyfully riding a network expense account, descending on five-star hotels and hanging with the so-called beautiful people, movie stars, fashion designers, English nobility, cigarette-puffing French intellectuals and reporters from *Paris Match*, local camera crews racing about madly on our bilingual and often contradictory instructions.

Ari "Daddy O" Onassis died suddenly while we were there and by some fluke, Jackie O's occasional dress designer, Roman couturier Valentino was staying near us at the same hotel. We wheedled information out of his partner Giancarlo about the dress Jackie was ordering to wear to the funeral as the grieving widow. You know, black but not "too" black. A slightly expurgated version of all this may well appear later in Mr. Primo's story, including the fact Lindsay left us flat at the last moment and I was thrown in to host the damn show. Several Hemingway sisters; Alden Whitman, the man who wrote obits for the *New York Times*; a glorious French movie star; an English milady; and other colorful characters made the final cut.

I soldiered on, working my way through the hour without too many blunders and slyly arranging to get myself kissed by the Hemingway girls. Our ratings may well have been the lowest ever recorded for the time slot, and Primo admitted Mr. Carson lost no sleep over our impertinence.

These days Al lives in Old Greenwich and works out of a terrific home and office fronting Long Island Sound, running a successful kid's news TV show, which airs over American Forces Network and on stations around the country Saturday mornings. His stars aren't Geraldo and Tom Snyder. They're the teenage kids of broadcast icons like Meredith Vieira, Frank Gifford, Paula Zahn, and Rosanna Scotto. And when he loses them to the competition, it isn't to a rival show or some rich network; it's more likely to freshman year at Yale, Harvard, and Vassar.

The guy's still breaking fresh broadcasting ground. "El Primo," indeed.

*Mr. Brady is an author (**Why Marines Fight** is his latest book) who writes weekly for* Parade *magazine and for Forbes.com and used to be a foreign correspondent, an editor, and publisher. He has a New York Emmy for his TV interviews.*

Chapter One

"If you suspend me, I'll have ten thousand Puerto Ricans lying side by side, elbow to elbow, all the way down Sixty-sixth Street, and you will have to drive the news cars over them before anybody could get to work."
—*Geraldo Rivera, 1972*

I couldn't help but remember that line as I walked down that same street through the frigid air of Manhattan, envisioning Geraldo's threat. But it was just one of many bizarre incidents that had marked my career in television news. I had dealt with Howard Cosell and his hair in a box, traded a weatherman for Tom Snyder, inadvertently launched Joan Lunden's career with a misplaced light, and wore the black hat when I had to fire a cartoon character that was actually a member of a New York City news team.

You couldn't make up stuff this good.

But then again, that's part of the attraction of the television news business. The stories from behind the scenes are often a lot more interesting than the news we broadcast.

Especially when you're in charge of the most popular local newscast in the entire country.

At the time, I thought that fact would make me the hottest commodity in broadcasting. You would think the network would be grateful to someone who had not only fixed the newscast at its flagship station in New York but the newscasts at four other local stations around the country. You would think that ABC, its network news languishing in third place, would let me have a crack at turning things around. And you would be wrong.

Because television news is unlike any other industry. As many anchors are fond of saying, where else can you rise to the top of your profession and have to work nights?

I couldn't help but think of the wild ride I'd endured reaching the top of my profession in local news. With the help of some of the country's most famous journalists and technical geniuses, we'd managed to turn the television news industry upside down and create a newscast format that exists to this day in dozens of large and small cities around the country.

But I had discovered that reaching the top has its perils. It's a long way down.

It was a far cry from my days in the mailroom in Pittsburgh, Pennsylvania.

The old St. Nicholas Arena on West Sixth-sixth Street stood as a forgotten monument to Willie Pep, Sugar Ray Robinson, and the Raging Bull, men who settled things with their fists. This long gray building now housed ABC Television, but the battles inside were just as bloody and ruthless. Fear and intimidation were routine punches in the gut thrown by men in thousand-dollar suits. And I felt like a weary battler without a cornerman as I headed to the office of Bill Sheehan, the newly named president of ABC News. He was a short, barrel-chested fireplug from the Midwest and as cold as that brutal winter of 1976.

Elmer Lower, ABC News, Laurence Grossman, NBC News with the author

Sheehan had broken into radio broadcasting in Detroit and became an ABC radio news correspondent when no one really wanted to work for what they called the Almost Broadcasting Company. He was hired by Jim Haggarty, the former press secretary to President Dwight David Eisenhower. Haggarty was known as a political powerhouse who was said to be actually running the country for Ike. A desperate Leonard Goldenson, who *was* ABC, tapped him as its president of news when Ike left office. But Haggarty, a former newspaper reporter, was like every other print journalist who tried his hand at television. Completely inept. (Rupert Murdoch was the sole exception to this rule.) In this case, Haggarty's failure would be Sheehan's opening.

Haggarty quickly shot himself in the foot with his bizarre idea of presenting a newscast without an anchorman; stories haphazardly strung together with voice-over reporting by ABC correspondents, at the time the weakest link at the network. It was basically just one step above radio, a ship adrift on the airwaves without a rudder. He was replaced by Elmer Lower, who ABC recruited in 1963 and truly was a world-class journalist who had worked at *Life* magazine, CBS, and NBC. Lower began the reorganization of ABC News, and Sheehan immediately hitched his wagon to the network's brightest star. He was moved up through the ranks quickly after endearing himself to Lower.

I had met Sheehan ten years ago when I was the news director of KYW-TV in Philadelphia. I had created the *Eyewitness News* concept there, and with the help of a terrific staff had achieved great success. We changed the world of broadcasting and armed with that, I arranged a trip to New York to see what the big guys at the network might have to offer a young guy with fresh ideas.

In 1966, the execs at CBS, NBC, and ABC only vaguely knew about *Eyewitness News* and really nothing about local television or a Pennsylvania kid named Al Primo. Sheehan thought I might be a good candidate for the national assignment desk at his network, a thoughtless remark made to basically blow off someone who had somehow made it into his office. It was a disparaging suggestion transparently designed to take me down a notch. But I recognized it for what it was. I left wondering how network news organizations functioned with executives so out of touch with the real world. But then, being young, I didn't yet know how the old boy network took care of its own. It wasn't boxing at all but tag team wrestling and very often, two against one.

But on this day, ten years later, Sheehan was the new president of ABC News. He still looked like a Midwest farm boy in an expensive suit. He had so much chest hair it actually stuck out above his necktie like a cornstalk. This, combined with a bad brown dye hair job, created an unusual appearance. All those years of large paychecks in the Big Apple still couldn't buy him a stitch of class to go along with the gray flannel. I was the executive producer of the newly cancelled *Reasoner Report*. I walked into his long office filled with a bank of television sets. He moved away from the desk and invited me to sit on the sofa. He said he was putting his own people in place. He turned on the flattery and told me I was to become a key part of his new management team; my pulse quickened and I sat up straight, trying to hold back a smile as I waited for him to hand me the brass ring containing the keys to the kingdom. Then he told me I would be vice president of the ABC Washington news bureau.

In a split second, the excitement drained from my body. I knew this job was the journalistic equivalent of manning the boiler room. The Washington half of the evening news had just been cancelled and there was very little work of significance there. DC bureaus of any news organization are completely dominated and run by the correspondents; managers were simply administrative pencil-pushing eunuchs. (Just imagine being Sam Donaldson's "boss.") The offer was both an insult and a shocker. The guy who had invented *Eyewitness News* and brought every ABC-owned television station to first place in news and was responsible for 25 percent of ABC's profit was being offered a position where he would never be able to bring the format to the network. Dick O'Leary, my boss and president of the division would say of those stations, "We got five aces." O'Leary had put the *Eyewitness* format in as general manager of WLS-TV in Chicago where a *Variety* correspondent named Morry Roth unfortunately dubbed it, "Happy Talk News."

It seemed to me the old boy network had found a way to shove a major threat into the basement since they didn't understand *Eyewitness News* and were unwilling to change their old ways. I detected a bit of fear behind the intimidation that always dominated Sheehan's steely smile.

A million thoughts flashed through my mind. Was it because I had been pushing ABC News execs a little too hard with my idea to turn the network newscast into the national version of *Eyewitness News*? I had once showed Sheehan a tape of every ABC News correspondent and suggested that most of them had to be replaced because they were inept, even if they were his pals. They were the face of a third-place news division, one that had held that position for years. But my comment probably didn't sit too well with Sheehan. He smiled and said he disagreed with my opinion and thought our correspondents were "great."

Or was it because I saw him sneaking out of the Madison Hotel in Washington with one of our female correspondents and didn't look the other way fast enough?

Maybe it was the CIA. Agents of the Central Intelligence Agency had been masquerading as ABC newspeople for years and most executives looked the other way when it came to that sensitive subject.

The reason didn't matter. I said, "No thanks." I would take my chances in New York. He said there was no other job for me with the network. I thought I detected a slight smile as he figuratively showed me the door and realized he'd offered me the job knowing I'd turn it down. The four-letter words formed in my throat, fighting for a place in line. I swallowed them hard.

But for the first time in my professional career, I lashed out. I unloaded all my frustrations and promised him this would cost him his own job in six months, no matter how many times he flew ABC President Elton Rule to London and Paris for a good time.

I was only off by a month on the day ABC finally fired Bill Sheehan. He ended his career as a PR flack for the Ford Motor Company.

But on this day, I couldn't believe my eyes or my ears. A flush of heat rushed across my face and body. I had to really reach down to stay positive as my anger did battle with my common sense. It reminded me of another day twenty-two years earlier . . .

Spring, 1953—not the best time in the seventeen years I had spent on this earth. My guidance counselor at Perry High School in Pittsburgh was a pleasant enough chap whose primary job was teaching metal shop. His name was Mr. Berry and he wore the same drab gray suit every day, only you didn't notice because a full black apron scarred with grease usually covered it. He operated in a very noisy room with fifteen lathe machines. It was the class where the tough guys from Pittsburgh who were not "college material" were trained to fill the thousands of jobs that supported the Steel City's huge manufacturing base.

Grease and dirt left a thin film that covered everything in the room. It matched the city of Pittsburgh. Mr. Berry had a flushed face; visible capillaries were roadmaps running across his nose. He topped it off with a mouthful of crooked teeth that seemed to promote mumbling. Mr. Berry seemed classically depressed and quiet. He said very little. He spoke with his hands in the same agile way he ran a lathe and taught us how to make steel plumb bobs and screwdrivers. On this day, his grease-scarred hands held my transcript and background papers as he looked across his desk at me.

"What's your father do for a living?" Mr. Berry asked.

"He works in a factory," I replied.

Armed with that information, metal shop instructor Robert Berry decided that Albert Primo, a C+ student from the north side of the city, should get a job. Right now. "Help out your family and don't take the place of someone who should *really* go to college." His words ground me into shavings like the metal in the shop. It was the kind of humiliation that cuts deeply, but at the same time fortifies you with resolve.

I'd seen my father and grandfather work themselves to the bone, and I knew there had to be something better than a life of endless physical labor. This was the land of opportunity for which they'd come to America from Italy. They'd risked everything for the future, and that future was staring me down.

My father had learned early on that he could literally work himself into an early grave if he didn't improve himself; he worked as a gravedigger. And when the Great Depression hit like thunder and sent the country to the unemployment line, he ironically kept his job, thanks to the certainty of death and taxes. The death part, anyway.

At age fifteen, my dad had come through Ellis Island with my grandfather, who quickly found work at the cemetery. Grandpa started out mowing lawns, then was promoted to gravedigger, and got a job for my father. I spent one summer working with my dad, and landscaping in the broiling sun only fueled my spirit to find a better future.

My mother, the eldest of ten children, was the proverbial coal miner's daughter but didn't enjoy the storybook life of Loretta Lynn. Her parents had settled in the hard coal region of Pennsylvania and lived the life-on-the-edge existence of those whose loved ones toiled in the bowels of the earth. My mother often told me that no matter what they were doing at home, they would always keep alert for the dreaded whistle at the coal mine. The high whine repeating in special code, which shrilled through the community and caused hearts to skip, happened often enough to keep everyone in constant fear. When it sounded, the whole town quietly went down to the head of the mineshaft to wait and pray. The women walked slowly, wearing their aprons as tears filled their eyes. They stood vigil with the priests, ministers, and town officials. Sometimes the whole crew of miners, faces blackened by the coal dust, would emerge safely to be embraced by a flood of emotion; other days, the always present row of black hearses from the funeral homes, usually kept to the side of the mine shaft, would pick them up. When the boys in the family grew old enough to start work, my grandmother demanded they leave in search of a better life. There was no way she was going to let her boys work in the mines. My grandparents managed to take the whole family to Pittsburgh, first living with friends long enough to get established and then moving on to their own place.

Albert and Jeanette Primo

Since my mother was the oldest, she became a "second mother" to her siblings, helping to care for her nine brothers and sisters. And when she married my father, nothing really changed. He just moved in and became a part of the family. The extended family all lived in the same house, brothers in the attic, my parents in part of the second floor. We had our own kitchen, a bath, one bedroom, and a wonderful porch off the kitchen that served as a dining room on hot summer nights.

Meanwhile, my father had been working to improve his skills and it paid off. He had learned to speak English, passed the driver's test and got a promotion at the cemetery to the position of driver. During the Depression, his was the only paycheck for the entire household so he became the "second father." In those days responsibility trumped all; I never heard my father complain or saw any regret in his dark, soulful eyes. He was very proud that his income saved the entire family. He stood only five feet five but managed to carry the weight of supporting us all.

We all slept in the same large bedroom. Mom and Dad shared a double bed while my sister and I used two cots that were placed at the foot. Brother Joe was in the crib. Baby Janet slept between Mom and Dad in their bed. A gas stove heated the room, and I can remember most nights sleeping with the flames of the stove licking out of the vent, a pot of water steaming atop it.

I can remember coming home from playing baseball at the field looking for my mom. My aunt Mary said she wasn't there. "You've got a new baby sister," she said. I was dumbfounded. It was a new experience for everyone since Mom went to the hospital this time to have the baby. My sister and I were born at home in the same room in which we all slept.

But the house, which by today's standards would be considered incredibly crowded, was also overflowing with love. Since I was the first grandchild, I was showered by constant attention from grandparents, aunts, and uncles. We may have been broke, but we were never poor. I learned there was a big difference.

Rose Ann Primo, Janet Primo, Joseph Primo

Sundays were dominated by church and food as they were, and still are, in most Italian families (though the obsession with food never goes away during the rest of the week). I became an altar boy, which instilled a sense of pride in me and the family. But in those days, the Catholic Church required strict fasting before Holy Communion, which meant my mouth began watering for my mother's weekly feast sometime around the reading of the Gospel. My mother was a beautiful woman and could stop traffic on Sundays; she'd fix up her dark hair and slip her best dress over her tall, slender frame, go to early mass, and run home to start cooking. Within five minutes she'd turned into Sophia Loren in an apron. The house would be dominated by the smells of her fresh bread and steaming tomato sauce filled with sausage and meatballs. The entire family would pile into our kitchen for a feeding frenzy that lasted for hours. My uncle Vincent, who started a construction company so his brothers would have work, would eat so many hot peppers that beads of sweat would run down his forehead. He'd simply mop his brow and continue eating.

It was a three-story house of love and strong family bonds. I never felt deprived. I was too happy to know we had little money. There was always good food on the table, always a hug from a parent or a relative, always laughter and endless stories of the land they'd left behind. But it never occurred to me to talk with my father about life. He always had two jobs and you didn't want to bother him with trivial stuff because his free time was so precious. Most of it was used for sleep. He simply led by example. His face looked like it was carved out of granite, and it may as well have been; to me, the man was a rock.

And the lessons he taught told me something important on this day in shop class. The teacher who was telling me I wasn't smart enough for college was dead wrong.

Still, one week after graduation, I swallowed my pride and set out on a systematic job-hunting assault in Pittsburgh. College would remain on the back burner for now. I began at the point of the Golden Triangle, where the Monongahela and Allegheny Rivers meet to form the mighty Ohio, entering each office building and applying at every company that would see me. The answer was the same from each personnel director, although one took a few extra minutes to tell me, "A willingness to work, dedication, energy, and desire aren't enough. You have to show someone how you can help the company." But I knew it was just a matter of persistence, and I wouldn't fail. I'd been built up by my parents and family; the first son was always told he was smart and would do great things. In my mind, I knew I could be a leader in business, just as my father led the family.

Six weeks of pounding the pavement can be discouraging. A foot in the door, any door, was what I needed and the buildings loomed taller and seemingly impossible to climb, like concrete-and-steel Everests. Then I looked up at the last, very last, skyscraper, the art deco Chamber of Commerce building, a recognizable part of the Pittsburgh skyline. It was the home of Koppers, a large chemical company. I took the elevator to the tenth floor, turned left, and headed for the personnel office. The reception room was very small and I hit it off well with the woman at the front desk. Suddenly, groups of giggling young women paraded by every few minutes, making quick eye contact and then covering their grins. By the time I was admitted to the personnel director's office, the mystery began to clear up.

The application form read, *DuMont Television Network.* I had made a wrong turn off the elevator. I was not at the Koppers Company, but rather at WDTV, a local television station. We didn't even own a TV set in our family, and it never even occurred to me that local television stations existed. The only television I'd ever seen was Saturday afternoon wrestling and *Captain Video* and only if the one rich kid in the neighborhood invited me over to his house. He was also the most popular kid on the block; cross him, and no TV. It never occurred to me there might be opportunities in the industry. But I was already there, so I started to fill out the form.

It turned out the receptionist had gone through the office and, as a practical joke, had told everyone an actor was in the lobby. And I was the "young Hollywood star." The incident provided everyone with a good laugh and saved me the embarrassment of not knowing where the hell I was. More importantly, they also remembered me for being a good sport about the whole thing.

I was hired as a mail boy a week later. While that may sound incredibly boring, it was just the opposite. It was a thrilling experience being around creative, happy, motivated people, working in an environment a world apart from the drudgery of the business offices I had observed over the prior six weeks. And compared to the backbreaking work of the cemetery, it was like a vacation. I couldn't spend enough time at WDTV and to this day never considered the work a job.

My salary was just thirty-five dollars per week, but what I learned was priceless. Life in the mailroom teaches you critical skills for survival in the business world. In a short period of time, you learn which mail held the free tickets, how well the company was doing by reading the amounts of checks in envelopes held up to the light, how to read upside down while standing in front of your supervisor's desk, who is carrying on with whom, and all the various office intrigues which reveal themselves late in the day when you're posting the mail. I didn't know it at the time, but my tendency to be nosy is a quality common to every news reporter. This was one life skill they didn't teach at Perry High School, but it was much more valuable (and a lot cleaner) than shop class.

One big benefit that came with the position was that the mailroom staff always knows who's being fired or promoted. The mail boy has the task of running off the memos and press releases, saying the fired exec wants to spend more time with his family, well in advance of the action. At eighteen years of age, I learned information is power, and it is a wise person who makes it a point to know well the mail boys of the world.

By the time September rolled around, the world of television consumed me, and I thought, *Who needed college?* I'd take a shot at the brass ring in television.

My life as a mail boy was a heady experience. It seemed almost as though people in the television business were constantly having a party and not working, quite a contrast to the other hushed and reserved offices I had visited while looking for a job. The men and women at WDTV also seemed rather loose, and no one ever watched the clock. I was told later that this was in large measure because back in the 1950s, the people employed really couldn't get regular jobs. They had been hired in television because no one else wanted to work there as it was considered too risky. The medium was taking on the kings of radio, and no one was sure if it had a future against the likes of Jack Benny and George Burns.

The stagehands had all been union theater workers when Pittsburgh was a "must stop" for national touring companies, and several retired members were reactivated to work in television. Some television studio cameramen were former steelworkers who had been on strike at the mills for such a long time they would take any kind of work at all.

The general manager of the station, Harold Lund, was right out of central casting. He had come from a very small and unsuccessful advertising agency. He was a bachelor who'd spent his life taking care of his mother until she died. Immaculate in dress with white hair that was quickly receding, he had a rosy complexion and was quite small in stature. But I noted he walked and carried himself like a giant of a man. The success of running a television station radiated from him and touched all those around him. It was a mental note I filed away. He married a sweet young thing very late in life, but she took him

Harold C. Lund
General Manager, WDTV

for a spectacular ride and almost bankrupted him before running off with a stable boy.

His secretary, Maria, was the unofficial head of the company. Dark, mysterious, and a powerful ally, she was a tough mother superior who held strong sway over the various departments. Maria had her special squad of secretaries who took no prisoners and dutifully reported all the activities of their managers. That's power!

One such secretary, Doris Armstrong, seemed to have a close relationship with my boss, Louis Kiernan, a good-natured middle manager who was a bit long in the tooth. He was a strict Roman

Catholic, the guilt-ridden altar boy who never grew up. He knew the station inside and out and commanded the respect of all the secretaries and those who knew where the real power in the station was.

Doris, on the other hand, was a typical fun-loving party girl. What she lacked in appearance she made up in personality. She was constantly smiling and cheering up the entire office. She would do anything for a laugh.

On my second day at work, Doris walked into the mailroom, looked deeply into my eyes, locked the door, and proceeded to chase me around the postage meter. While this small soap opera was going on in the locked mailroom, my boss and half the station employees were outside listening to the commotion and roaring with laughter. I had been initiated.

Her major claim to fame came months later. The station was owned by the DuMont Television Network in New York, a company whose main interest was in the manufacture of television sets. DuMont got into the actual broadcasting end of things for the sole purpose of selling more TV sets. DuMont's corporate management was better equipped to run manufacturing plants than broadcasting stations. Executives from New York would come to town from time to time to let the employees know how important they were to the company. Of course, the station would always take advantage of those occasions to show off the local talent and entertain the visiting brass with receptions and parties to which everyone, including the mail boy, was invited.

One party was held in the main studio on the first floor of our building. We heard the usual rah-rah speeches and enjoyed the very best of entertainment. The senior VIP on this occasion was a vice president of engineering. He was overweight, wore glasses, and had that New York City arrogance that rubbed some people the wrong way. He spoke little but drank a lot and carried himself with the power of the DuMont Television Network. I thought he was Mr. Cool; that is, until Doris took him down a notch. I noticed Doris leaving the party followed shortly thereafter by our visiting VIP. About an hour later, she returned and gave a, ahem, blow-by-blow account of the last thirty minutes up on the tenth floor executive conference room. When our VIP returned, a round of applause and cheers greeted him.

It was heady stuff for an eighteen-year-old. It took a full year to get over the notion that one could succeed in this or any other business without a college degree. I was getting an education in the ways of the world, stuff that couldn't be found in any book. But I wanted a lot more and it became obvious I needed a piece of parchment to get it. I might do well but knew no one would ever consider me for a top position with just a high school diploma.

I went to our personnel director that following summer and asked for permission to attend the University of Pittsburgh. Paul Palangi, who always had a nice tan that set off his steel gray hair, was a tough but compassionate manager who had come from a DuMont factory in New Jersey. The only contact I'd had with him was on my first day in the mailroom when he told me to get rid of my powder blue suit for a more businesslike outfit. It struck terror in my soul since it was the only suit I owned. But he was nice enough to accommodate my request to coordinate my classes with my job. He offered to move me over to the night switchboard job, which would allow me the daytime hours to attend school. It was tough to give up the mailroom, which had become a gossip clearinghouse. But it was time to take the next step.

In September, I quietly enrolled at the University of Pittsburgh as a full-time student. My confidence level in academics was low, not surprising when your shop teacher tells you that you're not college material. In fact, it was so low that I never really told anyone I was going to college to get a degree. I thought it best to simply keep a very low profile until I felt I could make it through Pitt. Only in my junior year did I tell anyone I was attending classes.

But by then, I knew a lot more about the television industry and my plan was beginning to take shape. All because I switched to the night shift.

Chapter Two

"I'll give you seventy five dollars a week. Do you want it?"
—*Program Manager Byron Doty, offering me my first newsroom job*

In 1954, the DuMont Television Network claimed that an incredible 94 percent of the TV sets in Pittsburgh were tuned to WDTV. Just before the network went out of business, it sold the station, using that fact in its sales pitch, to the Westinghouse Broadcasting Company. Donald H. McGannon, the Westinghouse president, traveled to Pittsburgh and presided over the company's first staff meeting in the big studio. He told the staff something I've heard so many times in my career and did so with a straight face.

"There will be no changes, everybody's job is safe."

In the world of television news, that statement is right up there with "the check is in the mail."

While I noticed several worried looks rolling like a wave through the room, I was just the college kid who ran the switchboard, and surely Westinghouse wasn't going to turn off the phones. I knew if any heads rolled they'd be the ones cashing the big paychecks. My thirty-five bucks a week wasn't going to make a difference to any bottom line. So I turned my focus back to school during the day and the news department at night.

In 1955, the news program at eleven o'clock was just fifteen minutes long and the anchorman did everything: the news writing (about ten minutes of copy), the film editing (local clips plus national film clips flown in each night from Fox Movietone News in Washington to the Greater Pittsburgh Airport), the beat checks of the police and fire departments, and updating of the AP and UPI wire stories by telephone. And the anchor was alone in the studio, a veritable television news one-man band.

It was a massive job, one that would send today's specialized newspeople into vapor lock, but nobody did it better than Bill Burns. The man had learned the news business the way most journalists did in the early days: from a mentor, in this case a KQV radio broadcaster named Louis Kaufman who eventually became so popular he was elected a judge of Allegheny County courts.

Judge Kaufman believed in what he termed *people news* and had a colorful delivery. He instilled in Burns a burning curiosity about events and the people who were an integral part of them. This meant not just interviewing a dry official on the scene spouting the company line but actually seeking out the people affected by the story. The folk, as he called them, were the backbone of America and Kaufman knew that if television cared about them, actually asked their opinions, they'd care more about television. And especially the channel that talked to the real people, which included just about everyone in a hardscrabble town like Pittsburgh. Kaufman reminded me of New York Mayor Fiorello LaGuardia, a real man of the people who instinctively knew what they were interested in simply because he was so real himself. He did things on the air like opening his broadcast with "Happy Birthday, Pope." That's how he started his newscast on the pope's birthday.

Burns remembered this simple lesson well when he joined the young television station in 1953, without a single day of training in television. His Irish good looks and manner were an instant hit in Pittsburgh. When Burns took over the main chair, the audience quickly forgot the previous superstar news anchor, Dave Murray. Murray had left WDTV to join a group that wanted to set up a second television station in Pittsburgh on an ultrahigh frequency band (UHF channels 14-83) rather than the conventional very high frequency (VHF channels 2-13) band. At that time, television sets were not equipped to receive UHF stations and viewers quickly discovered that neither a rooftop antenna nor a coat hanger and tinfoil would pick up the station. They were required to buy a special converter just to see it and television sets themselves were not cheap in those days. The enterprise was a colossal failure.

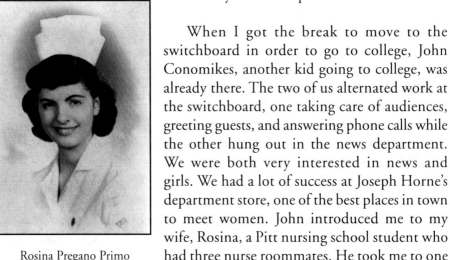

Rosina Pregano Primo

When I got the break to move to the switchboard in order to go to college, John Conomikes, another kid going to college, was already there. The two of us alternated work at the switchboard, one taking care of audiences, greeting guests, and answering phone calls while the other hung out in the news department. We were both very interested in news and girls. We had a lot of success at Joseph Horne's department store, one of the best places in town to meet women. John introduced me to my wife, Rosina, a Pitt nursing school student who had three nurse roommates. He took me to one of their parties and I asked her for a date on Saturday. We have been going out every Saturday night since. And John and I are still close friends forty years later. John eventually went up to the sales department. It was the right choice for him; he became president of Hearst Broadcasting and a trustee of the Hearst Foundation, a multimillion-dollar lifetime job.

In those early days of vacuum tube television, there were always some technical problems and the switchboard would light up like a Christmas tree whenever that test pattern with the Indian in the middle hit the air. Somehow, I managed to squeeze in my homework while being inexorably drawn into the news world. Though incredibly busy, Burns found extra time to show me his work and how he performed each task. He would occasionally complain about the amount of the work but never about the nature of it, and the sheer joy he demonstrated was infectious. I tried to find every opportunity to be of some assistance to him. It was a great trade-off; he was the beneficiary of free help and I was getting an education I couldn't buy at any university.

Lucky for me, there happened to be a typewriter at the switchboard. I convinced him that he should allow me to use it to write up new scripts. In television, timing is essential and I needed to learn to write copy that timed out to the second. Every element is written on a single page. The anchors words were written on the right, the director's notes on the left. I started with typing boilerplate scripts like standard newscast openings that read, "Good evening, in the news tonight . . ." on the right side of the page while the left read, BURNS: (on camera). This was followed by more stories, then a page that led into the commercials that read, "We'll be back with more news in a moment," while the other side of the page told the director he'd be going to a commercial. Bill's closing was always the same: "That's the news, this is Bill Burns wishing you good night, good luck, and good news tomorrow." Every news anchor has his or her own signature sign-off and Burns was no exception.

He encouraged me to get more creative since I wouldn't learn much, typing the same words night after night. So I expanded those few pages into six or seven by adding more elements. I called the U.S. Weather Bureau for the latest forecast and would type it into the script, saving Burns the call while trying to make the copy more interesting. As I gained confidence, I began to improvise. The serials at the theater got people coming back week after week with cliff-hangers, so why couldn't television news use the same concept? Instead of the standard commercial introduction, I added elements that enticed viewers to stay tuned, such as "Tonight, man bites dog, we'll have that story in just a moment." Burns instinctively liked it and though not exactly a cliff-hanger, it hooked the viewer into sticking around till the end of the newscast. Today, this device, known as the news tease, is an integral part of all newscasts; the standard that was born from a switchboard operator's desire to make a place for himself in broadcasting and an anchor who took a new idea and ran with it.

Slowly but surely I kept building up my involvement in the news operation. I tracked down airplanes carrying our vital film shipments from Washington and made the beat calls of the emergency services to save time for Burns. He really appreciated my help, but I wasn't sure anyone on the day shift knew I was becoming a valuable part of the news department. So one night, when I thought the time was just right, I stayed late at Pitt and called in "sick." I was later told the newsroom was in turmoil that night and Burns was overwhelmed with work. The next day, he marched right into the general manager's office, demanded additional help at night, and added that the assistance should come from the kid at the switchboard.

That's how I got into television news on a full-time basis. Burns and I had become fast friends and I had timed my move perfectly. When I got "well" the next day, Burns came up to me and said, "Kid, I've just gone up to see the GM, and he's going to give me help. He's going to call you to his office today. Don't settle for anything less than a hundred dollars a week." He was really emphatic on that last point. I was earning bare minimum wage at the time.

Sure enough, the program manager, Byron Doty, called me into his office. Doty was a slow-talking man with dark, Coke-bottle glasses who hailed from New Orleans. This Cajun had somehow made it to Pittsburgh, about as far out of water as a southern fish can get. He was trained in programming but was also the boss of the news department since prudent management would never allow newsies to be in charge of anything beyond petty cash.

I sat down and he looked across his desk. "Mr. Primo, you've been here a couple of years. I don't know if I should fire you or promote you," he said rather seriously. "Bill Burns wants you down in news. I'll give you $75 a week. Do you want it?" A rush of relief came over me and I accepted on the spot, completely forgetting Burns's advice. Burns was absolutely furious when I told him my salary. But I was delighted to get the opportunity to get into the news business full-time, so money wasn't really a factor.

Bill Burns had been, of all things, a typewriter salesman from Philadelphia. He was born in the "hard coal" country. He tried college for a while and went off to war like most other young men his age. Like many others, he came home with a Purple Heart after catching a load of shrapnel in his left leg. It forever damaged the nerve that controlled the bending of his ankle and he had to wear a brace to walk properly. At six feet five inches and striding with his special style, he was an impressive figure walking along the streets of Pittsburgh.

He was the embodiment of the fact that you can replace a good anchorman with an even better one and the audience will forget the first one faster than you can imagine. It's a concept that I have never forgotten and have used effectively at ABC and dozens of other television stations. Viewers can have a short memory when you give them something better.

While his leg didn't work properly, there was nothing wrong with the man's liver. Bill Burns could drink an entire bottle of whiskey with no visible effect, and he did that many nights but only *after* the eleven o'clock newscast. He never, but never, took a drink during the daytime hours or while working. I had either lunch or dinner with him every working day for ten years and never saw him drunk or visibly affected by alcohol. And every time we'd go out, people would stop to talk or ask for an autograph. He was friendly and patient with everyone, often letting his dinner get cold. I asked him if it bothered him and he said, "Hell, no! I know what the folks want and I give it to them. They watch every night 'cause they know I'll give it to them straight." He taught me the importance of connecting with the average Joe and being "one of them." He had an easy smile for everyone, and the people saw him as the friendly neighborhood Irishman with the curly hair and the wisp that always hung over his forehead; he just happened to be the local anchorman. He was the opposite of my father: a teacher who *told* me everything I needed to know.

We often went out after the eleven o'clock news to, in the words of Bill Burns, "Learn the town and meet news contacts." Though some of those, uh, "contacts" were not the type you'd hear about in journalism school. These "beat checks" were usually done at various bars since alcohol often loosens lips and we'd end up with some good scoops. But one after-hours joint in particular was Bill's favorite, Club 30. (The number 30 incidentally is journalism code for "the end.") We knew all the hookers, con men, and police brass that would arrive invariably after midnight. These were Damon Runyon characters one and all, Pittsburgh style.

Bill Burns—KDKA Election Night Coverage

One of my favorites was a prostitute named "Cockeyed Joanne," and you don't have to stretch your imagination to figure out the origin of her nickname. She was a wonderful woman of the night who fell head over stiletto heels for the top-ranked city police lieutenant, a Club 30 regular. Unlucky in love, Cockeyed Joanne learned to her dismay that the police lieutenant had another woman on the side. This, of course, in addition to his wife. One night we went to the bar only to find it filled with chaos and police. Cockeyed Joanne had turned out not to be the proverbial hooker with a heart of gold and while hell hath no fury like a woman scorned, it can't hold a candle to a pissed-off prostitute. Joanne shot her police lieutenant in the place where he would cause her or no other woman any further pain to the heart. At her arraignment, she said what so many others have said, "I shot him 'cause I loved him." Her story could have easily been part of the movie *Chicago*. In her eyes, *he had it comin'*.

All of this was an eye-opening experience for a kid still living at home with his parents. (Imagine hanging out with hookers at night and watching your mother iron your shirts in the morning.) The stuff I picked up in those bars was intoxicating but had nothing to do with alcohol.

But just like booze, it had the same effect. Once news got into my blood, I was hooked.

Chapter Three

"Working for the union gave me the idea that politics might be my future."
—Ronald W. Reagan, 1955

"Due to technical difficulties beyond our control" was the most often used phrase in the early days of television. But the reason a station was off the air at any given time was not necessarily technical. It was an all-purpose excuse that explained any problem to the public. TV was such a new technology that the general public had no clue as to how it actually worked, so "technical difficulties" became the universal apology when the switchboard lit up with callers wondering why their program was not being broadcast. Star of the program didn't show up? Sir, we're having technical difficulties. Engineer late coming back from dinner? Sorry, ma'am, technical difficulties. In the early days of TV, that Indian on the test pattern got more face time than Uncle Miltie.

Television in the fifties was all "live." Videotape had not yet been invented, and everything the audience saw on their tiny black-and-white Philco screens was happening at the very moment they were seeing it. Film was the only exception, primarily consisting of old movies, cartoons, and canned commercials. Well, not the only exception. A heavy large contraption called a "slide chain" could take a basic everyday photographic Ektachrome slide and broadcast it so that a still picture filled the screen. Riveting stuff.

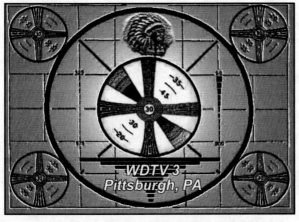

Pittsburgh's Window on the world

The programming on WDTV in Pittsburgh started at six o'clock in the evening with a simple program called *Concert Gems*, which consisted of one slide of the city's skyline accompanied by classical music. Even then, I found it hard to believe anyone would listen to a half hour of music while looking at the same picture for thirty minutes. In my mind, the real broadcasting began at six thirty when the DuMont Television Network news was sent down the line from New York. The newscast was anchored by a man named Morgan Beatty, who read the AP newswire stories with an occasional silent film clip or still photograph. We called him Morgan Beauty. Because there were still so few television stations on the air, the news producers in New York would switch "live" to Pittsburgh to get additional stories read, a device used to change the pace of the program.

Bill Burns would get a list of stories by telephone from New York and then sit on our local news set and read the material. Beatty would say, for example, "There was a disaster in Kansas City, Missouri, today and for that story we switch to Pittsburgh." We had no more information available to us than Beatty did in New York and, of course, no pictures of the event. Once, Beatty had a day off and a substitute read the news. He introduced a film clip which failed. The cameras stayed on him for an eternity. He became so upset he actually crawled under the desk to hide. And yes, the camera followed him down. That was the extent of how much passed for network news in the early fifties.

The newscast was followed by a series of fifteen-minute local entertainment programs that were all "live" and the television station was constantly filled with the excitement of show business. I realized the night shift had all the action and it wasn't always in the news department.

Actors, directors, musicians, singers, and dancers were always rehearsing, auditioning for programs like *Buzz and Bill*, a song-and-dance team; *Joe and Elaine Mann*, whose program was sponsored by a furniture company (their favorite song was "Three rooms, $398 . . ."); *Slim Williams and the Wildcats*; and a big favorite, *The Wilkins Amateur Hour*. But the real treats came when the Hollywood stars would wander by. You could feel the excitement in the air when Lucille Ball was in the building. I remember a wonderful conversation with Shirley Jones, now best known as the singing mother from *The Partridge Family*. This incredibly gorgeous woman who would win an Academy Award in 1960 for playing a prostitute in *Elmer Gantry* was just a nice normal person who didn't mind talking to the starry-eyed kid at the switchboard. The movers and shakers had figured out that television had a future, and the parade of big names left me in awe.

Even advertisers could become local celebrities if they had the cash. Louis Silverman, the owner of a jewelry store, spent so much money on his program every week he was like a god in the station. Executives jumped at his every command. Long before *American Idol*, the talent contest was a staple of television and for pretty much the same reason it is today. Without any big stars to pay, it is cheap to produce. Silverman started one in Pittsburgh. He offered prizes for the winners like a wristwatch or a ring, items he obviously couldn't sell in his store. Silverman figured out he could make a name for himself and his business while unloading the inventory taking up space in his back room. Silverman got bitten by the showbiz bug and soon thought of himself as a local media mogul. He actually started importing talents from New York to bring pizzazz to the show. His first hire was Gloria Okon, a model from New York whom he renamed "Jane Wilkins." She did all the commercials within the show. His announcer was a man named Brian McDonald, who was at the time a big star and announcer for the *Ice Capades*. Uncle Lou, as the insiders called him, was very possessive of his talent. No one talked too much with his stars except him, and he demanded total loyalty, including the knowledge of all details of their personal lives and careers. When he finally tired of *The Amateur Hour* program, he canceled it in a single week and fired the whole lot. In that respect, he did have one thing in common with a lot of Hollywood and television news executives.

Uncle Lou decided what Pittsburgh television needed was a big-time country and western show, and he went out and got the best. Major stars like Eddy Arnold actually moved to Pittsburgh to appear on the television show every week.

Some of the other programs were sponsored by local beer companies, and one group of local thespians included a young man by the name of Fred Rogers. He teamed up with Josie Carey (Josephine Vicari, from Butler, PA), and with Joe Negri on guitar, and Johnny Costa on piano, they created "The Children's Corner," on WQED, the predecessor of America's most popular children's show, *Mister Rogers' Neighborhood.*

The real stars of early television were the staff announcers who were brought to television from

Josie Cary, the puppets, Fred Rodgers, 1954.

radio. I can remember looking in awe at these deep-throated Lotharios as they walked through the station, resplendent in their dark, expensive suits and extravagant ties. Because of the American Federation of Television and Radio Artists (AFTRA) union fees, these announcers could make $50,000 a year or more, an incredible amount of money in 1953. All because they'd simply been born with great voices. They had to stand by during their shifts because they were called upon to go on the air at a moment's notice and creatively fill time when trouble occurred. Whenever those "technical difficulties" popped up, the announcer would deliver program notes, weather information, and even news headlines while people scurried about behind the scenes to fix the problem. These days the only pure "announcers" still used by networks are few. Don Pardo, who has been the voice of *Saturday Night Live* since its inception, is synonymous with that show. Alan Kalter of the *Late Show with David Letterman* and *The Tonight Show* still make use of the traditional announcer as well.

And the announcers in 1953 had filler material at their disposal as well. Because of the imprecise timing of television in the early days, one of the most popular programs was *Snaders,* three-minute films of popular vocalists singing their songs. There were stacks of them in master control, and when a movie ended a few minutes early or the network made an unscheduled ending, the film chain would chug into action and our local announcer would ad-lib his way into something like, "Here's Nat King Cole singing that all-time favorite, *Chestnuts Roasting on an Open Fire.*" When MTV became a staple of cable television, it was hailed as a historic moment, but it was a concept that was more than thirty years old.

In fifties television, everything was a major event. Even the commercials were attended to in a high-production fashion because executives realized they were as important as programming. After all, they paid the bills. One of my first chores was to make certain the yellow cab driver got paid properly after going out to the country to bring back a bale of hay or cornstalks used on the set for the live beer commercials in the news. One minute I was writing copy for Bill Burns, the next I was peeling off bills for carloads of produce.

One of early television's major network productions, *The United States Steel Hour,* was done "live" in New York, but the commercials were fed from Pittsburgh. Legions of producers, agency representatives, and technicians would pour into the Steel City to build the massive sets needed for the commercial production of the program. One Christmas, an entire Old English Tudor mansion drawing room was constructed in the main studio, and the president of *USS* sat before a roaring fire to give his message to America "live" from the steel capital of the world. It was Hollywood on a smaller scale, and I was right in the middle of it. No two days were ever the same and I realized that was part of the attraction of the industry. This was no assembly-line job. You literally never knew what your next day would bring.

At about that time, a big-time actor came to the station to promote his commercials for the *General Electric Theater*, a production right up there with *Playhouse 90, Hallmark,* and *The U.S. Steel Hour* as the most important of all the network dramatic series. Ronald Reagan was the spokesman for GE, and as part of his job, he toured the important television stations across the country, appearing on the local programs to promote General Electric and its products. The future president of the United States made a good deal of money, telling viewers about the wonders of the GE toaster.

Even then, I was impressed with Ronald Reagan who had begun his own broadcasting career as a sports announcer at WHO in Des Moines, Iowa. He actually did recreations of Chicago Cubs games (they weren't broadcast live) before becoming an actor. His visit was an opportunity to pick the brain of someone who had "made it" by starting in broadcasting. He spent at least forty-five minutes in the reception room talking with me about life on the road, Hollywood, his union activities with the Screen Actors Guild and the future. There was a glint in his eye when he talked about the possibility of politics. I remember telling a coworker, "You won't believe this, but Ronald Reagan actually wants to quit acting and become a politician!"

Chapter Four

"Over there, you, what's your question?"
—*President John Fitzgerald Kennedy at a White House news conference*

One of my favorite people in television at the time was a J. Walter Thompson advertising agency producer named Jim Gallagher. The Fort Pitt Brewing Company had decided it should have a major New York agency to create and supervise its one-minute "live" commercial within the eleven o'clock news broadcast, so Gallagher was sent to live in Pittsburgh five days a week, returning to his New York home only on weekends. He was a lonely guy who found solace in a bottle, a former journalist who had succumbed to the big money of advertising. He never seemed to forgive himself and it was clear he missed "the business" since he liked to hang around with me. He had a great influence on me in those long hours on the switchboard when we would talk about journalism. He was a natural teacher with a great eye for history.

He would devise tests on what was the most important news story of the day and what it meant to history. This was more than just a current events quiz. It was an important learning experience as it forced me to look beyond the story and consider its ramifications. Gallagher and anchorman Bill Burns both had a keen sense of news, but Burns knew exactly what appealed to a broad mass audience.

The news department consisted of just three other people. Burns served as both the news director and anchor, George Thomas was the news editor, and cameraman Chuck Boyle shot the film. I had by now grown comfortable with the thrill and excitement of television. I had set my sights on a career in journalism and knew in my heart this was my destiny.

I learned the way most reporters do by making mistakes, some of them laughable. Once assigned to get the facts on a bank robbery, I proudly presented Burns with a script that detailed the incident, the suspects, the getaway car, and the ensuing manhunt. The anchor got to the end of the copy, furrowed his brow, and gave me a puzzled look. "So, Al . . . how much did they get?" I sheepishly headed back to the telephone to find out how much money the bank robbers had taken. The errors were silly, rookie mishaps but once I learned the lessons, I never repeated the mistakes.

In the days that followed, I got to go on my first news story, and it was a big one. I had just arrived from my day of classes at Pitt and was casually crossing the lobby when Burns and cameraman Chuck Boyle rushed out. "Come on, kid, we've got a news story and we need you," Burns said. I was thrilled, but only until I had to climb into a waiting helicopter. There had been a coal mine disaster in Steubenville, Ohio, and this was the quickest way to get there.

I had never been in an airplane before and had never even seen a helicopter. As we took off, I noticed this particular model had a plastic cockpit that allowed you to see the full vista of earth beneath you, watch it grow small and flit in and out of the clouds in front of your very own eyes. The excitement I'd felt about my first story had been rudely shoved to the back burner by heart-pounding fear. My pulse seemed to be keeping pace with the beating rotors of the chopper.

We landed on top of a mountain above the coal mine. Chuck and I dragged the huge camera box down the hill while Burns slowly maneuvered down the mountain with his bad leg.

It was a devastating scene at the coal mine pit. It looked exactly like every old movie about mine disasters and also brought my mother's stories to life. Only this story was staring me in the face.

Because I was there to see it.

I was an *eyewitness*.

Steubenville, Ohio Coal Mine Disaster

The families gathered just inside the gates. A specific number of men were trapped in the mine, but at that moment, I realized there was a life behind every number. The numbers all had names; they were sons and fathers and brothers and best friends who each had a life that touched the people holding vigil. The mothers and wives and children stood silently with quivering lips and looks of despair on their faces. There were priests in attendance and a numbing quiet broken only by the whirl of the fans and elevators. I realized television news gave me the opportunity to weave a tapestry of emotion through the facts by showing and telling the viewer what people felt, not just what I saw.

The press corps, mostly newspaper reporters, was kept behind police lines. One enterprising reporter from the Associated Press, who had obviously covered these kinds of stories before, had ordered up a telephone line from Bell Telephone. He was in constant communication with his office. Something told me that I should be very nice to this guy. I was, and it turned out to be very beneficial as Burns had sent me back up the mountain to hang out near the only phone in the area.

After many, many hours, there was a break in the story. Burns and cameraman Boyle had been recording interviews with family members and were in the right place at the right time. They had managed to get close enough to the mineshaft to hear first that rescue workers had reached the trapped miners and they were coming up. Burns was running up the hill toward me, signaling the AP man to come down. I, of course, volunteered to hold his telephone since he obviously had to go down the hill to get the story. As soon as he was out of sight, I hung up and called the scoop into KDKA just minutes before the eleven o'clock news. Burns then recorded an on-the-scene radio report. I then went down to "help" the AP man as I saw him heading up the mountain, actually falling on top of him to give Burns a few more minutes to finish his feed.

The miners had all been found and were emerging safely one by one. The dam of emotion burst as the families rushed forward to meet them. As I trailed Chuck Boyle, he captured the moment, and I realized that film and sound could convey what words couldn't. The footage of a sobbing woman burying her head in the chest of her coal-dust-covered husband, hanging on for dear life as the tears rolled down her face was an image that burned into my brain. The viewers didn't need to hear a reporter for this part of the story. Words could add nothing more.

That very night I saw the future of the medium and I wanted to be a part of that future. Television news could take the marriage of pictures, sound, copy, and reporter involvement and bring story coverage to a new level.

Because television could make the viewer an *eyewitness* as well.

That night I also learned another valuable lesson. When I had called the station on the AP phone line to pass on the news of the rescue, George Thomas who answered the phone apparently didn't want to rewrite the entire newscast. He and Ray Scott, the sportsman who was filling in as anchor, decided to simply broadcast the first ten minutes as originally scripted, telling western Pennsylvania and eastern Ohio that the miners were still trapped when they weren't. He finally went to Bill Burns's taped report at ten minutes past the hour.

He'd broadcast a story that wasn't true. And in my mind, he'd committed a horrible affront to the people who were hanging on every word for news from the mine. He'd let those people believe their loved ones were trapped or dead when in fact they'd been safe for nearly a half hour. Letting viewers endure the sheer agony of thinking their loved ones were dead for ten gut-wrenching minutes was an unconscionable sin.

It was no surprise that after this experience, my burning desire was to get on the air to become a star news anchor like Bill Burns. And while I knew that would take time, I found a back door to build a reputation and increase my take-home pay. This ambition led me to call up CBS News so that I could sell telephone radio reports on one of Pittsburgh's many steel contract negotiations and strikes. The only CBS radio affiliate was a small daytime station located in nearby McKeesport, and it had no news staff. The network needed someone in Pittsburgh and was happy to buy my reports.

Since I was usually involved in the coverage for KDKA-TV, I was always able to take the extra time to feed for radio. It was a thrill to hear my reports on the *CBS World News Roundup* and other network radio programs, and I beamed with pride on the occasions my family heard them at home. Besides, they paid $25 for each report and on a breaking story, that could add up quickly and often exceed my weekly salary. I was able to establish a good working relationship with the network desk, and they used me often on stories. When a story got really big, CBS News would send in one of its own correspondents and it would be my job to give him a briefing and introduce him to all the principals in the story. I saw these visits as opportunities to observe different techniques of news coverage, even though I learned about 90 percent of everything I know about the business from Bill Burns.

Once, Harry Reasoner was sent in to cover a threatened strike at United States Steel. Naturally, I was thrilled at the chance to work with a network correspondent. I met Reasoner and took him to be introduced to David J. McDonald, the president of the United Steelworkers of America and one of the most colorful labor leaders of the time. I was hoping to pick up some nuggets of journalistic knowledge, assuming that Reasoner would be as inspiring a mentor as Bill Burns. But Reasoner spent most of his time complaining to me about having to come to Pittsburgh. He exerted little or no energy and showed hardly any enthusiasm for his work. But he was so talented it never showed in the final product; the viewer had no idea he was "phoning it in" when he was on the air. It was a major disappointment for me, like meeting a childhood hero only to discover he was a fraud. Many years later when I became executive producer of the *Reasoner Report* at ABC News, his style of being on "autopilot" never changed and it became part of my daily life when we worked closely together.

Meanwhile, I kept asking KDKA-TV to move me up the ladder, all the while being careful of News Director/Anchorman Bill Burns's sensitivities. Bill, like all on-camera talent, protected his turf and kept a wary eye on my involvement with CBS and his news program. He was so kind to me I never wanted him to think I was after his job, which I wasn't. It was a balancing act for both of us, but we had such great respect for each other and there was little if any difficulty over my working in both roles.

The author on set for the first time

I finally got the opportunity to anchor a five-minute newscast on Sundays just before noon. CBS had an excellent program, *Camera Three,* which was formatted to end at eleven fifty-five so that CBS News could insert a five-minute newscast. I went to the general manager, Jerome "Tad" Reeves, and convinced him to preempt the program in favor of our own local newscast with Al Primo serving as the anchorman. He reluctantly agreed. It was a wonderful realization of the driving ambition I'd had since the coal mine story.

But sometimes having is much different than wanting. Oddly enough, after several months of this work, I began to feel let down by the routine and was no longer being challenged. I really couldn't believe my emotions after wanting so desperately to become an anchorman, but it was true. The action was all out in the field or in the boardroom, not behind an anchor desk. Having this feeling helped a few months later when the station was able to sell the newscast to a local gas company, which insisted that its own announcer, Carl Ide, be made the anchorman. I put on an act of extreme disappointment but was secretly pleased. I had made my decision. I wanted to keep reporting and eventually move into management.

The steel strikes in Pittsburgh were the opportunity for me to get some national exposure and the chance to get beyond the city for coverage. Bill Burns suggested I to go to Washington during a strike to attend a presidential news conference, once again breaking new ground for a local television station. John Fitzgerald Kennedy held it in the huge state department auditorium. Burns had taught me the importance of being in position at the coal mine story, whether it is to get the money shot or hold the phone so naturally, I made certain I got there really early and stood as close to the podium as possible. It was one of the great thrills of my life when the president of the United States looked me squarely in the eye and pointed at me to ask the next question. Though my heart was desperately trying to escape my chest and my mouth instantly filled with a bale of cotton, I kept my cool.

I asked JFK whether he would intervene in the strike and invoke the Taft-Hartley Act. The first true master of the television news conference, Kennedy responded with great charm without answering the question, but his style was more than enough to satisfy a young reporter from Pittsburgh experiencing Washington DC and a presidential Q&A for the first time in his life.

I returned to Washington some months later for a state department briefing. Secretary of State Dean Rusk conducted an off-the-record analysis of the world situation over a period of two days. He wanted to give newspeople from smaller cities in America exposure to the inner workings of federal government. It was a very effective program, as the style of putting a positive "spin" on things was starting to be the way of life in Washington. Everyone had good things to say. The reporters were sold. This was a different time, before Vietnam, when the media had more trust for the government, more of a good working relationship. JFK had hot and cold running women in the White House and everyone in the media knew it, but in those days, reporters looked the other way. We needed Kennedy as much as he needed us since America was fascinated with the family. Besides, Jacqueline Kennedy was too good of a story in her own right. The schmoozing of the media also seemed to have an unlimited budget. In the evening, we were treated to a cocktail party at State, touring the magnificent facilities that only world leaders were shown. Great

Vice President Richard M. Nixon

treasures in paintings and furniture decorate the quarters. The First Lady was the hostess for this particular event and she was magnificent; Jackie was the embodiment of charm as she easily disarmed the hardest-nosed newsmen. I was close enough to *Camelot* to touch it, which for a kid in his early twenties was an incredible rush.

When VP Richard Nixon came to Pittsburgh, I met him at the Airport. Cameraman Boyle was late, arriving as the motorcade was pulling away. Nixon stopped the caravan and got out of his limousine to give me an interview. I never forgot him for that act of kindness to a young reporter.

While in the Capitol, I observed firsthand what is now known as the "power lunch." The Sans Souci Restaurant was a favorite for Kennedy administration insiders, and I was able to get there early enough to get a table from which to view the likes of humorist Art Buchwald, David Brinkley of the famed Huntley-Brinkley anchor team, and other powerful journalistic figures who made a strong impression on a rookie reporter from Pittsburgh. I discovered that the connection between newsmakers and those covering the news is a very close one, and there is a constant effort by politicians to keep the media on their side.

I've always had a fascination for people, particularly those whose actions affect our lives. We tried to find ways to see them firsthand rather than just talk on the phone, and luckily, Burns always supported story coverage that took us out of town. Once, I was sent to Gettysburg, Pennsylvania, to see the gentleman farmer, former president Dwight David Eisenhower, who had retired to his home there. The farmhouse was pristine and the herds of cattle were Black Angus, mostly presents given to Ike by world leaders who knew he would retire to his beloved homestead. The state Republican Party had a candidate for office who needed some serious campaign help and had asked Ike to endorse him. KDKA-TV sent a cameraman with me to Gettysburg to film the news conference. The former president came out and cheerfully greeted reporters. It was very routine, but you could tell that Ike missed the attention of the news media. I was impressed that President Eisenhower had a complete staff with him and was in good health. I managed to get there early enough to be allowed inside the farmhouse, and the president's butler showed me through the first floor, including the kitchen where he was preparing what he said was Ike's favorite lunch: chopped steak, loaded with minced onions. I was surprised it wasn't something like lobster. Ike was the opposite of JFK in many ways, but most notably in image.

I felt like I was living a dream. Rubbing elbows with presidents and movie stars while doing work that I loved. It was a noble profession, one that could inform and change the world for the better. It wasn't a job; it was a privilege, and one that came with an incredible amount of influence and responsibility. And while the work could sometimes be long and hard, it didn't come close to the backbreaking jobs my father had endured. I felt blessed that I would never have to spend a day digging graves or working in a coal mine.

Instead, I would soon be up to my neck in alligators.

Chapter Five

"I don't know you, Al, but I must tell you I don't have enough money to buy a plane ticket."
—Tom Snyder, 1965

By 1963, the job I loved had been kicking sand in my face for nearly a decade. Perhaps it was because I had started so young or maybe some people always thought of me as the mail boy, but I was continuously passed over for promotions. I'd managed to work my way up through the ranks to assistant news director by doing every possible job in television news. Reporter, anchor, producer, film editor, you name it. So when the position of news director opened up that year, I thought, *They have to give it to me this time.*

They did, but they gave the title and salary to someone else.

I had now been working for Westinghouse for eight years and ridiculously assumed that loyalty meant something to the company. But instead, they hired a newspaperman, Dave Kelly, who'd been a political columnist for the *Pittsburgh Press*. It was bad enough that they didn't hire a guy with television experience, but the news that came with the announcement was almost more than I could bear. General Manager Jerome "Tad" Reeves called me into his office to break the news and nearly broke my spirit. "This man knows absolutely nothing about television," Reeves said. (I wanted to say, "So why did you hire him?" but bit my tongue.) If that wasn't bad enough, his next sentence nearly sent me over the edge.

"And your job is to teach him."

Jerome R. Reeves,
General Manager
KDKA TV

I nearly cried. I clenched my fists as I left the office, my emotions running the gamut. Anger, frustration, sadness. The industry I loved didn't love me back. The GM had all but admitted I was qualified for the job and *still* didn't give it to me. But I was too hooked on the news business to clean out my desk. I swallowed my pride and did my best to lead a veteran journalist through the minefield of broadcasting. Kelly was decent throughout the whole experience and always acknowledged he didn't know a thing about television.

Marie Torre,
Anchor Woman

The next project from GM Reeves was to train a woman who was to become one of the first anchorwomen in America. Her name: Marie Torre changed from her real name Marie Torregrossa. She was a Brooklyn girl who got her first job in journalism by pretending to be a student and asking the editor of the *New York World-Telegram and Sun* for an interview for the school paper. When she got to his office, she confessed she was really looking for a job. He hired her. In 1959, Marie was the TV columnist for the *New York Herald Tribune.* She wrote a story about Judy Garland and quoted a network executive. She was sued and refused to name her source for the story. Marie Torre spent ten days in jail protecting the freedom of speech amendment to the Constitution and became a household name. But now she wanted to be in the industry she was covering. She chose KDKA, and my job was to, in GM Reeves's words, "make her the toast of Pittsburgh." Her journalistic skill was a huge help in teaching her the tools of the trade. Her real name was Marie Torregrossa, an Italian, and she needed help. It worked. Every cameraman gave her his best. We covered hundreds of stories on the street and even worked presidential candidate William Scranton's campaign plane. The Pennsylvania governor was trounced by Barry Goldwater for the Republication nomination. Hours and hours of practice reading on camera got her the anchor spot she desperately wanted. She was teamed with radio anchorman Al McDowell on one of the first morning news shows for which I was the producer. She spent many years at KDKA, truly becoming the toast of the town. She rewarded me once by letting me write a magazine article under her byline for which we got paid a thousand dollars. While Marie was on her way, Dave Kelly was so married to the written word he couldn't fully direct the news operation.

Incredibly, that lack of knowledge on his part led to my break into top management.

Shortly thereafter, the Westinghouse bigwigs came to Pittsburgh, so I was asked to make a presentation that normally would have been the news director's job. Everyone knew Kelly simply didn't know enough about the industry to pull it off, even if I'd written him a script.

Apparently, someone in corporate finally noticed. One week later, Westinghouse called, offering me the news director position at KYW in Cleveland, Ohio. The Mistake by the Lake. Not the most exciting place in the world, but a chance to cut the apron strings. Bill Burns was as sorry to see me go as I was to leave him, but he knew I had to move on if I were ever to move up.

But the news was even better. Westinghouse Broadcasting said the television station would be transferred to Philadelphia in sixty days and I would not have to move to Cleveland permanently. Westinghouse was swapping stations with NBC, trading Cleveland for Philly. That suited me fine because my wife, Rosina, was pregnant with our second child and wasn't up to a major change. The Cleveland gig turned into six months and by the end of February 1965, our baby girl Valerie was born, so the company let us move to Cleveland to be together.

However, there was a catch. (In this business, there always is.) I was dropped into an angry newsroom that had undergone union strikes and held no great love for management. Generally, when you find a station that is heavily unionized it is because the employees have been mistreated in the past. And of course, the staff knew I was only temporary and would soon be heading to a better job in Philadelphia. I called Bill Burns for advice. He told me the only way to win these people over was to act as if my future job in another state didn't exist. So I threw myself into my work and somehow managed to create a team atmosphere. Some of the union rules were quite odd and luckily, I had a secretary who often stopped me before I could commit a violation of the contract and end up with a grievance. On one occasion, the entire staff was out of the newsroom and the phone rang on the assignment editor's desk. I was about to answer it, only to hear "Nooooo!" from my secretary. Incredibly, the news director was not allowed to answer phones in the newsroom. The biggest story in the world could be on the line, but I'd have to get my secretary to take the call before handing me the phone.

My secretary, Louise Tacks, was a mature woman who had been beaten down by the horrible newsroom atmosphere. She dressed like a grandmother, complete with shawls and dowdy dresses that would suit Miss Ellie on *Dallas*. Her desktop was covered with pictures of JFK, Jackie, and the kids. She answered the phone with a lifeless "newsroom" in a tone that surely told the caller she hated her job. I told her to go out, get some new clothes, and jazz things up. And to let callers "hear" her smile. "Answer the phone like you're working for president Kennedy," I said. She started coming in wearing the latest styles and answered the phone with gusto. She was a new woman.

When I left six months later, she wept and thanked me for giving her a new outlook on life. And all I had to do was send her shopping and let her know she was important.

But things weren't that easy for the rest of the news department. Right off the bat, the main anchor, Jim Axel, told me he wanted to leave. He'd been in Cleveland for a few months, he and his wife hated it, and they wanted to move back to Atlanta. I gave him the standard manager's response, telling him that he had a contract and had to honor it. He said, "That's true, I do have a contract." Then he smiled as he dropped a bombshell. "But I never signed it." I couldn't believe the ineptitude of my predecessor. How could you not sign the man who was the main face of the station? Legally he could walk at any time. So now we had the task of finding someone willing to take the main anchor job at a station that would have a completely new management team and be under new ownership in a few months. In the news business, you can't exactly call a temp agency. I worked the phones, contacting other news directors, talent agents, and every contact I had. I was given several names of prospective replacements, but everyone knew about the management swap so there were no takers. I couldn't blame them.

Luckily, a guy named Tom Snyder needed a port in a storm.

Snyder was "on the beach," a television industry euphemism for being out of work. Since he lived in California, he actually *was* sitting around watching the ocean. The man had an incredible reel, showcasing his terrific interviewing style and a tremendous comfort factor on camera. He'd been let go from his reporting job at KTLA in Los Angeles due to a personality conflict and needed a job. The conflict arose because the station owner, Gene Autry (yes, *that* Gene Autry, "the Singing Cowboy") had a wife who simply thought Snyder was too liberal, too arrogant, and kept bugging Autry to "fire that SOB." And just like that, Snyder was out of job.

Our first conversation told me how much he needed one. I called him and asked him to fly to Cleveland to do an audition. I'll never forget his response: "I don't know you, Al, but I feel I must tell you that I don't have enough money to buy a plane ticket."

I sent him a ticket, thrilled that someone so talented would even consider working under these circumstances. It was the perfect symbiotic relationship. Snyder flew in and knocked everyone's socks off with his in-studio audition. Then we took him, a camera crew and a remote truck to the waterfront. Snyder did a series of stand-ups and interviews, never missing a beat. The man was obviously born to be on television and had an excellent track record as a reporter and anchor. I rushed to see the general manager and the program manager to tell them of my find, confident they'd be as excited as I was. But the program manager, Bill Wuerch, was adamant; he did not want to hire Snyder and was not shy about telling GM Fred Walker. I couldn't believe it. Here we were, a station in a state of turmoil with no anchor, an out-of-work guy with loads of talent willing to take the job in a location where no one wanted to live, and these two managers wouldn't pull the trigger. But Snyder would have been my top choice even if he were competing with other applicants. And right now, there was no other option. I was as desperate as Snyder. Finally, I managed to convince Walker to let me hire Snyder. "If this doesn't work, Al, it's your ass," Wuerch said. I swallowed hard, but I had no choice and felt Snyder had star quality. Years later, it seems incredible that two managers desperate for an anchor, any anchor, didn't want Tom Snyder.

Snyder became an instant hit in Cleveland. With that problem solved and the managers off my back, I decided to experiment. For the only time in my life, ratings were not a concern since we'd be trading the station in a few months. And Westinghouse knew I was up against a dominant station in Cleveland to begin with, so the company had little in the way of expectations. It was the perfect opportunity to try new things and take the ones that worked to Philly.

The one thing I hadn't planned was my relationship with Snyder. In just a short time, our families grew close and our professional relationship was terrific. Only problem was, I was going to be moving soon and Snyder was not. When the word came down in June of 1965, it hit both of us hard. Fred Walker called me at home and said, "We leave for Philadelphia on Friday, and we take over the station Saturday at midnight." While I had been anxiously waiting for this day to come, it was bittersweet in regards to Tom Snyder. Then my Catholic guilt got a workout when Snyder told me the bad news that Neal Van Ellis, the only person to ever fire him, had been named program manager of NBC and would be his new superior. "Al," he said, "you've got to find a way to take me with you, or I'm dead here."

Snyder had become my friend, and I owed it to him to try though I really thought the chances were slim. Apparently, Saint Jude, the patron saint of hopeless causes, was listening. Incredibly, a few days later, a bizarre turn of events turned into gold.

On our first day in Philadelphia, the general manager who was being transferred to Cleveland floated an idea. "I know our FCC agreement says we can't take any talent with us. But I was wondering if you'd consider . . . a trade." I'd never heard of such a thing in television news, but I was new at this news director thing. My interest was definitely piqued. The GM had apparently gotten attached to Wally Kinan, the weatherman, who'd become a household name in Philly after many years. Kinan felt the same way about his boss and didn't want to work for Westinghouse; he wanted to stay with NBC and go to Cleveland. So the GM offered to trade Kinan for our weatherman, Dick Goddard, who was just as popular in Cleveland as Kinan was in Philly.

Suddenly I felt like a general manager for a major league baseball team. I'll trade you my weather guy for your weather guy . . .

And a player to be named later.

I knew this was a golden opportunity and I had to maintain a poker face even though I was thrilled at the prospect of getting rid of Kinan. I'd seen his work and didn't care for his schtick. But the Philly GM didn't know that. I said, "Wally Kinnan is a real popular guy here. And much as I love Goddard, he'll be an unknown in Philly. I'm thinking if you're serious about this, then it has to be an even trade."

Jim Leming, Dick Goddard, Vince Leonard—
The short lived anchor team

"So what are you suggesting?" asked the GM.

"Well," I said, "to me, an even trade would be Wally Kinan for Dick Goddard and . . . oh, how about Tom Snyder."

Incredibly, he agreed to the deal.

It was the television news equivalent of the Yankees stealing Babe Ruth from the Red Sox. But in an ironic twist, it was Mrs. Dick Goddard who decided within weeks she had no love for Philadelphia. She wanted to go back home to Cleveland. Dick Goddard resigned in the parking lot of KYW to GM Fred Walker. We quickly picked Bill Kuster from the announcing ranks to become our weatherman. He was an instant success, reporting the weather for 16 years before being lured to Denver where he finished his career.

Chapter Six

Westinghouse Broadcasting selected its top managers to run the Philadelphia operation and most had been promised general manager positions after long years of service. For this important task, however, they were once again asked to put their personal goals aside and come to our new flagship station KYW-TV in their old positions. None of these managers was thrilled at the prospect since most had considerably more television experience than Fred Walker, the radio manager from KDKA, who'd been sent to Cleveland. Westinghouse simply couldn't get anyone else to go to Ohio for a short period of time because of the situation.

Keeping the GM job when Philadelphia cleared the FCC hurdles and restored as a Westinghouse station was Walker's reward. Unfortunately, he had to contend with a business manager, a program manager, and a general sales manager who all thought they deserved the position. It was a management nightmare, like having four head coaches on a football team, each with his own game plan. The office politics went off the scale with so many cooks in the kitchen and I knew it would be hard to fly under the radar that sought me out from all directions.

The staffs from the Cleveland and Philadelphia stations gathered at the Sheraton hotel a few days before the takeover to meet each other and question our counterparts about the operations, contracts, and the basic information about the station. "Yep" and "nope" was about the most we could get from these interviews, as it was a very unhappy group preparing to leave the cosmopolitan City of Brotherly Love for Cleveland, an unfortunate gateway to the Midwest, a city which had polluted its Lake Erie to the point where the Cuyahoga River emptying into the lake actually caught fire. I had been used to working in a helpful atmosphere with Westinghouse, but the NBC people had no reason to assist us. We were literally taking their jobs and sending them off to broadcasting Siberia. My counterpart, Irv Margolis, had begged NBC to give him a position in New York to no avail.

At that time, the news director reported to the program manager who had the ultimate responsibility for the entire "look" of the station. All production people (directors, artists, and creative personnel) reported to the program manager. The news director had editorial control and dealt directly with the general manager but reported to the program manager. Fortunately, the corporate politics of KYW kept the major department heads so busy I was able to operate somewhat independently, thanks to Fred Walker who gave me tremendous support. Unfortunately, my other supervisor wanted nothing to do with me, thought I wasn't qualified for the job, and wasn't shy about letting me know it.

The first time I met Winthrop Baker, the new program manager fresh in from Baltimore by way of Peoria and Boston, was at the bar of the Sheraton Hotel. The new management team was asked to gather there in order to develop a plan for our meetings with the NBC management. Baker, a blue blood who traced his roots back to the mayflower, was puffing on a pipe and looked me over severely through steel-framed glasses as we were introduced.

Winthrop P. Baker,
Program Manager KYW—TV

Here I was, the son of a gravedigger named Al about to talk with a man named Winthrop who was a descendant of Massachusetts's first governor. I sat down feeling like I'd been summoned to the principal's office and began talking rather enthusiastically about the historic change that was about to begin. Baker said nothing so I kept running down my list of ideas. After a while, it became obvious that this man had already made up his mind about me and my concept of a newscast. I felt as though I was talking to a wall.

I eventually ran out of things to say. He kept up his intense stare without speaking while puffing deeply on his pipe. When he finally spoke, he said, "I want you to know I had *nothing* to do with your coming here as news director. You're too young and inexperienced to handle this job. I'm very worried. There's too much at stake." The words just sliced right through me. Somehow, I gathered the courage to respond, "Well, I hope you will give me a chance to show that I can do it."

Baker just shook his head from side to side, puffing what was clearly a silent but emphatic "no no no." I realized that trying to plead my case was pointless until my actions spoke louder than my words. I went back up to my room and literally got into bed, hid under the covers, and took a long, long nap. The stress of that transition was unbearable. I knew the only way to convince Baker I could do the job was to deliver the ratings. Good numbers always gets everyone off your back.

After a few weeks operating the station, executives from Westinghouse headquarters in New York, a little more than an hour away by train, began visiting for various meetings. Walker, an old radio promotion guy, loved it. He was the ultimate host, holding cocktail parties, lunches, and dinners for the brass.

On one occasion, I was unfortunate enough to find myself standing next to Baker at the bar of the Warwick Hotel, crowded with station and corporate people. The national program manager's deputy came up to Baker and made what seemed like a harmless remark about how well he liked a program move. Baker exploded, took his drink, hurled it to the roof, and cursed, "Don't you come in here and tell me what you like and don't like!" The whole room fell dead quiet in an instant as liquor dripped from the ceiling. Walker came over, quickly made a joke to diffuse the situation, and the party went on. Happy that I wasn't the only one on Winthrop Baker's shit list, I nicknamed him the Boomer. The name stuck with him through the years, even as he moved along to become a general manager in Pittsburgh and then the president of television for Westinghouse. I later learned that Baker had actually been a drummer in a band known as the Dukes of Dixieland before breaking into television. Not having any percussion instruments to bang, he simply beat people into the ground.

It was during our strained conversations with NBC executives when I discovered that the entire Philadelphia newsroom, with the exception of copy boys, belonged to the American Federation of Television and Radio Artists (AFTRA). I cringed, remembering the tough union situation in Cleveland. I asked News Director Irv Margolis for the contract and discovered a key phrase in the agreement which stated that AFTRA members could write, report, and perform news stories on air for their base salary and no "talent" fee. It was the silver lining. No, make that gold.

The real reason there were no reporters on television in the fifties and sixties wasn't because there was a lack of talented people. It was that the performers' union required the station to pay an appearance fee if any part of the anatomy appeared on television and a larger fee if the voice was heard. So if a reporter's hand was seen holding a microphone and it was seen on the early news, it cost about $25. If the story was repeated at 11:00 p.m., it cost another $25 and on the morning news the next day, still another $25. TV writer/reporters were paid about $300 a week in the big markets and could double or triple their pay by literally "sticking their noses" into the camera shot. If you're a news director, all those fees could add up in a hurry and all of a sudden you're well over your budget. Consequently, there were no reporters on television. I can remember asking questions as a reporter in Pittsburgh then telling the newsmaker to pause before answering so an editor could cut out my voice.

But in Philadelphia, some smart NBC lawyer had negotiated the clause in the contract, eliminating "talent fees" and that's what jumped off the page when I looked at the contract. The entire newsroom, with the exception of copy boys, belonged to AFTRA. Because the station was owned by a network, the unions had great power. And the last thing you want on your record is union trouble. The slightest grievance filed by a union member, even for doing something as innocent as answering a telephone, can damage a career. Before you know it, you're a marked man.

But in this case, a union rule could actually work in my favor. There was a clause in the AFTRA contract which read, "Any member could write, report and perform news stories on-air as part of their duties without extra compensation." I couldn't believe my eyes. I checked with the corporation's lawyer just to make certain I wasn't reading the contract incorrectly. "Does this say what I think it says?" I asked. Sure enough, said the lawyer. He told me I could legally use anyone I wanted on the air and not have to pay an extra dime. It was the breakthrough I needed to create television's first "beat" system.

But I didn't come up with the idea solely because of a quirk in the contract. It all came about because a Pittsburgh photographer had forgotten an important part of his camera in 1955.

Chapter Seven

The concept of *Eyewitness News* had its seed from a piece we'd done at KDKA in 1955. A story had moved on the Associated Press wire about a Filipino war bride who had been put in jail. She'd allegedly killed her husband who had been physically abusing her. The story was located in Franklin, Pennsylvania, about a hundred miles from Pittsburgh. Chuck Boyle, a true visionary of a cameraman, saw the story the same time I did and he knew it was a lead, something that would now be called a "watercooler" story. Boyle, who spent his weekends going to the movies and studying the craft of great Hollywood cinematographers, also had a pilot's license so the distance wasn't a problem. The man was always looking for a way to fly at the station's expense, and this looked like a natural. We loaded his gear into a rented plane and took off for Franklin through sleet and snow. When we arrived and started to unpack the gear, I saw Boyle's face drop. He'd forgotten the magazine for his Auricon sound camera, which meant we couldn't record the audio portion of any interviews. Still a kid, I was worried I'd get the blame for spending so much money on the trip and not coming back with a story. But Boyle, like most television photographers, knew how to improvise and gave me an assignment. So at nine o'clock at night I tracked down the owner of a hardware store at his home and begged him to sell me a tape recorder. Incredibly, the man trudged down to the store and sold us one.

So now we had audio but no way to sync it to the film. Once again, the wheels were turning in Boyle's mind. He knew it would look like one of those badly dubbed Victor Mature sword and sandal movies so he'd have to shoot the interview of the woman from different angles, keeping the woman's lips out of frame or out of the light.

At the jail, we found a gentle tiny woman who had filled her cell with religious pictures and candles. She was praying for the soul of her dead husband. Boyle used the flickering candles to create an ethereal scene; the audio of the woman's voice augmented the powerful images Boyle captured of the cell and the religious "shrine" she'd built.

But Boyle had little in the way of what is known as "b-roll" or "cover video" to fill in the story so he included me in a few shots. It was another way to avoid the woman's lips. When we returned, Bill Burns found the story so compelling he decided not to edit me out of the story, thereby making me an "eyewitness" for the station. It showed our viewers one of our people was actually there. They knew it was *our* story.

Boyle's piece caused such a public outcry for justice that the case against the woman was dismissed.

For ten years, I'd wondered what would happen if every story had an eyewitness. Thanks to that union contract, I didn't hesitate to find out.

There were nearly twenty people in the news department, all AFTRA members who had signed the contract that would permit them to appear on the air without extra compensation. We took the five people who had what is known in television as "a good face for radio" and made them producers. Everyone else became an instant TV news reporter. And just like that, on the very first day, we had the biggest reporting staff in town. No new hires, no increase in budget at all. They would be eyewitnesses to every story we broadcast. The viewers would see them getting involved and know they actually covered the story. And since I *wanted* them to be seen in every story, I made it a rule that with the exception of funerals, reporters had to appear in every piece that hit the air.

The staff wasn't the only thing getting a face-lift as the current dreary state of the building reflected the mood of the employees. On takeover weekend, we joined a team of workmen busy repainting every office white with blue trim. (AFTRA rules apparently didn't prohibit managers from wielding a paintbrush, moving furniture, or throwing out trash.) We got a few raised eyebrows from the few staffers on duty that weekend. When the station staff came to work on Monday, everything would look new: clean walls, nice carpet, attractive signs, and bright logos, desks rearranged. It was a fresh start for everyone, and I wanted to create an atmosphere that would convey that fact. Even the other department heads got into the act. Dave Henderson, the sales manager, planned to raise the rates for the thirty-second commercial before the eleven o'clock news from $300 to $1,100 on the first day.

On Saturday night, though, we were dog-tired from a day of painting and impersonating a cleanup crew. We gathered in the master control room of what was to be called WRCV for the last time. The cool bank of television monitors flickered in the dark room of the NBC-owned television station in Philadelphia. It was June 19, 1965, a few minutes before midnight. It may as well been New Year's eve on Times Square for me.

The technicians manning the controls were annoyed at the small group of suits that filled the room even though we wore our paint splatters and dirt smudges as blue-collar badges of honor. None of us was surprised at the animosity that permeated the room. At the stroke of midnight, the monitors transmitted the new station ID, designed by artistic genius Ken Philo, while an announcer boomed, "This is KYW-TV, Channel 3, Philadelphia." Champagne flowed while grown men hooted and howled. One of the union engineers blurted, "Get the hell out of the control room." We did, smiling all the way and drunk with a sense of accomplishment.

The takeover was as strategically planned as D-day. Every man in the room was handpicked by Westinghouse to work in the largest station it would own. Fred Walker, in his first job as a TV general manager, incredibly got to choose only two people, both in the promotions department. The rest were from business, sales, and programming at other Westinghouse stations. It was my first real news director's job after working twelve long years at KDKA, Pittsburgh. In my mind, the six months in Cleveland were just part of the training.

Fred E. Walker, General Manager,
KYW—TV Philadelphia

Our first order of business was to put the title *Eyewitness News* on the sign-off and sign-on newscasts. WCAU, the CBS-owned station, actually had the rights to the name but never used it. They had broadcast a prime-time program hosted by Charles Kuralt called *Eyewitness to History* and everyone was worried that it was close enough to cause a problem. Even though WCAU didn't have any locally produced shows containing the word *eyewitness*, our lawyers felt the right to use *Eyewitness News* belonged to them. We were terribly disappointed. I'd been working with station executives in meeting after meeting in Win Baker's office, unsuccessfully trying to come up with another title for the newscasts. *Eyewitness News* was, up to that point, just a promotable title for a news program. But we had to take a shot that WCAU wouldn't care. Walker and Attorney John Steen quietly filed to register and trademark the title in Philadelphia, and we all held our breath for the thirty days we had to legally wait to give anyone a chance to file an objection.

But for some reason, Jack Schneider, WCAU's general manager, never raised a challenge and we reserved the exclusive rights to the name *Eyewitness News*. It didn't seem to hurt Schneider's career. He went on to become the president of CBS and heir apparent to Bill Paley. But like Frank Stanton before him and others after, no one ever succeeded Paley. Years later, Paley screamed at a CBS meeting, "Why the hell don't we have the name *Eyewitness News?*"

The title clearance was a relief and by this time, I was on a first name basis with the lawyers. They were genuinely interested in helping since KYW-TV in Philadelphia was now the biggest station in the group. By the time the name was approved, I was well into organizing the news operation. On that first Monday, an apprehensive news staff arrived, trying in vain to hold back their smiles as they saw the clean, remodeled studio which was also the newsroom. One by one, the staff members came into my office, which was the control room looking over the studio, for their new assignments. While the reporters were thrilled at the prospect of telling their own stories on television, not everyone was happy about the idea. When thirteen people gain face time, somebody's gonna lose it, and you guessed it: the main anchorman wasn't happy. Vince Leonard, real name Homer Venske, came by to quietly say he was absolutely not going to become a "news jockey." He was polite about it but simply refused to introduce reporters with their own stories. Now, normally a longtime anchor drawing a line in the sand can be a big headache for a news director. But Leonard didn't have the hand for this kind of high-stakes poker because of one factor.

I had Tom Snyder waiting in the wings.

Chapter Eight

"A woman will do news over my dead body."
—NBC manager's response to Marciarose Shestack,
who later became a longtime anchor for the KYW-TV.

Though I created the concept of *Eyewitness News*, credit for the name actually belongs to an unknown at WCCO, a radio station in Minneapolis where it originated. The name could only be copyrighted and reserved in each market that it was used, much like any other business. In other words, if you wanted to open a bagel shop across the street from Joe's Bagels, you needed another name for your bakery even if your name happened to be Joe.

When I first heard the name *Eyewitness News*, it fit my idea of a newscast perfectly and was also an incredibly promotable name. The term *branding* was not used at the time, but that's exactly what it became. *Eyewitness News* wasn't just a name but a style, and by bringing both to KYW, we gave the newscast real meaning. We wanted to set it apart from the traditional newscasts that consisted of news anchor, sportscaster, and weatherman (or "weathergirl," as female weathercasters were known at the time). The name *Eyewitness News* would tell the viewer the reporting staff would be on the scene and personally involved in every story. We would ask the questions the viewer wanted to ask. We'd be their eyewitnesses while they were going about their daily lives.

At the very first staff meeting in the newsroom, I tried my best to inspire them. "Up until now when most people looked at the news, they'd see the anchor in a studio sitting there, reading stories to them," I said. "However, when you're on the street and you turn to the side and ask somebody a question, you become a human being. You become someone just like the person you're interviewing and more importantly, you become just like the television viewer. And this will not only add to your reputation, this will support your character and credibility and make you a more popular and effective newsperson. If people can see that you are telling the truth, they will of course believe you." I looked around the room and saw some approving nods.

That first day we had thirteen reporters and four film crews at our disposal, a veritable journalistic army to turn loose on an unsuspecting Philadelphia. But sending a baker's dozen reporters off to find stories every day without any direction would result in a lot of wasted time and energy and many retraced steps, so each one was assigned a "beat." Each reporter was asked what his interests were. One reporter had a lot of contacts in local government, so he became the city hall reporter. Another loved to read about medicine and space exploration; he got the science beat. A union town like Philly demanded a labor reporter, so I assigned that beat as well along with several others. For the first time ever in television, we had a small battalion of specialists covering city hall, transportation, medicine, education, politics, science, entertainment, and for good measure, a special reporter for nearby New Jersey, just minutes over the Delaware River from Philly. My hope was to gain a strong foothold in the New Jersey part of the market largely ignored by all the local stations. This idea was initially met with apprehension from some members of the staff. "People in Philly don't care what happens in Jersey no matter if they are just over the bridge," said Bill Dean, the most senior newsman NBC had left behind. But despite his misgivings, he was loyal and devoted to KYW-TV and willing to give it a shot. He became the executive producer of our news and became sold on the concept that ignoring half the viewers who could pick up our signal wasn't a good idea. Besides, just because people lived in New Jersey didn't mean they worked there; plenty of people commuted to Philadelphia. (I would bring that concept to New York with me since everyone in northern New Jersey and southwestern Connecticut watched New York City affiliates for their news.)

After we handed out the beats, the staff was told they were expected to cultivate sources within those beats and we gave them money to do it. This wasn't checkbook journalism but a few bucks to take people for coffee and get to know them. They were also told this was not a nine-to-five job and were expected to work more than eight hours a day while keeping their eyes open for stories during their time off. Their new responsibilities combined with getting face time on television energized them. The staff charged headlong into the beat system, and as they began to get their own stories on the air, their sense of pride in what they were doing swelled like a tick. They began breaking story after story, making the competing news stations look like they were always running behind.

When we launched the new format, it worked like magic, but we were doing more than just beating the other stations. Our reporters were coming back with news stories days ahead of the competition, sometimes even weeks, because of their daily contact with sources they'd developed on their beats.

We were regularly beating other indirect competitors that didn't show up in a ratings book: the local newspapers. And one of the methods we used was so simple I was surprised no one in television had ever done it.

It all centered on a press release term known as an "embargo." For instance, a company might not want the news of a merger released to the public until 6:00 p.m. on a certain day, so at the top of the press release you'd read, EMBARGOED UNTIL 6:00 PM in bold big letters you couldn't possibly miss. Our reporters saw it as an opportunity to get the story shot, edited, and ready to air before the embargo then broadcast it on our 6:00 p.m. newscast. We weren't breaking any rules since the company had already released the information and asked us as a news organization not to broadcast it until a certain time. This simple tactic helped us stay a day ahead of the newspapers and stuck in their craw. They started attacking us in print, saying we were not responsible journalists and calling us "powder-puff" entertainment. But they couldn't deny the reality that we could get the story on the air faster than they could get it on the newsstands; they lashed out because there was absolutely nothing they could do about it.

KYW-TV began to shine as the news authority in Philadelphia. The editor of the *Philadelphia Bulletin* began to attack us publicly in speeches and in the paper's news columns; proof positive we were making great progress.

The extra benefit to all of this was that the reporters were gaining great confidence, and it was beginning to show on the air. Being on the set gave their stories more importance and provided more face time. And now they were being recognized in public which did two things: it fed their egos a bit and their recognition provided an opening to the public that now approached them with story ideas. Their interaction on set with the anchorman brought a special dimension to the newscast never before seen on television. The warmth and genuine camaraderie was apparent and gave viewers a comfortable newscast to watch. They got in the habit of getting real people involved in the news events. And putting those "real people" on camera in every single story began to pay great dividends. People can tell their own stories much better than reporters writing down their impressions. The material presented on *Eyewitness News* was clearer and much simpler to understand because the people telling the story were mostly average Joes.

Philadelphia had a significant minority population. I wanted to find reporters who mirrored the community. There were few available so I turned to the newspapers. I hired Claude Lewis from the Philadelphia Bulletin, a young black reporter with a fine writing hand. We tried desparately to turn him into a broadcaster and he almost made it but the lure of the written word drew him back to newspapers. He became a nationally syndicated columnist and made a real impact on the world around him. I could find no women reporters so I turned to the legendary talent agent, Shirlee Barrish. Her fee was 25% of the first year's salary but who was counting when the fourth largest market in the country had few, if any, minority reporters. She sent me a radio reporter from Detroit, Trudy Haynes. Her audition was spectacular. I offered her the job at $13,000 a year. Before I could get the figure out of my mouth she said, "I accept." We made her the featured reporter on the 11 PM Eyewitness News. The next time her contract came up, I had to deal with her lawyer, the same guy who represented the infamous Father Divine. He made up for the first year's contract and Trudy was on her way to becoming a very rich woman. And a good reporter. Malcolm Poindexter, an original hire at KYW Newsradio, came to me one day asking for a chance to join the Eyewitness News team. He had the fire and spirit and quickly became one of our most valuable reporters. Another radio reporter who we brought to TV was Dick Stockton as our weekend sports anchor. Stockton is still working NFL Football as one of its biggest stars, 45 years later.

We also needed to create a "family atmosphere" in which (in appearance, at least) the news staff got along. For people who were living away from home or those without any relatives in Philly, like me, we provided a "family" for them—and made them a part.

Even though the plan was in place for the content, that wasn't enough. It would be like putting a diamond ring in a paper bag. The station needed a nice package for its product, with pretty wrapping paper and a colorful big bow.

In other words, bells and whistles.

Not being an artist or a director, I needed a lot of help to make it all come together. *Eyewitness News* needed "a look" that would set it apart from other news programs. Luckily, the station had some serious talent when it came to art and directing.

One of our directors was a skinny guy named Art Fisher, who had taken creativity to a new level when it came to job hunting. He'd been hired in Baltimore by Win Baker after sending him a resume and a ten-page letter containing "one hundred reasons why you should hire me." But Fisher's talent went way beyond writing clever cover letters. The man had some incredible ideas, so he took the concept and ran with it. He brought two major changes to the newscast: lighting and movement. He created an opening in which the studio lights were dimmed just before the newscast began. As the theme music played, he'd bring up the lights. The effect was really dramatic and conveyed a feeling of excitement to the viewer. Fisher's second rule was that cameras should not be stationary. Most newscasts in the fifties could basically survive with an unmanned camera and a single anchor. But with so many people now involved in an *Eyewitness News* newscast, Fisher saw an opportunity to create several different shots. He would move cameras, use pans and zooms, and created an energy that seemed to take the newscast to another level. For instance, the anchor might be introducing a reporter and Fisher would direct the camera and would pull out to include the reporter instead of just punching up a static two-shot. The content was the same, but his use of movement, lighting, and music gave the newscast a sense of urgency and just made it seem more compelling. The camera operators, who could have eaten a sandwich during a newscast under the previous administration, were now part of Art Fisher's thirty-minute aerobic workout. In addition, he used what are now known as "beauty shots" at the end of the newscast. Instead of just rolling credits and music over a static shot of the anchor desk, the viewer might see the anchors and reporters smiling, talking, or joking around. That gave the viewers the feeling that our reporters and anchors were real people even when they were still on the clock. Fisher might also end the newscast with a pretty shot of the city, cute animals, kids playing in the park, or anything that left the viewers with a smile. The man was such a huge creative force that *Eyewitness News* would not have become a success without him. I consider it an incredible stroke of luck that our paths crossed at this critical time in my career.

Advertising Promotion Campaign 1965

Fisher's talents were more suited to Hollywood than the news business, and his work at KYW did not go unnoticed. He eventually headed to California and ended up as the director of the *Sonny and Cher Show*. Once that show ended, producers were beating down his door to hire him. One such producer wanted to impress Fisher, so he picked up Art in a helicopter to take him to lunch. Tragically, Art Fisher was killed when the chopper crashed. I often wonder what incredible breakthroughs he would have come up with had his life not been cut short. Fortunately, his legacy lives on to this day in hundreds of newscasts around the country. We wouldn't have achieved the success without his vision.

The other key player in the creation of our newscast look was a guy named Ken Philo, who was an artistic wizard. Philo, whose main job was the design and graphics of *The Mike Douglas Show*, created the first "working newsroom" in studio B. The front held the anchor desk. So Philo built three levels of desks behind it which made up the newsroom and the background of the set. It was a "big" look. He placed the *Eyewitness News* logo in each corner and rows of the powerful "3" in repeat fashion. That Channel 3 logo has lasted more than forty years.

Eyewitness Newsroom Set on election night, shot from a reverse angle

Philo designed the studio newsroom look and graphics for *Eyewitness News* that set us apart from the other local news programs. Before that, viewers had no idea what a newsroom looked like; for all they knew, it was just another office. But Philo's vision provided them with a room that was a beehive of activity. It was a news revolution to which the audience responded immediately, and it gave Art Fisher a ton of possibilities for camera shots. His camera movements along with the continuous activity in the background made it seem as though newspeople never stopped working even while the newscast was being broadcast. As with the case of Art Fisher, having Ken Philo cross my path was another incredible stroke of luck.

But the buzzards were circling over my head because there were so many of Win Baker's people in the building. Another guy who was also one of his Baltimore connections was a fellow named John Baker, who was made public affairs director. Baker (no relation to Win Baker) was the subject of a hilarious story involving actress Veronica Lake, she of the Alan Ladd movies and peek-a-boo blonde hairstyle that covered one of her spectacular eyes. Win Baker had wanted to jazz up movie nights on his Baltimore station, so he hired Veronica Lake to introduce the movies, usually ones in which she was starring. One night, Miss Lake showed up after hoisting a few at the bar and was teetering back and forth on her heels. She could still speak perfectly but could barely stand. In a move that has become legendary in the annals of Baltimore television, John Baker actually duct taped Veronica Lake to a lamppost so she wouldn't fall over and framed her up so the tape wouldn't show. She read her lines

The Movie Legend Veronica Lake

perfectly and the audience never knew this petite Hollywood star was being supported by ten cents worth of stuff from a hardware store.

John Baker was put in charge of a show called "Philadelphia on Parade." Though one of Win Baker's "boys," he really had no influence on the news department but served as a reminder that Baltimore, and my replacement, was just a short drive away.

Win Baker had been threatening to bring his old news director friend from Baltimore, Mel Bernstein, to "help" me get the programs organized. He'd had me and everyone frightened to death most of the time. But he immediately backed off a bit after the first newscasts hit the air. This allowed him to go back to sharpening his knives and concentrate on the political struggles in the executive corridors, as well as deal with *The Mike Douglas Show* staff, which was rapidly eroding his program empire. He didn't have to worry as much about the news.

Tom Snyder had arrived and had hit the ground running. Vince Leonard was under contract and generating strong ratings so we couldn't give Tom the main anchor job. So we created a brand-new newscast and called it *Eyewitness News at Noon*, figuring a whole bunch of housewives might want a break from their daily soap operas. Snyder's coanchor was a woman named Marciarose Shestack, whose husband was a prominent attorney. His many clients included NBC.

Marciarose was a pioneer as far as women in broadcasting were concerned as she would eventually become one of the first woman in America to anchor an evening newscast in a major market. She'd dipped her toe in the water as a regular panelist on an educational discussion show. She'd moved to Pennsylvania to work on her PhD but was bitten by the broadcasting bug and wondered if there might be other opportunities for her in the news department. So she marched into an NBC manager's office one day in the late 1950s and asked if she might do some work in the news department. She was told, "A woman will do news over my dead body. They are not authority figures and they don't have very good voices."

Well, she obviously hopped over a corpse as she became an instant hit when we did the unthinkable and actually put a female on the news desk for the first time in Philadelphia, just as we did with Marie Torre in Pittsburgh. And by doing so, we actually created a brand-new audience we didn't expect.

Snyder, of course, had no problem with this concept. When he first met Marciarose, he stuck out his hand and said, "Hey, kid! I understand we're going to be working together." As it turned out, they became fast friends and stayed that way for a long time.

Tom Snyder and Marciarose on set of Eyewitness News at Noon

The newscast premiered on August 30, 1965, and it caught on quickly. When the first ratings came in, we were surprised to find out a lot of the viewers were men, shift workers, and we wanted female viewers between eighteen to thirty-four years of age. We'd simply assumed the only people watching would be housewives. So we sat down with Tom and Marciarose and came up with a plan to give the newscast a woman's touch while maintaining the hard news segments at the top of the newscast. Subjects such as fashion, motherhood, children, and health were now part of the newscast, but we didn't automatically hand Marciarose all the women's topics. She and Tom both agreed it would be best to split those and the news of the day right down the middle. Some days she'd handle the Vietnam coverage while Tom might do something on parenting. There were plenty of light moments, and our anchors were not above throwing snowballs at the weatherman during his segment. The ratings grew and we began to attract our target audience—along with some other "viewers."

Some of the stories on the noon newscast were so innovative that the local newspapers began to monitor the broadcast. They'd "borrow" our story ideas and with a 6:00 p.m. deadline, found enough time to knock out a feature in time for the next day's newspaper.

Meanwhile, more good luck arrived via the stork as Marciarose found out she was pregnant. Walker and Baker took her to an expensive lunch, hoping to convince her to let the station promote her pregnancy. She was very receptive, and we decided to let her document her experiences with a weekly series called *KYW Is Having a Baby*. The topics ranged from breast-feeding (not exactly a casual topic for television during this time period) to choosing baby names. Marciarose had found a book of photographs that chronicled the development of a fetus, and she put the pictures to music. This was a big hit with most viewers, but she did get one phone call from a woman who told her, "That was blasphemous! God is going to punish you! God is going to take that baby away from you!" This was naturally very upsetting to Marciarose, so we didn't let her take any more viewer calls during the pregnancy.

But overall, the promotion was a huge success. The ratings went off the charts and brought us more than 50 percent of the audience. We of course wanted her to stay on the air as long as possible. (She remembers one manager telling her, "We'll boil water in the newsroom if we have to.") Since the show had an audience that by this time was predominantly female, the attraction of an expectant mother was irresistible. When she gave birth to her daughter Jennifer the day after Valentine's Day, she was deluged with gifts from viewers.

Tom and Marciarose became household names in eastern Pennsylvania and New Jersey. At one point, we sent them both to Pittsburgh to participate in a panel with my old mentor Bill Burns and other Steel City news icons. As they were going out the door, I yelled, "All right, you guys . . . eat 'em!" Marciarose sweetly replied, "Al, we don't *do* that." (It should also be noted that Marciarose's father told her that her language had deteriorated since she'd joined an all-male newsroom.)

We'd eventually moved Marciarose to evenings, and thanks to an ad-lib, turned her into a football prognosticator. At one point, our sports director was having a horrible time picking winners and one anchor said, "Good God, Marciarose could do better than that." We saw an opportunity to have some fun since she knew absolutely nothing about sports, so she was assigned to make football predictions. She'd make her picks based on things like uniform colors. Years later, she was asked to make a prediction on the Super Bowl and asked, "Who's playing?"

Snyder, meanwhile, had turned into the lead reporter for the six o'clock newscast. We had a running joke in which I'd tell him, "You have two minutes to make Vince Leonard look like *yesterday*." Snyder quickly proved he was head and shoulders above the other reporters in town. And as a bonus, we had someone who could teach our new staff of reporters how to perform on camera. At first, the reporters started doing what they'd always done—writing a list of questions on a clipboard and getting the answers. But now, they weren't giving those answers to the main anchor; they were using them in their own stories. During their first few days, they would stand in front of the camera and read their story from the clipboard. I quickly called a meeting to share the finer points of field reporting, and at one point just threw up my hands and said, "You know what? Just watch Snyder. And do exactly what he does." So I turned the whole meeting over to him since he knew a lot more about reporting than I did. Snyder patiently shared his tips and knowledge and the other reporters soon ditched the training wheels known as clipboards and notes. Tom also served as a friendly bridge between new management and the old staff. The new reporters saw that a guy I'd brought with me was a talented reporter and decent person and began to believe they'd be treated fairly by me. To win these people over, they had to believe I was going to help their careers. The on-camera opportunity convinced them and

Vince Leonard, The single anchorman of WRCV with strong ratings

slowly broke down the wall that had been put up between the union and management. With Snyder's help, they developed the muscle and art of asking the probing questions that resulted in sound bites that jumped off the screen. They also learned to *listen* instead of *waiting to speak* and became adept at the follow-up question. And of course, all of it was captured on camera.

Meanwhile Vince Leonard, the apprehensive anchor, needed to be appeased. Vince had been with the station for twenty years and was not in the mood to change now. So he had to be convinced the new format would not only help the station but take his career to a different level. "People have been watching you look straight into the camera for twenty years, and they've only seen that one dimension of your personality," I said. "I'm going to put reporters on set with you and let the viewers see you in a different light. They will also know that you are in charge, you're the head guy, that all these other people report to you." I'm not sure if Vince totally believed me, but he agreed to give it a shot. He had to know the station wouldn't hesitate to put Snyder in the main chair.

Since KWY-TV Anchorman Vince Leonard had become so established in Philadelphia, we built the program around him, though, to be honest, Tom Snyder was far more talented. (Of course, in fairness to Leonard, it should be noted that Snyder was more talented than just about everyone in the industry.) So we had to create a bigger role for Tom in the six o'clock newscast. I took his slot as "big story reporter" and expanded it a bit further, making him what today has developed into the role of "field anchor." On major stories, Snyder was the principal reporter, but he also might introduce stories by other reporters from the field then toss it back to Vince Leonard in the studio. He also didn't miss a chance at a practical joke. Marciarose remembers him coming back from a zoo story with a canister of film and a box of elephant droppings, which

Tom Snyder's Contact program led to the legendary
Tomorrow Show on NBC.

he quietly placed on someone's desk. And when Tom Snyder finally turned it off for the day, he went home to play with his model trains.

We found another way to get Snyder out in public in a more relaxed situation. Philadelphia was a location where Broadway producers would try out their new plays and were always reluctant to have them reviewed. We decided to send Snyder to these productions not as a reviewer, which he was not, but as a regular guy. He would do a report after the performance and interview people coming out of the theater. It was great television because the audience members really unloaded if the play was a disaster. But one producer, David Merrick, was livid that we were doing this; how dare we let people who weren't card-carrying New York theater critics actually *voice an opinion*! Didn't matter that these were the people who bought the tickets and paid his salary. On the opening night of his play, Merrick got more publicity than he wanted when he actually cut the TV cables on Snyder. Bingo, we had a national story. *Director yells cut! and takes it literally. Film at eleven.*

Tom Snyder was a pioneer when it came to different styles of reporting. He perfected the walking stand-up that would add energy to his reports. Snyder did an outstanding job looking straight into the camera to give his reports without notes and was one of the key people in developing the *Eyewitness News* reporting style that has become the standard in today's journalism. And he was a wonderful mentor to anyone who sought help.

We all felt guilty having such a talented newsman in a secondary role, so Walker and Baker created yet another new venue for him. It became one of America's first telephone talk programs, *Contact*. Snyder was a natural for the show, which was a simple interview program that allowed time for the audience to call in their questions—basically, a radio talk show on television. Viewers especially liked to call in on "gripe day" and just vent while Snyder moderated, and people in Philly love to complain. It became a huge hit and laid the groundwork for his talk show career. *Contact* was the forerunner of hundreds of programs on television today.

Meanwhile, I was also holding frequent one-on-one meetings with every member of the staff, all the way down to the copy boys, to explain the big picture. It made each one feel important and showed them that every member of a newsroom is a key player. It was true that we really needed the help and complete dedication of every single person if *Eyewitness News* was to be a success. Letting these people know we cared about them on a personal level and about their future made them take pride in their work.

We also changed the way we broke for commercials. In the past, the anchor would simply say, "We'll be back with more news." Now, the anchor did more than just tease an upcoming story; we also sneaked in some information using graphics. These little tidbits of information were called data banks. For instance, just before a commercial the anchor would say, "Just ahead, find out why the mayor went on the rampage at city hall," while the viewers saw film of Hizzoner yelling at people. Then we'd cut to a wide shot of the studio and run an informative graphic at the bottom of the screen. It might read, "Polls are open tomorrow from 6:00 a.m. until 9:00 p.m." or "Philadelphia is home to more lawyers than any Pennsylvania city." Little stuff that kept the viewer sticking around a few more seconds and quietly added more information to the newscast. Incredibly, few stations do this anymore. It doesn't cost anything and just makes the newscast more interesting.

Ironically, it was a duty that everyone considered to be a real pain in the neck that helped push me out of the building and get my finger on the pulse of the community. At that time, the company required executives to meet with community organizations. We had to fill out forms about who we talked to, what was discussed—paperwork that would no doubt go into a drawer and never see the light of day again. It turned out to be a good way to both get feedback on our news format and also find out what was really important in Philly besides cheese steaks.

But while things were off to a good start in the news department and I was developing a wonderful relationship with people in other departments like Ken Philo and Art Fisher, dealing with the station's managers was another story. Staff meetings on Tuesdays were such a nightmare that every Monday night my stomach would start to churn until it was tied in a Gordian knot. Fred Walker had to deal with every department head and each had been promised a GM position at his last Westinghouse station. Now they found themselves with their old titles in Philadelphia, they weren't happy about it, and weren't shy about letting anyone who would listen know how they felt.

These days, the news director is always included in department head meetings, but back then I wasn't supposed to be there since the program manager, Win Baker, was the department head for programming and news. Early on, Fred Walker knew that news was the most important program at the station and to his everlasting credit, invited me to every meeting. Much to Baker's dismay.

An atmosphere of tension permeated those Tuesday meetings, which often resembled a courtroom filled with hostile witnesses. Walker would go around the room and ask for reports from various department heads. Each manager grudgingly filled the air with information laced with sarcasm and disdain. Their attitude toward Walker was "Why do I even have to talk to you? I'm supposed to be a GM." Fred Walker was the perfect executive, as he managed these superstars with ease even though when he turned his head or took a phone call from New York headquarters, these grown men would act like immature schoolyard bullies with gestures and disgust. Walker could stroll down the hall and end up with enough cutlery in his back to host a dinner party. While I had Walker in my corner, I still had to keep a wary eye on Win Baker. The man was simply waiting for me to screw up and didn't miss an opportunity to jump on me anytime there was the slightest glitch in a newscast. He still wanted to bring in his own people from Baltimore to run the news department. And he wasn't shy about letting everyone know that as well, especially me.

One of the first things you learn in the news business is be sure to watch every program because the boss is certainly doing so. That might sound like a pretty obvious thing, but many news directors still don't watch their own shows each day. With Win Baker poised to drop a guillotine on my head, I wouldn't dare miss a single minute, much to the displeasure of my wife and kids. And this was well before the invention of VCRs so dinner with my family at six o'clock or going to bed early was out of the question, even on weekends and holidays. One night, Baker called me at eleven fifteen in the middle of the sports segment. Jim Leaming had come to work with a brightly colored sports coat even though we had made a rule that everyone on air was to dress in dark blue blazers. Baker reamed me a new one over the phone. "Who the hell is running the newsroom? You or Jim Leaming? Get in your car and go down there and fire him!" It dawned on me that Baker was using one of broadcasting's oldest ploys: trying to make me so miserable that I'd quit or find another job.

I also figured Baker would be monitoring my every move for at least six months since ratings tend to lag behind for that length of time. You might be hearing good things about your product from the public, getting positive mentions in the print media, but it still takes six months for it to translate into good numbers. Despite the shots from the local newspapers that we were hearing rave reviews about the new format, but it wouldn't matter (at least to Baker) until it actually showed up in a ratings book and translated into dollars from the sales department.

His animosity continued to wear on me and unfortunately resulted in my venting at one of our best people. One night Tom Snyder was substituting for Vince Leonard and he ended the program with "Good night from all of us at *Eyewitness News*." I quickly called him and screamed, "No one can ever close the station down like that!" I made a rule that we always promoted the upcoming show or tomorrow's newscast, but the anchor should never, ever just say, "Good night." Snyder just took it because he didn't want to rock the boat, but years later he said it was something he never forgot. It was a lesson for me as well; take a minute and calm down before you say something you'll regret, especially to someone who is a good employee and a friend. Just because your boss is treating you badly, that's no excuse for you to do the same to your subordinates.

Upon my arrival, KYW was a strong performer, always neck and neck with the CBS affiliate. But our main competition was really one guy: John Facenda, their suave, noble, and highly competent anchor. Facenda, best known nationally as the "Voice of God" for NFL Films, was literally the Walter Cronkite of Philadelphia. (When Chris Berman of ESPN lowers his voice and says, "The frozen tundra of Lambeau Field," he is imitating John Facenda.) Unlike our anchors, Facenda didn't promote other shows and ended his newscasts with "Have a nice night tonight and a good day tomorrow. Good night, all." We all knew there was little hope that Vince Leonard could ever build a dominant lead over Facenda going head to head, but if viewers could simply sample the *Eyewitness News* style, they might give us a shot as a news *team*. The best way to do this was to lure viewers when Facenda wasn't around; namely, the weekends. Few people realize that Sunday has more television viewers than any day of the week. People have the day off, everyone is home with the family, and no one goes out on Sunday night. So we needed someone to grab their attention before heading back to work on Monday. One of our reporters was a ruddy-faced guy from Maine named Joe Harper. He was a solid newsman but very quiet during my first days, often sitting in the back during our staff meetings. I did a little checking into his background and found he'd been married several times and was "hiding out" in Philadelphia from his ex-wives and their lawyers who attached themselves like leeches whenever he'd narrate an NBC feed and make a few extra bucks. Every time the poor guy did something for the network, it actually *cost* him money. No wonder he didn't seem enthused about going on the air. Despite his valid argument to stay in the background, I managed to cajole him into taking the weekend anchor position. That gave me two venues for viewers to sample our product: the weekends and the noon newscast with Snyder and Marciarose.

Harper, ex-wives and bloodsucking attorneys be damned, dove right into his new duties and embraced the new style of reporting. He had enormous credibility and a captivating presence to go along with fabulous writing skills and started to grab viewers on the weekends. While people were creatures of habit Monday through Friday, they were more relaxed on the weekends and Joe Harper created an atmosphere that fit the mood. Hearing good feedback on his newscast, we started using the weekends to promote special stories we were going to do during the week. We were, in effect, now using the "news tease" to bridge one newscast to another. In a short time, Harper's weekend newscasts had charged into the number one position.

Sadly, Joe remained unlucky in love. One of the local "gals" who hung out with the newsies became the new Mrs. Harper. Softhearted Joe married her and took her to Maine. The rugged life didn't suit wife Pat and she managed to get a weekend job at WPIX-TV in New York. NBC, still reeling from the onslaught of *Eyewitness News*, hired her away to anchor its newscast. She dumped Joe and became a huge success in New York. Always innovative, she once dressed like a homeless bag lady and produced a powerful news series *Homeless in New York*. It won her an Emmy and a big new contract.

I'd happily signed Tom Snyder to a new five-year deal when we brought him to Philadelphia so we had a solid backup for Vince Leonard as well as the city's best reporter. But when I went to ABC in New York three years later, that long contract came back to bite me. I was unable to bring him along because the contract was written in stone and there was no legal way for me to get Snyder out of it. By the time he was free of his contract to join me, I had launched the new *Eyewitness News* format and didn't need a main anchor. The ones I had were well on their way to capturing the New York audience. Timing can work both ways when you have talented people in your employ.

Looking back, it is hard to believe the turnaround happened so quickly, but I was blessed with a very talented staff and some incredibly creative people in Philo and Fisher. They all took my basic idea and built it into something I could never have dreamed of.

Eyewitness News became Philadelphia's dominant number one-news program in just eighteen months.

KYW TV Philadelphia, PA
Eyewitness News Team, 1967

Chapter Nine

"What the hell is an elephant doing in the elevator?"
—GM Fred Walker, who discovered one of The Mike Douglas Show's
"guests" in the station's only method of avoiding the stairs.

During the 1960s, viewers of afternoon television discovered the variety talk show. These all but disappeared around 1980 but have made a comeback of late, with shows hosted by people like Ellen DeGeneres bringing back the format. In 1965, KYW was the flagship station of a broadcast called *The Mike Douglas Show*. (If you've ever seen that video of Tiger Woods as a two-year-old playing golf with Bob Hope, that's from *The Douglas Show*.) In any event, Mike Douglas, a singer who served as host, would always have big-name cohost. He would command a huge national audience by 1967. At that time, Douglas had been best known for providing the singing voice of Prince Charming in the 1950 Disney classic, *Cinderella*. Unfortunately for all of us in the news department, his show originated in the same building as *Eyewitness News* and from our point of view, turned the place into a pumpkin on a daily basis.

The Mike Douglas Show was a constant thorn in the side of Fred Walker. He had to supervise the construction of an entire TV theater in the basement of our antiquated building on Walnut Street. The cost overruns, as well as the growing influence of this first of America's talk shows, put a lot of stress on Walker since his background was really in radio. He eventually got tired of the headaches and moved to KPIX in San Francisco, a newly acquired Westinghouse station, but ran into a micromanaging situation with his superiors. The problem there was that the original owners still resided in the building and wanted to continue to run things even though they got a ton of money for selling the place. Walker ultimately went on to Cincinnati to run a TV station there.

The executive producer of the Douglas program, Woody Fraser, and his assistant, Roger Ailes, wielded great influence over the station, much to the dismay of the station's executives. Very often, *The Douglas Show* interrupted the flow of operations. Once there was a baby elephant stuck in the elevator that brought the place to a halt. Fred Walker came into the building, hit the "up" button and got a loud, trumpeted greeting from the smelly pachyderm when the doors opened. Needless to say, most people in the newsroom took the stairs for quite a while.

The news department frequently clashed with Fraser, Ailes, and Jack Reilley. They would book top news makers on *The Douglas Show* and we would send a reporter to do an interview or at least get some film, showing the guest arriving with a lot of excitement from the local media. Barry Goldwater, fresh off his presidential run of 1964, was scheduled to be on the show and we sent a crew to film his arrival and snag an interview. Roger Ailes tried his best to get in the way of the photographer. Since the show was taped and sent via mail from one station to another in a process that was known as "bicycling," it would often be weeks before the entire country had seen the episode. So the producers of *The Douglas Show* would try to keep the news department from running the story. They didn't seem to understand the story was also in the newspapers. Most of the time the news department won these ridiculous battles, thanks to Fred Walker.

After three years at KYW, I was thrilled to be running the number one-news department in town despite elephants in elevators and blue-blooded vultures circling over my head. But I was beginning to wonder if anyone outside Philadelphia had taken notice of our success. It was time to run our ratings up the flagpole and see who might salute. I decided to make a road trip to New York City in the hopes of bringing *Eyewitness News* to the number one market in America. With Fisher and Philo's help, the total package was complete and ready to transplant. Because of KYW's track record in the ratings books, I'd managed to schedule appointments with high-level executives at each of the three big networks.

But I may as well have been the mailroom boy in a powder blue suit all over again. In addition to the rude treatment by Bill Sheehan at ABC, I was blown off by CBS and NBC as well. A corporate suit at CBS asked, "So what would you propose to do with yourself *now*? Be a correspondent?" The question came out like a teacher asking a child what he wanted to be when he grew up. I proudly stated that I had helped turned around KYW, which was, by the way, now beating *his* CBS affiliate in Philadelphia. But not only was the guy ignorant of that fact, he really didn't seem to care. NBC was no different, showing no interest in what I had to offer. Shot down at all three networks, I passed up a taxi and despondently trudged back to Penn Station by way of Times Square.

Along the way, I was struck by the sheer energy of the city, people moving at a fast pace in a determined fashion. There was little eye contact as everyone seemed incredibly focused. I saw the real New York: black, white, Jewish, Italian, Hispanic, Asian, and most of them working class. These people had nothing at all in common with the Ivy League-educated corporate wasps that had deigned to grant an audience to a blue-collar Italian kid from Pennsylvania. And the people reading the news from the teleprompter reflected those in the ivory towers. Pure white bread with the crusts cut off. I wondered, do these people in charge of the networks have any idea what is going on in America? Good newspeople are supposed to have their fingers on the pulse of the audience, but these guys seemed totally out of touch. They were insulated from the turmoil of the late sixties and their products reflected that fact. This was 1968, a watershed year in American history, arguably the apogee of common man and it could be argued, the common woman. This was the time of Vietnam and moon shots when the country was at a turning point. It was the height of the antiwar movement, when the Democratic National Convention would be overrun by radicals and erupt into violence, when Bobby Kennedy and Martin Luther King would be assassinated. But to the network suits, the blood from the American streets or Southeast Asia came from people who lived on the other side of the tracks.

In Philadelphia, I'd seen the results when a newscast was geared toward these people who were the backbone of America and reflected *their* lives. I saw what happened when you transformed a reporter from an invisible off-camera position and turned him into an active participant in the story, making the story seem more real. I knew I was in sync with the world around me. But as I got on the train back to Philly, I thought, *I guess this is it. I'll be in Philadelphia the rest of my life.* It wasn't really a big deal. I liked the city and loved my job. If KYW was the top rung of my personal ladder, that would be fine.

The next day I decided to appreciate what I *did* have instead of thinking about what I *didn't*. I spent some time drinking in the surroundings that made up my office and had become my home away from home. I realized I had a lot to be thankful for because without a lot of fortuitous breaks, I could be a blue-collar guy back in Pittsburgh. It was cool inside the long, narrow control room that had been converted for me. The one lamp on the white-topped modern desk I had managed to commandeer before Mike Douglas could lay his hands on it provided a halo of light in the working area and gave the room a peaceful atmosphere.

A floor-to-ceiling bookcase behind the desk held the freebie reviewer copies of books and the mementos journalists pick up wherever they cover stories. It was pleasant to look at though I never read any of the free books. Awards and plaques were strategically placed on each level to create the subtle message of success, and each one brought a fond memory for me. Once, after a corporate vice president from New York had come to visit, he said of me, "Primo's a good news director because he's got all those great books behind him." I've been meticulous on the subject ever since!

A comfortable low black leather sofa was set against the wall opposite a large glass window. It looked out over the huge KYW radio studio that had been converted into Philo's working television newsroom. I looked down at it with pride, knowing that what we had all created was something special even if it wasn't in New York. The room was an oasis and not a bad place to work if Philly was indeed to be my final stop.

Three months later, I'd all but forgotten my trip to the Big Apple. On this day, I was spending my lunch hour in the office with reporter John Pierron. We were dreaming out loud, as most newspeople outside of New York do, about getting to the networks and seizing the brass ring. In an effort to keep the reporter's spirits up, I shouted, "One of these days, John, that damn phone is going to ring, and it's going to be New York calling because they finally got hip to *Eyewitness News* and we'll be out of here!" I swear that not a minute later the telephone rang. I was so carried away trying to amuse John, I only paid casual attention to the strange-sounding voice on the other end.

The wheezing tones belonged to Richard Beesemyer, the vice president and general manager of WABC-TV in New York. He wanted to know if I would be interested in talking about coming to work for the ABC-owned station in New York City. I knew exactly who Beesemyer was, and I knew he had a lot more clout than Bill Sheehan, whose condescending treatment still bugged me. But I was so shocked at this amazing bit of timing that I joked around in front of John Pierron. "Yes, I'm the news director. That's right, *Eyewitness News*. You're from WABC . . . what's your name again? Dick Beesemyer . . . and you're *who*? The general manager. So how did you hear about me?"

Beesemyer answered my questions because he didn't know I was feigning the recognition of his name. But he quickly got to the point. He had a local newscast with anemic ratings that was being promoted with the bizarre slogan of *Roger Grimsby and the Noisemakers*. He needed a news director and he needed one yesterday. He'd been told that I might be the only person in the country who could put a team together that would turn his newscast around. Finally, someone had noticed, and it was someone who obviously understood the concept.

If you'd turned on WABC-TV in 1968, you would have seen a newscast in several incarnations, all of which could possibly qualify as the worst in New York City broadcasting history. The station had hired an anchor named Roger Grimsby from San Francisco, where he'd built a solid reputation as an anchor, news director, and journalist. As the sole anchor in New York, he took care of the news segments. The "noisemakers" were a collection of contributors who were supposed to add spice to the newscast. New York *Daily News* columnist Jimmy Breslin would do three political pieces each week; Alan did theater reviews and reports on the arts; newspaper columnist Cindy Adams took care of society stuff and gossip; and Howard Cosell nasally crooned a sports commentary, but incredibly didn't bother including scores of local games. At one point before my arrival, WABC had tried an all-female newscast with Cindy Adams and her Hollywood gossip counterpart Rona Barrett. Though I didn't see that one, I can only imagine it was something like having Mary Hart fill in for Ted Koppel. The format thankfully lasted just a few months before dying a grisly death.

I'd watched WABC's latest attempt during my earlier trip to New York and was flabbergasted that it was being presented every night in the number one market in America. Grimsby, a decidedly average-looking guy with a terrific voice, sat on a clumsy, claustrophobic set wearing a brown shirt and black tie. He looked like a character out of a Damon Runyon tale in search of a two-dollar window just before post time.

Beesemyer, who could have sold the proverbial icebox to an Eskimo, had more energy than the newscast and went over the top with his pitch. I repeated his question aloud for John Pierron's benefit and said, "Would I be interested? Well, I'm very happy here in Philadelphia, but sure, I'd be interested in talking about it." For good measure, I added, "But I don't know if ABC has enough money to pay me." I was smiling at John, whose face was filled with amazement by now. Beesemyer sounded like a decent guy and was at least familiar with our success, so I agreed to come to New York for an interview.

Richard Beesemyer
General Manager, WABC-TV 1968

In Dick Beesemyer, I found a likeable very large man with a raspy voice that must have lived in a bar and smoked four packs a day. He talked in what might best be described as a "shouting whisper" and sounded like Burgess Meredith (trainer Mickey from the *Rocky* movies) with laryngitis. He was pure salesman, a bon vivant who ate sixteen-ounce steaks for both lunch and dinner, known around WABC as "the Beeze." But he was also brutally honest about his newscast right off the bat.

"We have an embarrassing news show," he said, shaking his head. Then he told me how important it was that he overhaul the entire concept. "And if I don't fix it, I'm going to be fired. So if it is really true that you're the only guy in the world who can fix it for me, obviously I'd like you to come here ASAP and take charge."

I had rehearsed my own sales pitch, and it had no room for negotiation as I didn't want to go to such a dysfunctional situation without total control.

"There are two things you need to understand about me," I said. "If I come here, I have to have full mandate to do anything I need to do. And if I come here, I will use this format we created in Philadelphia. It's called *Eyewitness News*. But it is very complicated. It is an intricate system of broadcasting that requires team cooperation and more importantly, precise timing and coordination of the on-air people and technicians. There's no room for people who don't understand it or resist it. This means I have to be able to fire people if necessary. If they can't cut it, they have to go and I get to reassign or hire anyone I like."

Beesemyer nodded as he raised his hands in submission. "Fine, you can do that. As long as you work with the unions. And you *have* to work with them."

"Dick, I'm not talking so much about technical people as about talent. Reporters, anchors . . ."

He was taken aback for a moment, but considering the ratings, he really had no choice if he wanted to save his own skin. "Al, let me put it this way. No talent is sacred."

"I'll hold you to that," I said, knowing I had the job if I wanted it.

He got a wicked gleam in his eye and I knew the dreaded salary negotiation was all that remained. Suddenly I found myself in a car dealership talking to a guy who wanted to sell me some undercoating. "So how much are they paying you down there?" he asked.

If I'd told him what I was making, $15,000 at the time, he would have lowballed me. So I threw out a figure. "I'll need $30,000 to be able to move here."

Beesemyer looked as though he'd been slapped in the face. He leaned back in his chair. "Come on, Primo. No news director in this company makes that kind of money."

I shrugged but was determined not to budge. My wife Rosina had made me promise we wouldn't move again unless we earned enough to pay our bills and I'd done a little homework. Living in the New York area wasn't cheap. But for once I was negotiating from a position of advantage. "I'll need thirty, Dick, or I can't even consider it."

"Well, I can't pay you that."

I got up and extended my hand. "Then it has been very nice meeting you."

He got up and shook my hand, but there was little life in his grasp. "Likewise," he mumbled. I turned and headed for the door but not before he tried one last-ditch sales attempt. "You know where to find me."

I could only think of Bill Burns's frustration with me when I'd accepted that seventy-five bucks a week so long ago. I turned and smiled. "You know where to find *me*."

And the game was on.

Once again, nothing happened for a month and I put the meeting out of my mind. Then during the first week of August, Beesemyer called again, begging me to take the job but still not budging on the money. I stood firm. "If you change your mind," he said, "call me back within twenty-four hours."

I said I couldn't call him back because I was on my way to Miami. Westinghouse had assigned me the role of organizing the coverage of the 1968 Republican National Convention for all of its television stations. I was still somewhat dazed by the conversation but absolutely thrilled that Beesemyer was still interested.

In Miami, we got down to the work of covering Richard Nixon's GOP coronation, my conversation with Beesemyer shoved to the back burner. I had a tiny office in the Group W trailer in the rear of the convention hall. I was coordinating the coverage when Beesemyer tracked me down on the phone. "Primo, I'm at the Doral Beach Hotel. There isn't another goddamned room left in this city. Come on over and have a drink at the pool." I told him he'd have to wait until I got all the feeds out for the six o'clock newscast and I had a short break before I had to start on the eleven o'clock newscast. As soon as I got the couriers off to the airport and the crews of reporters and photographers off to their assignments, I hailed a cab and hurried over to the hotel.

It was a typical Florida summer weather, so hot and humid it felt as though you were breathing liquid air. I was bone-tired when I got to the Doral pool. There wasn't a single person there and I assumed I'd arrived early. I collapsed in a deck chair. A few moments later, I heard a swooshing noise and saw an enormous man breaching out of the water. Beesemyer emerged from the pool like a great sea creature.

"Hello, Al. Let's have a drink," he said as he toweled off. The man had the look of a salesman who wanted to close the deal quickly, and he got right down to business. He moved through each motion with great ease. "I really want you to come to New York," he said, wrapping the towel around his waist and sitting down. "I don't think I can get you the money you want, but I can get close."

I shook my head and glanced at my watch as my dinner break was quickly disappearing along with any hope of getting something to eat.

"Look, I have to get back to my feeds. I wish you hadn't brought me here. I already told you I can't do it for anything less." I said I really wanted to come to New York, but I was firm on the money.

He smiled at me. I really didn't think he had any more cards to play, but he had a trump up his sleeve. "You know, Al, I really don't think it's the money so much as maybe you're really *afraid* to come to New York."

This precision arrow struck deep in my soul and I felt my blood pressure spike. I was about to react with anger, but took a deep breath and swallowed it, knowing Beesemyer was merely playing the game most managers play.

"Dick, you're a great salesman. You know how to push all the right buttons. But let me tell you again for the record, this is about money, pure and simple."

He ended our conversation with what by now seemed to be his standard line. "I'll be here for another day. If you change your mind in the next twenty-four hours, call me here."

I gave it right back to him again. "If you change yours, call me." I felt sure Beesemyer would be the one to blink first, and soon, since he was the one whose job was on the line and the November ratings period was just a few months away. I was in no hurry at all, and New York would still be there next year.

There was a break in the convention the next day and I *knew* he'd call, so I never moved from my telephone. It didn't ring. I couldn't believe the game of chicken we were playing but figured it was all part of the dance. I headed back to Philly wondering what it took to crack the New York market without getting shortchanged in the salary department.

About a week after the convention, Beesemyer called me again in Philadelphia. "Primo, get up here right away. I really want you to meet some people," he said.

I got a grip on myself and refused, giving him a compliment that I couldn't make it through another session of cat and mouse. "Dick, I just can't come up there and be *salesmaned* to death. You're going to make me do something I don't want to do."

"Come up here tomorrow," he commanded. Then he added with a note of exasperation, "I think we got a shot at the money. Come on up. You just need to meet two people and if they like you, you get the deal."

I was so naive that I thought it would be faster to fly to New York rather than take the train. The only value that came from that decision was the opportunity to be exposed to the phenomenon known as the New York cab driver. He seemed to sense I was from out of town and on my way to a job interview. The grizzled cabbie didn't beat around the bush. "Most guys in New York are phonies and you can make it in this town even if you have this much talent," he said, holding his thumb to the top of his little finger. "New York is no big deal," he said. "Everybody's equal, rich, poor, Rockefeller-rich. We're all the same here. No big deal."

I could feel the excitement of the city again and thought it was the most important place in the world. I arrived at the Sheraton Hotel in enough time to watch the early newscasts, and the disaster that WABC broadcast sent me straight to the hotel bar.

The next day, my meeting with Beesemyer went smoothly but the real purpose of the visit was to meet his boss, Ted Shaker, the president of ABC's owned television stations division. Shaker was also Group VP for ABC, the third most senior executive after Leonard K. Goldenson and Simon Siegal, who had run the company from its earliest days.

Beesemyer looked as though his clothes were filled with itching powder during our ride up in the elevator, quite a contrast to the smooth-talking TV executive I had been exposed to earlier. It reminded me that everybody has a boss. He kept cautioning me not to smoke my pipe because Shaker disliked smoke. I got the message and put the pipe in my pocket. When I was escorted inside, Shaker sized me up, smiling and circling me like a shark as he seated me at his sofa across the room from his desk which had absolutely nothing on it but polish. He asked if he might get me a drink. I politely declined. He seemed disappointed and insisted I have something. I realized he wanted to demonstrate the perks of his office, so I accepted a Coke.

The interview that followed centered around Shaker's question, "Why would you want to leave a successful operation in Philadelphia which has such a great reputation for news to run a disaster of a newscast? Why would you want to do that?"

"Well," I said. "I think there's a great opportunity here. You're ABC. This is a network and Westinghouse is simply a group of stations. I think I can make a change and help the station."

"Fine," he said. "But let's get one thing straight. This is the flagship station of the American Broadcasting Company and we cannot tolerate any more bad newscasts. Our image is such that we are the laughingstock of this city."

His attitude of corporate authority, combined with a cunning smile, should have frightened me to death, but I responded with the vigor of youth and enjoyed the exchange. I told him I felt I could transform the show in the same way we'd taken KYW to the top, that New York City was the perfect locale for this style of newscast. I also took full advantage of the opportunity to get a commitment from ABC to have complete authority to make whatever changes in channel 7's news operation I thought necessary, particularly after watching the previous night's newscast. I stressed the fact that the on-air talent would have to change. The answer was "You can do anything you want to get the news show moving. Leonard says he can't bear to walk down the street anymore." Apparently, Goldenson's country club buddies thought his newscast was a joke.

Next up, the top dog. When Beesemyer took me to meet the head of the ABC network, I found that Ted Shaker wasn't kidding.

"I don't know you, Mr. Primo," said Goldenson. "But all I can say is that I cannot be embarrassed a day longer with the local news on channel 7. I want to be able to walk down Sixth Avenue to the 21 Club for lunch without hiding my face. You don't have to be number one. You just . . ." His voice trailed off and he looked out the window at the Manhattan skyline at the city he desperately wanted to own. "I cannot suffer this humiliation any longer."

"I'll give you a program you can be proud of," I said. Goldenson looked back at me, nodded, and smiled.

It was apparent that Shaker had been putting great pressure on Beesemyer to get the New York station in shape because he felt it was eroding his own strength with Goldenson and Siegel. There was a look of relief on Beesemyer's face when we left the office, and the news director's job was mine. "When can you start?" he asked.

Westinghouse had also assigned me to coordinate coverage of the Democratic National Convention in Chicago in August. I told him I couldn't bail on the company until after that, so we settled on Labor Day as a starting point.

When I got back to Philadelphia, I went to KYW-TV General Manager Ken MacDonald, who had taken over for Fred Walker, and informed him of my decision to leave. Westinghouse did not take this sort of thing well, especially after the success of *Eyewitness News*.

"You just sit right there in that chair and don't you move!" said McDonald. Then he yelled to his secretary. "Get me Jim Allen on the phone, right now!"

Ken then talked to Allen, his boss in New York, while I sat glued to the chair. He put the call on the speakerphone.

"Jim, Primo is in my office and he told me he's been offered a job at ABC in New York. He's accepted the job and I will not accept his resignation."

Then the disembodied voice strapped me to the chair with duct tape. "Al," said Jim Allen. "You stay right in that chair and don't you move! I'm taking the next train down and I'll be down there in an hour and a half."

I politely said, "Jim, save yourself the trip. I've accepted the job. The ship has already sailed."

But I wasn't getting through. "Look, Al," said Allen. "You've been a Westinghouse employee for fifteen years. You're our main guy."

MacDonald always had the corporate acumen to handle situations like these in a way that would not come back to haunt him. Allen was the executive who liked the bookcase in my office and had given me great authority to develop the *Eyewitness News* format. I kept telling him it was too late, the money was too good, and it was the opportunity to move up the ladder in news, which was impossible at Westinghouse. But he still wanted a shot and was coming to Philly.

When he arrived, he walked into my office, sat down, and said, "You are the news director of the flagship station of the Westinghouse Broadcasting Company. We've got a lot of great plans for you in this company."

As is often the case in broadcasting, you're never really considered valuable until you threaten to leave. I had been with Westinghouse forever, fifteen years being an eternity in broadcasting, and I'd really been taken for granted.

"Jim," I said. "You've had a chance to make me vice president of News or put me in charge of all the Westinghouse stations. Instead, you gave the job to Jim Snyder, someone who worked in radio and has no television background. So from my point of view, you haven't really demonstrated anything. And second of all, you are paying me fifteen thousand a year and New York is going to pay me thirty."

Allen sighed and shook his head. "Well, goddamn it, I can't compete with that. I wish you luck."

You would think that would be the end of it, but I would get one more scary phone call before heading to New York.

While I was at the Democratic Convention, I got a call from Dick Beesemyer in my hotel room.

"Al, you're in good health, aren't you?" he asked.

"Yeah, why?"

"Al, there was one thing I forgot to tell you. You've got to pass a company physical before we can hire you."

The color drained from my face in an instant. "Dick, I've already resigned my job! I've quit! I'm coming!"

"Look, I'm gonna set you up with a doctor in Chicago. Don't worry about it. He's great, he passes everybody."

Considering the shape Beesemyer was in, I believed him. Still, I wondered, what if I have a heart murmur or something weird shows up on the physical?

So the next day I went to this doctor's office. The guy gave me the fastest physical in the history of medicine. When he said, "Breathe out" and told me I was okay, it was the biggest exhale of my life. He signed the papers, and I was off to New York.

And so I had to leave the scene of my greatest success behind.

As for the rest of the knife-wielding GM wannabes at KYW, well, eventually they all got their wishes and left with Philly in the rearview mirror as well. Win Baker got to be the GM of KDKA in Pittsburgh and subsequently president of television. David Henderson, the sales chief who raised the rates for a thirty-second news spot by nearly a thousand dollars on the first day, got to be president of Westinghouse Programming in charge of the Mike Douglas and Merv Griffin shows.

Tom Snyder, apparently not terribly fond of my replacement, Tom Bryson, actually dumped a plate of spaghetti on the new news director's head during an argument. Mr. Bryson was the first in a long line of executives hired by KYW-TV to fix something that wasn't broken. Tom eventually went to Los Angeles where his star shone brightly enough that he was given *The Tomorrow Show*. Tom Bryson lived to become the General Manager of the ABC station in Flint Michigan.

Roger Ailes, the kid producer with Mike Douglas, became his executive producer and a huge force in television. He became President Richard Nixon's trusted TV adviser and ran the campaigns of presidents and the leading Republicans in America. His first work was taking advantage of his political clout to make corporate videos for big American companies. Then he got lucky again. He was asked by Ed McLaughlin, the former president of ABC Radio, for help. McLaughlin had found a radio announcer by the name of Rush Limbaugh and helped build him into a powerful force on talk radio. He thought he'd be a natural on television. Rush desperately wanted to be a TV star. Ailes produced the conservative radio/TV personality's show, but the show flopped. Ailes was then hired by NBC to be president of CNBC, the new cable enterprise being started by General Electric. I like to think he took all the experience of his past and borrowed generously from *Eyewitness News* to create what has now become the leading financial news network. Then Rupert Murdoch decided he wanted to get into the cable news business and lured Ailes into becoming president of Fox News, which has successfully challenged CNN in the cable news field. Ailes figured out a conservative approach would find a big audience in the red states, and the Fox News approach became very popular with Republicans. His last published salary from FOX: 20 million.

And I was off to New York.

It would turn out to be an even bigger challenge than Philadelphia.

Chapter Ten

"We call this the snake pit. It's all yours! I gotta go!"
—WABC Production Manager Gordon Kuntze
upon bringing me to the newsroom for the first time

In the late sixties, ABC was called the Almost Broadcasting Company because the network truly had no commitment to news either on a network or local level. In New York, WCBS-TV, WNBC-TV, and even the independent stations had solid ratings for their newscasts while *Roger Grimsby and the Noisemakers* was barely registering a pulse in the Nielsen books. Cable didn't exist at this time, and New Yorkers only had a choice of six commercial stations; incredibly, with such limited offerings, no one was watching. Looking back at the product, that was probably a good thing.

Though the situation seemed hopeless, I never doubted for a second that it could be turned around. The *Eyewitness News* concept had worked in Philadelphia so it should prove successful in New York. And there was nowhere to go but up as far as the ratings were concerned.

Throughout the interview process, my only exposure to ABC had been my visit to the main corporate office at 1330 Avenue of the Americas, which all real New Yorkers still refer to as Sixth Avenue. The headquarters of the three major networks stood nearly side by side then on what was called Broadcast Row: NBC at 30 Rock, part of the spectacular Rockefeller Plaza which featured Radio City Music Hall—an ice-skating rink frequented by the Kennedy clan—and a giant Christmas tree; CBS, referred to as "Black Rock" for either its unique black granite facing or the film *Bad Day at Black Rock* in which everyone is trying to kill Spencer Tracy (your personal opinion of the nickname's origin depended on whether or not someone was gunning for your job); and ABC, either known as Little Rock, a nondescript high-rise named for ABC's then diminutive status among the Big Three, or Hard Rock, for WABC, its powerhouse top forty AM "Musicradio" station that featured Cousin Brucie, rockin' and rollin' inside.

At that level, no matter which one you worked for, you were literally between a rock and a hard place. Stress went to a different level in New York as the stakes could not be higher.

On my first day at work, I bounded into Dick Beesemyer's office ready to hit the ground running. I found him waiting with Gordon Kuntze, WABC-TV's production manager. Beesemyer was under so much pressure at that time his face was permanently crimson, but he at least looked relieved to see me. His voice was always hoarse, and he croaked that he had meetings that morning but that Kuntze would be happy to take me up to the newsroom. I later discovered why "the Beeze" didn't want to be around when I saw the hand I'd been dealt as it literally included a deck of cards.

It turned out the newsroom was located nearly a mile away on the West Side, on Columbus Avenue just north of Lincoln Center on Sixty-sixth Street. Kuntze, my tour guide, was tall and lanky, a grown-up Tom Sawyer who was now a typical New Yorker and he seemed amused for some unknown reason as we taxied up to the production center. I assumed that he, like Dick Beesemyer, was eager to see me turn things around and was simply in a good mood. He knew I had been to the network but had never seen the local station. I didn't think there was anything out of the ordinary as the cab pulled up to my new home away from home.

Kuntze hopped out of the cab like a teenager going to a prom. He gleefully led me into the first floor newsroom where Don Dunphy Jr., an assistant to the news director, was waiting for me, along with secretaries Carrie Van Zile and Gail Fluer.

Kuntze announced, "Here's the new news director!" and introduced me to this rather nervous group that was no doubt wondering if I'd start lopping off heads. I shook their hands and smiled, trying to act as casual as possible to diffuse some of the tension. Kuntze then took me on a minitour of the newsroom and my jaw hit the floor.

It looked like a teenager's bedroom to the tenth power. The clutter was incredible: towering piles of old newspapers were stacked on the corners of desks and on the floor, film canisters, piles of press releases, books, and magazines littered every piece of furniture. Typewriters (if you could see them) were buried under piles of junk. If you wanted to sit down, you had to clear off a chair. If you wanted to work, you had to shift things off a desk. The areas of the carpet that were actually visible were stained and filthy. I was shocked, just as Kuntze knew I would be. And if there had been a game show host in the room, he would have, at this point, yelled, "But wait! There's more!"

Realizing a total cleaning and remodeling job was going to be a top priority, I decided to move on to the studio. I figured it couldn't possibly be in any worse shape than the newsroom. I asked where it was, and Kuntze responded with a smile.

"Oh, that's down the street in another building." I thought, *You gotta be kidding me. It's not even in the same building? This is insane!*

But wait, there's more . . .

"What about master control?" I asked, wondering what was behind door number three.

Kuntze looked as though he were trying not to laugh, biting his lip before he answered. "Oh, that's down in the basement in the operations section behind the parking garage."

It was a logistical nightmare that even an army of couriers couldn't fix. I wondered how in the hell this news staff ever got anything on the air quickly, running film from building to building while shuttling anchors across midtown Manhattan. The answer was—they didn't bother to try.

Kuntze then put the cherry on top of this sundae from hell as he wrapped up his part of my tour. "We call this the snake pit," he said, looking across the newsroom. "It's all yours! I gotta go!" He slapped me on the shoulder, turned, and briskly walked out of the room. I shuffled into my office, collapsed in the chair, and just stared at the ceiling for the longest time.

Don Dunphy Jr., son of the famous fight announcer, was the first to peek into the room. "We're sure glad to see you," he said, obviously knowing that after my look at the newsroom it was his turn to lighten the mood. The

Don Dunphy, Jr. an assistant to the News Director who became The Assistant News Director and ABC News VP.

rest of the welcome wagon committee arrived, as Carrie followed right behind Dunphy, thoughtfully bearing a fresh, hot cup of coffee (though at this point I could have used something stronger). Dunphy sat down and I started by asking for all of the contracts, schedules, and a complete list of the staff members. Once he delivered all the paperwork, I began to immerse myself into the operation of the news department. Carrie took her place on the sofa next to a telephone, which was equipped with a listening device. I thought this was kind of strange, but I quickly found out the reason the secretary thought her workstation was on the couch.

ABC had second phones in every manager's office, apparently to allow secretaries to listen in and take notes. I noticed that Carrie seemed to like camping out on the sofa, answering calls and conducting her secretarial business from this position instead of her desk. Now, I may be quirky, but my office is my private space unless I choose to share it. Carrie's constant presence quickly got on my nerves, and I finally had to tell her that I preferred she sit at her desk just outside the office door.

Incredibly, it had only taken seven years for the news department to fall into its current state. ABC had waited until 1961 to start a local newscast in New York City. David Shefrin was recruited from CBS to be the station's first news director. He quickly assembled the anchor team of Bill Beutel from CBS Radio and Jim Burns. Rosemary Haley was the attractive "weathergirl," and Howard Cosell was brought over from radio to take care of sports.

"Early newscasts at ABC TV,
New York" Circa at 1963

That was basically the news department, a skeleton crew assigned to cover the biggest city in America. There was no eleven o'clock newscast, no film crew, and only one producer, Madeline Amgott, who had worked in the same capacity on the CBS news magazine, *Calendar* with Harry Reasoner, and Mary Fickett. She was very proud of being one of the first females in local news.

Amgott liked to tell stories of how ABC threw nickels around like New York City manhole covers in those early days. Her favorite story illustrated how little upper management knew about the inner workings of television. General Manager Joe Stampler had brought her to the studio and asked why the station needed two cameras when only one anchor was seen at a time. (Art Fisher is probably turning over in his grave at that one.)

After launching the newscast, management finally realized it would be nice to actually have reporters who could cover news stories. But when they actually got around to hiring a film camera crew, they forgot one small detail: they had made no provision to pick up the stories from the field. It would be ridiculous to have your only crew run back and forth to the station while dealing with New York City traffic, so film was initially sent back to the station by taxi. But that proved too costly. They decided to try a time-honored Big Apple tradition and use a messenger, so a film courier was hired. But instead of buying the poor guy a bicycle, which in those days probably cost twenty bucks, management made him take a city bus for *fifty cents* to meet the camera crews then another bus to get back to the station. Once, when a vehicle fell into the river and tied up traffic, WABC could not get its lead story on the air. The courier was stuck on a gridlocked bus.

It was no mystery why the station was still stuck in last place seven years later.

Amgott told me the whole operation was a disaster from top to bottom. News Director Shefrin went to her in 1963 and told her the top brass needed to fire someone, and he preferred that it would be her. Cosell, meanwhile, was said to walk through the newsroom snarling, yelling that everyone was incompetent, that he knew members of the board, and that the entire staff would all soon be fired. He was right. Shefrin got the ax in 1966, replaced by another ABC Radio veteran, Ed Silverman. He lasted just over a year until I came along. But he left quite a tradition as his legacy.

The first of many land mines I stepped on that morning exploded when I learned that my predecessor, a slick broadcaster with a pencil-thin mustache, and senior producer Larry Goodman, both inveterate gamblers, actually held a card game in the newsroom every day. These were high-stakes affairs, and our star anchorman Roger Grimsby was among the regulars in this green eyeshade club. The poker game would go on throughout the afternoon, up until an hour before the newscast. I couldn't believe it! Was it any wonder the on-air product looked so terrible? I tried to imagine newspeople who had actually made it to the number one market in America playing seven-card stud during what is known in the news business as "crunch time."

I'll raise you ten. It's twenty to you, Roger.
Hold my place, I gotta go anchor the six.

So my first official memo to the staff did not concern journalism, unions, budgetary items, or the name of the new newscast. The message was, of all things, that gambling on the premises was prohibited and that anyone participating in such activity would do so at the risk of his or her job.

But wait, there was more . . .

I had Don gather the staff together for our very first meeting that afternoon. By the time everyone was assembled, I had managed to gain enough composure to face this tough crowd of New York newsies, though I had to climb up on a desk to see everyone over the clutter and partitions. I began with a polite "pleased-to-be-here" speech that quickly escalated into an attack on gambling and sloppiness. Then I segued into what I thought

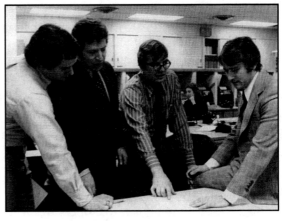

from L to R, Don Dunphy, Assistant News Director, Al Ittleson, Executive Producer, Steve Skinner, Producer 6 PM Eyewitness News

was a major problem with the news operation, a lack of self-esteem and initiative.

I needed to appeal to their pride as I was sure there were plenty of good people who had just been caught up in this vortex of negativity. According to Dunphy, morale wasn't a problem and neither was talent, but ABC's third-place standing among the networks bothered many of its proud employees. They had produced many award-winning documentaries in the past few years, but these fell into the "tree falls in the forest category" since no one was watching. I told the staff that if any of them felt unable to compete and work harder than they ever had before in their professional lives, they had an open invitation to my office where I promised I would help them find another job, someplace else. But I added that I wanted all of them to stay, and if they gave the new format a chance, they were in for the ride of their lives. I emphasized that we would be out of the ratings basement in no time if people simply worked hard and stuck to the plan.

I'd written a short memo about the basic concept of *Eyewitness News*, but I wanted to give them more details in person.

"People tell their own stories better than you can," I said. I told them how reporters were going to be involved in their stories, along with the average New Yorker. How it was possible to use this concept to transform their lives and make an unwatched newscast into the most powerful local station in the country. How we'd done *exactly the same thing* in Philadelphia and it had worked. How it had quickly become the top-rated newscast in the market. I began to see eyes brighten and a few smiles to go along with some approving nods. I told them they shouldn't be intimidated by the people at the NBC and CBS affiliates because they were just as talented. I told them that despite the reassurances they'd been hearing from upper management that things would remain the same, in reality, everything was going to change. I knew some people in the news department would resist or be unable to conform and they'd have to be left behind. But I sensed a spark of hope in the room, and I finished up my little talk with a strong message that it is possible for a group of dedicated, determined men and women to turn things around completely as long as they put their hearts and souls into it.

I returned to my office and called Dick Beesemyer at his downtown office. He was waiting for the call. He knew I would be in shock, and I took advantage of his guilt to get some immediate help. The "honeymoon period" was going to be a very real thing in this circumstance since Beesemyer's head was squarely on the chopping block and the executioner was nearby sharpening his blade. I knew I'd have carte blanche for a while with Dick so I told him the first step would cost money. We had to improve the work environment immediately and bury the "snake pit" as a bad memory. He agreed that I could spend what I deemed necessary to spruce up the place, and I was happy to learn we had a "building department" at WABC. I immediately called the supervisor and told him I wanted his staff to paint the place white, rip out the filthy partitions, and install new carpet. And I wanted everything done in three days. It wasn't a problem. Painters quickly arrived and slapped a fresh coat of white on the walls. New blue carpeting was laid down, and I had carpenters build cubicles around reporters' desks to give them quieter places to work. The staff had cleaned their personal work areas, filed what was useful, and thrown out all the junk. When the remodeling was complete, I wanted them to feel as though they were working at a completely new station. I have discovered that when you go to extra lengths to polish up the working environment and make a place appear more professional, it's a great morale booster and motivates people to start moving in the right direction. The clean new newsroom not only brightened up the building but the staff's outlook as well. They seemed to know we were turning the page and not looking back.

Since the painters were already here, I had them paint the studio white as well. But that wouldn't solve my main problem: space. The studio was relatively narrow but very long, and I needed a way to make it look bigger. I kept walking around the room, remembering all that I'd learned from Art Fisher and tried to apply his lessons to the current situation. I realized the only option to create the illusion of a huge studio was to place a camera outside the door and use a rolling long shot of the studio and reporters. A technical crew set it up and sure enough, it worked.

Back in my office, I stepped on another land mine in the form of a ratings book. The numbers for *Roger Grimsby and the Noisemakers* had, incredibly, slipped below a "1" rating. It was unheard of at a network affiliate, especially one in a market with more than ten million viewers.

No one was watching. The numbers were, as one of my future secretaries was fond of saying, "lower than whale shit."

Yet, incredibly, WABC had contracted with an advertising agency to "promote" this product. And there was an in-house promotions department as well. My eyes grew wide and my jaw dropped as I saw what had been spent on the project. I could have hired Walter Cronkite for that kind of money.

I called the promotions manager and asked him to come to my office. When he arrived, I told him to pull all the advertising for the current newscast.

He looked at me as though I had two heads. "But you can't do that. We've paid an enormous amount of money for these spots. We've just spent two hundred thousand dollars making these spots, buying billboards . . ."

It didn't matter. The *spots* (another term for *commercials*) were reinforcing the lack of credibility and the current newscast format and name would soon be dead. We needed to stop the hemorrhaging as quickly as possible and stop reminding people that *Noisemakers* even existed. "Take them off now," I said. "I don't want to see another spot. I want no promotion because we don't have anything to promote. We can't even call this a newscast. And if I see a spot hit the air, you're unfortunately going to have to answer for it."

He grudgingly nodded. "Fine, I'll pull the spots, but I can't tell the advertising execs at the agency. You're going to have to do that."

"No problem," I said, actually dying to meet the people who had come with such a bizarre advertising concept. "Let's get them on the phone."

The promotions manager called the ad agency and broke the bad news. In a very short time, the account manager and his two assistants came rushing into my office in a frenzy.

"These ads are over," I said. "They're done. I don't mean to offend anyone, and please don't take this personally, but this is the worst advertising campaign I've seen in my life." I nodded toward the promotions manager. "And it's being pulled off the air as we speak."

The agency people groveled, trying to save their big account. (Advertising agencies generally receive a 15 percent commission for ads they place, so for every $100,000 worth of ads they purchase, they pocket a cool $15,000.) They explained their "strategy" and even asked for input from me. But paying a huge amount of money to promote a newscast that didn't even register in the ratings book simply was simply throwing funds down a black hole. "What we really need to do is establish our credibility," I said. "Nobody believes we're a journalistic organization. No one will watch us because you have to trust the people you're watching and you've turned this into a circus, a clown show. So you cannot expect viewers to come to this circus we've been putting on every night at six and eleven. We've got to do credible news. So I don't want any advertising because we're not credible. We don't even have our organization in place. I don't want anybody watching us until we're ready. I'm sorry, but our business with your agency is *over*. Good-bye and good luck."

The advertising people turned and looked at the promotions manager as if to say, *Who the hell is this guy and what is he doing? Who does he think he is?* They finally left. Four hours into my new job, heads were already rolling, though none of them were in the news department.

But I'd made a statement, at least with the promotion guy who now knew he was working for me. In any leadership position, you almost have to seize power right off the bat.

I hadn't told Dick Beesemyer of my plan since I knew this action would send shock waves around the building and a few tremors among the higher-ups at Fifty-third Street. I was also using the old "forgiveness versus permission" concept. If I'd asked permission to fire the ad agency, it might have taken weeks or even months to get a decision, and the agency might have been some VP's untouchable sacred cow. With forgiveness, you just take your shot and wait for the fallout, then ask for dispensation if necessary. (It's actually a lot like going to confession, but you do the praying beforehand.) I wanted to test the waters right away to see if anyone was going to interfere. I held my breath for a few hours, but the phone never rang. No one ever called or said anything about the subject.

Because they knew what I knew.

It couldn't get any worse.

It reminded me of the days when Ralph Kiner played for my beloved Pittsburgh Pirates. This story came to me from my wife, Rosina, who was the team doctor's nurse and worked every night the Pirates played at Forbes Field. The future Hall of Famer was the only star of a perennial last place team. After one particularly good year, Kiner asked for a raise and instead was traded after a long salary dispute. General Manager Branch Rickey told him, "We finished last with you. We can finish last without you."

I felt the same way about the ad agency.

Knowing the amount of time it takes to create the production elements for a new look and set, I made it a priority to meet with artists and design people as soon as possible. I'd seen how valuable Ken Philo and Art Fisher had been in Philly, and I hoped WABC had people of similar talent and vision because I couldn't be successful without a lot of help. The name and the style of the newscast were already set. Now I needed a signature logo. ABC's art director was Jack Guest.

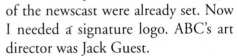

The *Eyewitness News* logo was actually designed on a paper napkin in a bar across the street from the station known as Chips. It was the favorite watering hole of the news staff and where Grimsby climbed into his liquid spacesuit before each newscast (though I'm not sure if this occurred before or after the poker game). In the interest of speed, we kept everything as simple as possible by ordering a repeat pattern of the title with News, Weather, and Sports followed by the number 7 with a circle around it and the ABC network logo. It done in gray and off-white, and the art department quickly created a pure logo that has become a classic industry standard among the many ABC stations that happen to reside on channel 7. We ordered "Circle 7" logos sewn into the jackets we bought for all the on-air people to wear.

The most important thing I did on my first day was to order the sign-off news capsule renamed *Eyewitness News*. I did the same with the sign-on news. I did this to protect the title in New York, a valuable piece of information we obtained while clearing it in Philadelphia. No one noticed but Westinghouse who called to complain. I just laughed it off. I knew they could do nothing legally since they didn't operate a station in New York City.

I looked at my watch and saw it was getting close to news time. In the past, I could just walk down the stairs to the studio.

Now I had to head over to an entirely different building.

The tiny studio in the 7 West Sixty-sixth Street building was crammed with equipment and brightly lit. A wall of heat hit me in the face as I entered the room during the newscast. The dozen or so people scrambling about in the high temperature, dripping sweat as they tried to operate teleprompters and other equipment, was like a scene from Dante's *Inferno*. I visited the studio in frustration for several days and as I was leaving one evening, noticed from the hallway that when the lights were being turned off after the broadcast, there was a change that gave the studio an entirely new look. As was the case in Philadelphia, I needed someone with a creative eye who could somehow transform a darkened studio into something special.

Enter "Big Julie."

While the name might sound like a character from *The Sopranos,* it actually belonged to Julian Barnathan, who was the director of broadcast operations. He was mostly interested in working on the Olympics, and his engineers were a great force in developing the technical equipment that is the basis of today's great sports coverage. A swarthy, stocky guy with dark features, he was also a proud man who didn't like being harassed by the brass because of the station's failure, so he didn't mind listening to any new options. He told me of the excuses used to explain the poor ratings of channel 7's news. They ranged from bad lighting to small sets, along with a third excuse I found most amusing.

It seems that in the early days of channel allocation, engineering consultants and government officials had told ABC President Leonard Goldenson that the lower numbered channels would be reserved for government use and that a safe bet would be to apply for channel 7. So he did that for all the ABC stations at the time, including a group in South America in which ABC had part ownership to be better positioned when global television would come. No one really thought that would ever happen.

As a result, Barnathan was constantly harangued with the theory that fewer people watched channel 7 because they turned on channel 2, switched to 4 and then to WNEW, now the FOX station on channel 5. By then they were supposedly too fatigued to click their dials up to channel 7. (You may remember that in the days before remote control, children were usually the "human channel changers," sitting next to the television while they took orders from their parents.)

The new concept for news coverage caught Barnathan's eye. He got the idea quickly. He became very cooperative in providing the help necessary to get the job done and thankfully was very up-front with ideas of his own. The man was a production genius and I was thrilled he was taking such an interest. After all, a successful newscast would get a lot of people off his back. We also discussed simple matters like having the same engineers work the program regularly. He felt familiarity with one's job being critical in avoiding technical mistakes. Most of the great engineers at ABC wanted to work on the *Wide World of Sports*, the Olympics, football games, and other exotic programming rather than the local newscast. Big Julie managed to get the same set of engineers for a minimum of three months on rotation, thus giving us the use of the best talent available to get *Eyewitness News* started. You can have the best content in the world, but if the newscast is a technical disaster, it can overshadow anything and make your program ineffective. Research clearly shows mistakes affect the credibility of the news with viewers. We were both determined that was not going to happen.

Since we had a new logo, we decided to standardize all the handheld microphones used by reporters in the field to make them distinctively noticeable as being channel 7's. In the old days, microphones were cumbersome, unattractive large sticks or they were attached to loops that actually hung around a reporter's neck. We needed some new microphones with a modern look that would set off our new logo. Those little things with logos that are attached to microphones are called "mike flags," and Barnathan helped us create the impression that *Eyewitness News* was special and exclusively an ABC product with distinctive new microphones and flags. Now when a reporter did a stand-up in the field, or when we covered a news conference, the "Circle 7" on the new microphone really stood out.

In retrospect, I think we spent less than $5,000 for the mikes and the flags but the local engineers couldn't get it done until Barnathan gave it his blessing. As a matter of fact, all the changes implemented to create *Eyewitness News* in New York were accomplished at no additional cost simply by redirecting money already in the budget. I did, after all, have a few bucks left over from dismissing that ad agency.

Thanks to Big Julie, all the cosmetic changes to bring *Eyewitness News* to life were set in motion in a very short time.

Then I got down to the most important facet of any news product: the people.

I discovered that many of the people at WABC had been "dumped" there after unsuccessful runs at the network level, whether it was on radio or television. These people were protected by the union so in those days if the network wanted to get rid of someone they couldn't fire, they would simply send them "down to local," knowing the atmosphere might make them miserable enough to quit. As a result, I inherited a staff of shell-shocked, depressed people who had to deal with self-doubt and the fear that the new guy would fire everyone.

As a manager, you'd like everyone to be a star performer, but not everyone is Babe Ruth. You still need your singles hitters, table setters. You can't expect everyone to hit a home run every time at bat. You need solid starters and a great bench. So you put people in the position where they are most likely to succeed.

I've always believed that if you surround yourself with people who are smarter than you are, they'll make you look good. It sure had worked for me in Philly with Tom Snyder, Art Fisher, and Ken Philo. Many television news managers feel just the opposite and are intimidated by a greater level of intelligence, so they make sure they're always the smartest person in the room. I wanted all the brainpower I could find in New York, and some brilliant people were already on the staff. But the puzzle had a lot of missing pieces, so I started looking.

I could not possibly guess that one anchor I would hire would end up in a courtroom and hear the phrase, "Will the defendant please rise."

Chapter Eleven

"The format is diluting the anchorman's effectiveness, it won't work."
—McHugh-Hoffman Research, 1970

When I arrived at WABC in September 1968, it seemed as though someone had gone on a nationwide search for the most unattractive television newspeople in America and dressed them in clothing from a thrift store. Yes, you want competent people on your newscast, but television is a visual medium so most of your people should be reasonably attractive and dress well. Just make sure they're smart or as I used to say, look smart. It is a delicate balance. These days you can even get away with a few average-looking reporters as long as they're credible. But when the entire news team looks like the road company of *Guys and Dolls* and everyone appears as though he's just rolled out of bed, you're in trouble.

Anchor Roger Grimsby was the leader of the people-who-look-like-they-slept-in-their-clothes club. He had a penchant for wearing brown suits, matching brown shirts, and white neckties, making him look like an off-the-rack extra at a mob funeral. I'm not even sure how he managed to find so many brown clothes. Howard Cosell, the original good face for radio, took the term *wardrobe malfunction* to an entirely different level. His main problem had nothing to do with apparel, though his closet didn't contain anything resembling Armani. Howard would do his sports commentary wearing a first-generation toupee on some nights and appear au natural on other occasions. Hair today, gone tomorrow. The weatherman, Tex Antoine, actually did his schtick in an artist's smock and an array of red suits to match his receding hair and moustache. He even did his weathercast while holding a large paintbrush. Of course, he had his cartoon partner that he drew, Uncle Wethbee, who may have actually been the best-looking character on the anchor desk.

New York *Daily News* columnist Jimmy Breslin, a fabulous writer and a real-life Oscar Madison if there ever was one, stopped in from time to time to read his newspaper column on the air. He'd literally hold the script in his hand and read it. Legend has it that Breslin, like most newspaper people, was truly uncomfortable being on camera and that his prerecorded segments always took several takes. Cosell would be leaning against the wall, smoking his ever-present cigar as he patiently waited his turn. Breslin would finally get a usable take and step aside for Howard. Cosell would then ask the producer, "How much do you need?" and would be told the time limit for his commentary. Cosell would stand in front of the camera and without any notes, eloquently launch into a wonderfully thought out monologue that had a climax and a pithy comment at the end. And of course, it timed out to the second. Breslin, frustrated that Howard could knock out something so perfect while on autopilot would yell, "Son of a BITCH!"

We also had contributors for the arts. Allan Jeffries did theater reviews after his announcer shift at the station and Martin Bookspan was the music reviewer. I liked Marty because he really knew music, but he had to go if we were going to change people's impression of the news programs. Bookspan went on to become the voice of the New York Philharmonic and *Live from Lincoln Center*.

And finally, there was Rona Barrett, who appeared nightly from Hollywood on film flown in especially for WABC-TV. She was more Brooklyn than Hollywood at this point in her life, with tightly coiffed blonde hair that looked like it could withstand a category 5 hurricane. Roger delighted in introducing her material with special zingers like, "And now here's Rona Rooter (in honor of the well-advertised drain router of the era) with the latest dirt from Hollywood." Johnny Carson later created a character for *The Tonight Show* called Rona Blabbit. Though not one of the guys, she looked ragged as well.

Do you remember that line of children's clothes called *Garanimals* with which kids learned to dress themselves by matching the animal tags so they'd know if their clothes matched? Our on-air staff needed the same thing for adults. Since that didn't exist, we took a simple approach. Well, actually we stole it from Catholic schools. We decided to create a uniform look and put all the men in tailored dark blue jackets.

This had the additional benefit of getting Tex Antoine out of that ridiculous smock though he wanted to impale me with his paintbrush when he got the memo. He marched into my office, claiming that doing weather without his smock would "spoil my image." I did my best not to laugh and replied, "Tex, we're either all going to wear blue jackets, or we're all going to wear smocks."

Though I caught some heat from Howard Cosell on the jacket issue, the anchors finally realized they were fighting a losing battle and became comfortable with their blue blazers. Clothing was one less thing for them to worry about. And the company was paying for them.

Now I had to deal with the people who wore the clothes.

One of the bright spots at WABC when I got there was weekend anchor, Gil Noble. Channel 7 fell right into line with CBS and NBC by having a minority anchorman on the weekend. Gil got the job six months before I got there and made enough impact to get his own program, "Like It Is," on Sunday afternoons. He was an aristocrat, a true leader in the African American community. We hired Charles Hobson, a Fulbright Scholar, as Executive Producer of the program and Marquita Poole right out of Columbia University. Together with Gil they managed to interview virtually every African head of state, top entertainers, Muhammad Ali and other sports stars as well as politicians ranging from Stokley Carmichael to Andrew Young. Gil Noble is still hosting "Like It Is;" Charles

Weekend Anchor Man
Gil Novel with Al Ittleson at the
Assignments Desk, 1969

Hobson owns Vanguard Documentaries; Marquita Poole went on to become Senior Producer of CBS Sunday.

Roger Grimsby had come to the station from ABC's affiliate in San Francisco, KGO-TV, where he was not only the anchorman but also served as the news director. So he knew all the management tricks of the trade: how budgets worked, what a station could really afford. Roger had a built-in prejudice against management, having seen it from both sides.

He was always convinced it was my job in life to fire him even though the thought never ever crossed my mind. As a matter of fact, a report was delivered to the station by McHugh-Hoffman Research, a television consulting firm, that recommended Grimsby be replaced on the anchor desk. Even though he'd only been at the station a few months.

Consulting firm? Oh yes, a few months after I was hired, I discovered door number 4 behind which stood a bunch of "news doctors" that would help me "fix the newscast." In January, I was casually informed ABC had hired a research company that was gathering information on our new format. I was told, "They are going to do a study of our program to measure its impact." Not thinking I'd receive anything but some paperwork, I thought this seemed like a good idea. Ratings don't always tell the whole story and some research might tell me how our new format was being received.

Then the consultants arrived, armed with data and some very strong opinions. At first they were very complimentary, setting me up with a few nice comments about the new look of the newscast. After I began to relax, Phil McHugh went into attack mode. "There's one thing you have to understand," he said, "and that is, you don't know *anything at all* about show business or this business, television."

I couldn't help but be insulted. Who the hell was this guy? Had he ever worked in a television newsroom? Before I could shoot back, he continued with his assault on me and the product. "Our basic premise is that you never supplant the star performer, and what you have done by putting all these reporters on the set is that you are diluting the impact of your anchorman."

I was truly ticked off, so when he paused, I fired right back. "*You* don't understand. It is exactly the opposite. All these reporters in the studio are going to build up the anchorman because the anchor can't do it all by himself."

McHugh tried to jump in. "Well, look, I'm just telling you what the research—"

I cut him off. "Where does it say that?"

Needless to say, the rest of the meeting was not pleasant.

A few weeks later, they returned with a report, showing that people were sampling *Eyewitness News,* had noticed a change, and thought it was a positive one. However, the consultants said that based on "popularity charts," Roger Grimsby would never succeed in the New York market and should be fired. They also recommended we discontinue putting reporters on the set.

In other words, kill the *Eyewitness News* concept.

I saw McHugh and Hoffman as advertising charlatans, intruders. Where I had once thought the idea of research might be a useful tool, I was now furious the company had been hired by the station to do this kind of work without my knowledge. Research was one thing, but this was something else. The old joke about consultants came to mind: they borrowed your watch and then charged you to tell you the time. Bottom line, WABC was paying me to turn the station around, now someone expected me to ask for advice from people who didn't even live in New York? McHugh and Hoffman's research was as big a waste of money as the ad campaign.

And I didn't agree at all with their feelings about Grimsby.

We ignored every one of the consultant's recommendations. (Later, after *Eyewitness News* had become a huge success, WABC, for some unknown reason, commissioned another study from McHugh and Hoffman. They responded with a glowing report, highlighting the fact that we had listened to their suggestions and implemented the changes. In reality, we hadn't done a single thing they'd suggested.) We also went around the country recommending our ideas to stations, building a very successful business.

Despite the nonexistent ratings and lack of support from the consulting firm, there was something in Grimsby's angry attitude and acerbic wit that would really appeal to New Yorkers. Roger had an on-camera delivery that might be best described as a combination of constipated and pissed off, but he *was* New York and could launch a hilarious quip in a nanosecond. In a city that dealt with things like broiling subway cars and garbage strikes on a daily basis, having a cheery rose-colored glasses anchor just wouldn't make sense. I took it upon myself to prevent his firing and at the same time get a shot at McHugh and Hoffman. ABC needed to know that some consulting company from Michigan was not running the news operation.

I was determined to give Roger Grimsby every opportunity to succeed. It is always easier to get an established anchorman to adapt to your own format and style than bring in a new person and start from scratch. Despite the fact he had more baggage than a sorority girl on spring break, the guy was a solid newsman and was truly dedicated to his work.

Roger was not really interested in change but like Dick Beesemyer, he too was desperate because of the poor ratings and realized he had to do something if he wanted to continue cashing paychecks. When anchors move from station to station, they often present any ratings successes on their resume. In Roger's case, he had nothing to show, so if he found himself out of a job it might be tough to find another gig. Who would want an anchor with a zero rating? Grimsby would channel his anxiety into the newsroom, as he tended to lash out at his coworkers. His fear seemed to manifest itself daily with criticism of just about everything going on in the news department. He hated the writers, producers, and virtually everyone he came in contact with. With the afternoon poker game gone, most of his time was spent inside his office talking with his old pals at ABC in San Francisco.

One day, I was walking by and heard him say, "These writers here are so bad I have to rewrite everything."

I stuck my head through the doorway. "I *want* you to rewrite everything," I said, stopping to chat. "As long as it's in your own words, not just a Cincinnati rewrite."

Many anchors routinely rewrite copy, even the stuff penned by very skilled writers. The thinking is that no one can truly write the way someone else talks, so anchors generally polish things to make the "conversational style" fit their delivery.

But lazy anchors do "Cincinnati rewrites." I'm not sure of the origin of the term, but in the modern world it would be known as cut and paste. An anchor might take a story from the six o'clock newscast that read, "Three men robbed a bank in the middle of Manhattan," and simply change it to, "A bank in the middle of Manhattan was robbed by three men." If Grimsby was going to rework the copy, I wanted it to fit his style of speech and delivery. Since I'd heard him say how much he hated the writers, he had no choice but to do it.

But giving Roger an attitude adjustment was a slow process. Grimsby's negativity reared its ugly head when I sent him to Cape Canaveral in the summer of 1969. I wanted our main anchor serving as an eyewitness to the launching of America's attempt to place a man on the moon. The plan was to fly him to Florida the night before, have him watch the Apollo 11 liftoff, then hop an airplane back to New York in time to anchor the eleven o'clock news and do a report. Local anchormen had rarely been given this kind of assignment, and it was our chance to "claim" a story that would get worldwide attention. We all thought it was going to be a great coup and would boost his spirits.

I was home in Connecticut that night watching the eleven o'clock newscast. The program began with the lead story of the space launch. I was angry that Roger made absolutely no reference to having been on the scene. I thought he was saving it for a big closing. Thirty minutes later, Grimsby signed off, never mentioning that he'd been to Florida and seen the launch. I was absolutely furious. I called him and screamed, simply yelling, "Why?" He said, "Well . . ." and his voice trailed off. I shouted, "No, don't give me an answer. You take the next three days off without pay and then you can tell me."

Roger Grimsby and the Author on set, 1971

I still don't have the answer to this day and Roger accused me of running the newsroom like a kindergarten for that incident. This was typical of the kind of actions Roger took to provoke not only me but all of his coworkers as well. And his attacks were usually on the air. His commentary was humorous but occasionally cutting. He once introduced Howard Cosell's sports segment by saying, "And now let's go to the president of the Howard Cosell Fan Club." (Cosell responded, "Once again, a laborious endeavor by the grim-faced Mr. Grimsby to be witty and impertinent has totally missed its mark.")

In one legendary incident that became a staple of television news blooper tapes for years, an on-set reporter named Mara Wolinsky apparently thought her story was still running and she extended her middle finger at someone behind the camera with great gusto. Much to her dismay, her studio shot had already been punched up and viewers caught a glimpse of her flipping the bird. Grimsby then ended the program with, "As Mara Wolinsky would say, we're number one."

While that one brought the house down, more often than not the quips were offensive and got us into big trouble. In 1972, the National Organization for Women filed a petition with the Federal Communications Commission charging sexism at WABC. They were particularly upset by the "snide comments" he made about women. They were referring to Roger's introduction to a report on the first national Women's Rights Day when he said, "And now for another item of trivia."

Panic in the executive corridor set in when NOW demanded a special meeting with Leonard Goldenson and Elton Rule to discuss the matter. Everyone who attended the meeting was shocked at what transpired. Rule, a tall, square-jawed man who was the epitome of corporate cool, had assembled his top vice presidents, along with two female ABC employees, around the dark oak conference table. He was confident, eloquent, and opened the meeting with a casual remark about how nice it was for the members of NOW to come to headquarters for a discussion. Gloria Steinem and a very angry band of women gave him a tongue-lashing that he could never have expected. It was humiliating for him to endure the verbal beating he got in front of all of his vice presidents. It was frightening just to be in the same room. The women meant business and let everyone know it. It was a real consciousness-raising session and as a result, ABC developed a series of practices that have proved invaluable over the years.

But Grimsby didn't change during those early years. He was an orphan who was reared by a Lutheran minister in Duluth, Minnesota. He told me once he searched for his birth mother for many years and when he found her, he went to her house, knocked on the door, and introduced himself. He simply said, "I just wanted to know what you looked like." Then instead of getting to know her and having some lifelong questions answered, he turned and walked away.

All this from a man who ended each newscast with, "Hoping your news is good news."

But Grimsby wasn't the only difficult personality on the anchor desk. Tex Antoine, the cheerful guy in the smock who drew cartoons while doing the weather, was quickly becoming a headache.

But not as big as the character he drew.

Chapter Twelve

On a minute-to-minute basis, the weatherperson is the most critical member of the anchor team. What he or she has to say appeals to every segment of the audience and often is the primary reason people watch television news. The perfect weather personality is a meteorologist, a person trained in the science of meteorology with experience working in a weather service. Someone who can truly help the viewers stay safe in times of severe weather. Most importantly, that person must be confident and comfortable in an electronic environment and have a well-developed sense of humor, especially for those days when nothing is happening weather-wise.

Despite his difficulties with me regarding the smock issue, I knew Tex Antoine could fit the bill. Tex, real name Herbert, had grown up in Texas so the nickname was legit. He had been the weathercaster on WABC-TV for two years when I arrived. He'd left the Lone Star State for the Big Apple in the late 1940s, like many young people in search of stardom. While he never made it to Broadway, his great voice landed him a job as an NBC staff announcer. On one Friday afternoon in 1949, the station asked him to create a weather show by the following Monday. Tex, who had a real flair when it came to art, whipped up a cartoon character he called Uncle Wethbee, a bald-headed little man who wore a variety of hairpieces and moustaches to create a visual effect that matched the weather forecast provided by the National Weather Service. If it was cold outside, he would draw Uncle Wethbee with earmuffs; if rain was in the forecast, the character would have an umbrella. If Tex got the forecast wrong, he drew Uncle Wethbee with a black eye the next day. The audience loved Antoine and he won an Emmy for best TV personality in 1961. Tex was an extremely nice man, knew what he was talking about, and had a sharp sense of humor that often got him in trouble.

It was difficult to find this combination because the ability to excel in an exact science seems to run counter to the development of a broad sense of personality. It is a rare bird indeed that captures all the elements necessary to superstardom. There are perhaps two dozen people who fall into this category in the entire United States. Television executives have been using gimmicks to fill this void for years. The first TV weather personality appeared in 1941 on WNBT (now WNBC.) It was a dancing cartoon lamb that pranced about while a voiceover announcer read the forecast.

You should also note that most of today's television weathercasters get their forecasts directly from the National Weather Service. A TV meteorologist may be the most brilliant in his field, but few television stations have the forecasting equipment that matches that of the federal government.

With that in mind, it was no surprise that Tex would show up about four o'clock in the afternoon (like a lot of television weathercasters), call the local weather bureau, (just as I used to do for Bill Burns in Pittsburgh) and get the forecast. This would give him enough time to "dress" Uncle Wethbee (or "Unk," as Tex called him) for the newscast.

Tex Antoine, Eyewitness Weather   Uncle Wethbee in Happier Times

While I'm sure kids thought this was cute, I knew that having a cartoon character as part of a newscast would seriously undermine the credibility we were trying to build. Uncle Wethbee would have to disappear down a portable hole just like the Road Runner. I just shook my head as, for the first time in my career, I was about to fire a fictional character. But after all those years playing straight man to a cartoon, Tex couldn't easily grasp my concept of providing the weather with as much credibility as possible, which of course, precluded the use of "Unk" or cartoons of any kind. I believed a star personality should not be lost over a philosophical disagreement and spent many hours talking him through the concept of the kind of weather I wanted him to do for *Eyewitness News*. He fought every suggestion.

I told him I wanted the principal portion of the weather segment to be the forecast delivered clearly and concisely with bold graphic illustration. I suggested he spend time on the national weather map to show the weather patterns which would affect the weather in New York. The myth that people in one city want to know the weather in their old hometown has bored millions upon millions of viewers over the years. Tex thought people wanted to know how hot their snowbird relatives were in Boca Raton. I reminded him that a simple temperature noted on the map could easily take care of the problem. In this case, he didn't have to state what the viewers could see.

I also wanted to take our winter weather coverage to a new level. The audience is always interested in weather video from almost anywhere in the country, particularly in places where it is unusual for a snowfall. Television too often gives coverage of snowstorms by showing standard video of traffic and snow removal equipment. I told Tex we would always get a cameraman to create a video essay, complete with music, on the beauty of the snowstorm that he could use during his weather segment. The audience can never get enough of this material. I told him that providing this coverage angle every time there was a snowstorm would build him and a weather franchise that would pay off in ratings dividends.

Tex still wasn't on board. He thought all of this took away from his face time on the newscasts. But we worked on it. Meanwhile, he grudgingly packed away the smock and paintbrush, had whatever funeral cartoonists have for their characters, and put on the blue blazer as if it were made of porcupine quills.

The cool clean look helped Tex and all of the *Eyewitness News* team. It even gave Tex a resurgence in popularity. I was about half right when I said it would give him another twenty years on television.

Bars and microphones would be his undoing as he couldn't keep his mouth shut near either.

He proved to be another perfect foil for Roger Grimsby, whose lead-in comments to the weather became something New Yorkers looked forward to every night. To mark his twenty-fifth anniversary on television, the station let Tex do the weather forecast in his old smock (he hadn't thrown it away) and brought back "Unk" for the night. One of our other weathermen, Gary Essex, brought out a birthday cake in the shape of the United States. It was all great fun on television. As time began to run out, Roger said, "We have to go now, Tex wants to eat Florida." Someone inadvertently stepped in front of Tex who said, "Get the fuck out of my shot." Fortunately, the laughter from the studio crew at Grimsby's comment drowned out Tex so that the audience couldn't hear him drop the f-bomb.

Tex didn't drink a lot, but in his case it didn't take much to put him half in the bag. Tex was a diabetic and proudly wore his silver bracelet. He would have dinner at the same German restaurant on the East Side virtually every night between news programs. He would sit quietly in the back with one glass of wine, but he was often recognized and someone would send over another glass. There was trouble every time it happened because he physically couldn't deal with much alcohol. Two or three drinks made him look as though he'd had ten. His presentation would be slurred, sometimes slightly, other times dramatically. Reporter Bob Lape recalls viewers occasionally asking if Antoine had a drinking problem, so he would tell them that Tex was a diabetic. But covering for his problem with the viewers didn't fix the problem.

It was impossible to talk with Tex about it. He was in complete denial. I finally recorded his segment one night and made him watch the entire three minutes in my office. It was painful but it worked. For a while.

The uncertainty led me to develop new ways to present the weather and build the news team at the same time. We would have celebrities come in when Tex went on vacation. I started with New York Mayor John Lindsay doing the weather. His political handlers knew Eyewitness News was on the rise and they were delighted to have him replace Tex for a few nights. We also used sports stars and even the anchors in front of the map, Geraldo, Jim Bouton and others from the entertainment world. It captured a great deal of press and our audience showed its appreciation with increased ratings

But his mouth, not his drinking, would eventually be his demise. Though Tex had a quick wit that rivaled Grimsby's, what he said on his last day wasn't the least bit funny. On November 24, 1976, Tex truly crossed the line with something so tasteless we couldn't possibly let him continue on the air. After an earlier news report about an attempted rape, Tex came on and said, "With rape so predominant in the news lately, Confucius say, 'If rape is inevitable, relax and enjoy it.'" To make matters even worse, the victim in this case was an five-year-old girl. My jaw dropped, and I'm sure every viewer had the same reaction before all of them picked up their phones to call the station. We immediately took Tex off the air and suspended him. Grimsby led the eleven o'clock newscast with a sincere apology. The public outrage cost Tex his job though, to be honest, he would have been shown the door even if we hadn't gotten a single complaint. Incredibly, Roger pushed the envelope a few days later when he introduced the replacement meteorologist. "Lie back, relax now and enjoy the weather with Storm Field."

But as is often the case in television, the public has a short memory and is often in a forgiving mood. In January 1978, Antoine was hired by WNEW, an independent station, but lasted less than a year. Tex complained he couldn't draw on the new weather maps that by now had become electronically generated. He was replaced by a former Miss New Jersey, Linda Gianella. Her spectacular success got her a position at ABC's early morning news and ultimately to the main weather position at KYW-TV in Philadelphia. Tex left the business and died on January 12, 1983.

Chapter Thirteen

"Nobody gives a shit about ordinary people!"
—Rona Barrett

While I was spending an inordinate amount of time arguing with people about wardrobe, a news staff had to be built. Some of the people who were already there would remain, but there was one segment in the newscast that seemed to torpedo any inkling of credibility.

Gossip, with Rona Barrett.

One of my first calls when I arrived in New York was from Hollywood's rumor queen. Leonard Goldenson, she told me, wanted her to come to New York to spend some time with me. She wanted to meet the guy who was putting together the news concept Goldenson hoped would lift the flagship station of his network out of the ratings' cellar. She sounded as though she wanted to be the one to lead the way.

I didn't want her anywhere near my newscast. I agreed wholeheartedly with Roger Grimsby about the value of Rona's reports though I never said it on the air every night. Grimsby had once followed a story about trash with, "Speaking of garbage, Rona Rooter has something ripe and odorous for us from Hollywood . . ." as he introduced her report. He would look at her segment earlier in the day so he'd have time to think up something clever in the way of an introduction.

Even though Grimsby rarely introduced her using her real name (which, by the way, was Rona Berstein), she brushed it off and said it didn't matter whether he called her "Rona Rooter" or not. She was going to make it as a gossip queen no matter what some anchor in New York City said about her. She did tell me her mother once fell off a stepladder when she heard Roger introduce her daughter that way.

When she strutted into our newsroom with her nose in the air, I could tell immediately that she wasn't just another newsie. She obviously had a highbrow attitude to go with her plan. She was only about four feet tall with a permanent smirk on her face. When the working stiffs in the newsroom barely acknowledged her presence, a troubled look grew across her face. Grimsby hid in his office and later walked right by her without speaking on his way to Chips bar. She was wounded but tried not to let it show.

Rona had flown all the way in from Tinseltown, as she wasn't about to throw her weight around on the phone. Her plane had been met by a driver and limo provided by the network. She was holed up at the exclusive Plaza Hotel, and now she found herself in what she considered a run-down newsroom. Meanwhile, she was surrounded by a collection of wretches who were in the business of surviving rather than noticing the superstars. Besides, they didn't consider her to be in that league.

"How can you work here?" she asked as she clicked her heels into my office. I was a bit offended but smiled. After all, I had just gotten the newsroom remodeled, the staff appreciated it, and I felt like a fledgling hero. I could only imagine what she would have thought about the place *before* its makeover. She began to talk about *Eyewitness News* and the future, but it was clear the surroundings were beneath her and she couldn't wait to get back to California, or at least her hotel room. Because even with the new carpet and paint, it wasn't a suite at the Plaza.

"Let's go somewhere where we can talk better," she said. Not wanting to create a scene in the newsroom, I agreed, and after the six o'clock newscast, she gleefully took the opportunity to take the new guy in town for a ride in the big black ABC limo. We raced off into the night, moving quietly down the Great White Way. She was the perfect backseat hostess with her home court advantage. She could operate much better here than inside a noisy newsroom. There was a large well-stocked bar and the stereophonic music filled the compartment. Holding a martini and looking through the tinted glass of the limo at the hordes of people moving through the streets of the world's toughest city gives one a feeling of safety and security.

"They love me out there," she exclaimed, sitting straight up with her nose uplifted as she deigned to look at the commoners through the window. "They don't want to hear any more about Vietnam and politics. They want to know what *my* people are doing," she purred. Rona launched into a sales pitch about how *Eyewitness News* could succeed on her coattails. Then she started dropping the big names. "I was telling Mr. Goldenson my theory when he was on the coast two weeks ago." I did my best trying not to look impressed. "Elton Rule agrees with the whole idea," she added. Thankfully, the limo pulled up to a theater and rolled to a stop. It seemed the driver was at the door instantly, having mastered the art of escorting the stars.

The bright marquee on the theater told me she was pulling out all the stops. I knew *The Great White Hope* with James Earl Jones was the hottest Broadway ticket in town, but Rona had two great seats on the aisle. It was a spectacular theater experience, and before I knew it, we had melted with the crowd over to Sardi's, the Broadway landmark restaurant off Times Square. Naturally, the velvet ropes disappeared everywhere Rona showed up, as she seemed to be intent on impressing me with her power.

It would all have been fine if I were the producer of a show like *Entertainment Tonight*, which didn't even exist at the time.

Vincent Sardi himself was bubbling over Rona as he escorted us to just the right seat in the front room of his establishment. We were in the middle of a sea of beautiful people who can manage to eat their filet mignons without looking, as their eyes search the room for acknowledgment of the famous and their elegant hangers-on.

Ms. Rona had the most wicked stories you could imagine about the notable customers, running through the list of famous names she spotted nearby. She always ended each story with "That's why he hates me" or, "That's why I have to be careful of her. She can't stand the fact I know that about her." Then she dropped a line that almost made me do a spit-take. "But that's what journalism is all about," she intoned, looking very serious about it all.

It almost worked, but gossip and journalism are two very different things. As a matter of fact, it's a matter of *facts*. I never felt so bad in my life about telling a person that it was all over. I calmly told her *Eyewitness News* was going to be television's first people-oriented news program, about regular people, the ones she so detested. The people whose sweat and hard work kept the city's pulse beating would be the subject of our newscast, not the celebrities she knew so well. No, I told her, we didn't want exclusives with movie stars, we wanted the wife of a policeman telling us about living with the fact that her heart skipped a beat when her husband was late coming home and how every morning send-off kiss might be her last. We would air hard facts, not rumors. We weren't to be confused with the paparazzi and would not be in the business of airing dirty laundry that may or may not be true.

We were going to have to work extra hard to earn credibility with the average New Yorker since we currently had none at all. WABC had made it even harder with the current format. Trying to succeed by paying personalities to appear on its news programs instead of using reporters to gather news didn't make sense. The ratings, or lack thereof, (with Rona as part of the current team) proved my point. She was Ralph Kiner with a microphone; we could finish last without her.

She wasn't hearing any of it, nor would she take any responsibility for the current ratings. The low numbers were someone else's fault. "It's a mistake," she said, detailing her disapproval of the new format. "Nobody gives a shit about ordinary people!"

Well, yeah, except maybe the ten million of them who live here . . .

"Does Mr. Goldenson know about this?" she asked, demanding an answer.

"No, he doesn't," I said quietly. I didn't want her to know that I'd only seen him twice in my life. I told her she would no longer be a part of *Eyewitness News.* "We're going to go in a different direction," I said. "You're the queen of gossip, but we can't even have gossip in a newscast because gossip spells no credibility."

She went right into attack mode and brought out the big artillery. "Well, Leonard Goldenson and Elton Rule *personally* want me on that program."

"I know. But *I* don't want you on the program. I want it to be credible."

The smile never left her face the rest of the evening. When the limo dropped her off at the Plaza Hotel, I got a kiss on the cheek, but it was more of the kind you'd get from a Sicilian mobster.

"I'm going to *get you* for this," she said, her eyes suddenly narrowing and taking on the look of a gunslinger. "I'm calling them. Good night." She turned and strolled back to her suite and I could only wonder if she might be someone's sacred cow.

But once again I didn't need any forgiveness. Just like the fallout that never came from the advertising agency dismissal, I never heard a word from anyone at ABC about Ms. Rona.

Years later, Rona Barrett did get the last word of sorts. I was walking through the first-class cabin of a commercial jet in Los Angeles. I was at the time vice president of News for ABC stations, making my way back to the tourist section where ABC executives are required to sit when traveling. She looked up at me from her stretched-out position in an oversized leather seat. She held up her wine glass, smiled, and said, "So . . . are you still *there?*"

In 1978, Rona Barrett published a book called *How You Can Look Rich and Achieve Sexual Ecstasy.* Not exactly the title you'd want from a member of your news team.

Many of the other "contributors" like Jimmy Breslin would no longer be used. If the station had been a dominant number one or a solid reputation, then an occasional visit from New York's most popular columnist would be a nice addition. Breslin was a brilliant journalist but just not a TV guy. As it stood, it seemed the entire newscast was nothing more than a parade of special contributors who dropped by to fill the hour with just about everything *but* news. They were all very talented in their field, but unfortunately, they weren't television news reporters or anchors.

In Philadelphia, I created an instant staff overnight simply by putting the reporters on camera. In New York, I'd have to pretty much hire all new on-camera reporters.

Meanwhile, I would still have to deal with Howard Cosell.

Chapter Fourteen

"Arrogant, pompous, obnoxious, vain, cruel, persecuting, distasteful,
verbose, a showoff—I've been called all of these. Of course, I am."
—Howard Cosell

In many ways, putting together a newsroom is a lot like drafting a football team. In this case, we had our quarterback, Roger Grimsby, but he had no blockers, no wide receivers, no defense. He needed a supporting cast to sit on the set with him. With all of the "contributors" on the way out, there would be a lot of time to fill with real news, and I needed a new army of reporters to hit the streets and find it. However, along with weatherman Tex Antoine, there was still one holdover from the *Noisemakers.*

Howard Cosell.

Noisemaker didn't even describe the half of it.

Everyone was familiar with Cosell's work, and most Americans who watched *ABC's Wide World of Sports* considered him a polarizing figure. He also liked to stir the pot on radio with his daily radio commentary *Speaking of Sports.* Sports fans either loved him or hated him, or just loved to hate him.

But they watched him and listened to him religiously.

And what they saw or heard was what they got. I got it on my first day.

I was sitting behind my desk shuffling through contracts. Cosell strolled into my office like he owned the place, unannounced, smoking a cigar while he turned and closed the door behind him. I was surprised at how tall and lanky he was, and I had often wondered what this man was like "in real life." I found out there was no difference between Howard the sportscaster and Howard the person as he launched into a monologue with the same delivery used to voice football highlights.

"Albert T. Primo . . . Un-i-ver-sity of Pittsburgh, nineteen sixty-five. K-D-K-A, channel 2. News director, K . . . Y . . . W. Inventor of the VAUNTED *Eyewitness News* format. The kid from the north side of Pittsburgh, facing the daunting task of improving the fortunes . . . of a third rate . . . LACKLUSTER . . . A . . . B . . . C station in the number ONE-television market in the world."

He was demonstrating his journalistic ability, letting me know that he had vetted me and that nothing would surprise him. Then as I sat there with my mouth hanging open, he took a page from the *Rona-Barrett-don't-screw-with-me-I-know-people-in-higher-places-than-you* school of intimidation.

Cosell came close to my desk, leaned forward, and whispered, "Leonard Goldenson considers me the son he never had."

I'm sure David Letterman could make a top ten list of comebacks to that line, but I was still blown away by his attitude. Howard sat down, leaned back, and continued to puff on his cigar. We chatted for a short time during which he placed all his cards on the table.

Howard Cosell
before Eyewitness News, 1963

"Arrogant, pompous, obnoxious, vain, cruel, persecuting, distasteful, verbose, a show-off—I've been called all of these," he said. "Of course, I am."

He then pulled out two letters from his breast pocket. "Look at this, the fans love me," he said. He always had the same two letters with him at all times.

He ended the discussion with a prediction regarding my fate. "Your job here is *impossible*. You *cannot* succeed. Children are *born* knowing that ABC is number three. A virtual loser when it comes to news." As I sat there wondering how the negativity had permeated a member of the news staff to this level, he got up to leave. On the way out, he said, "I like you kid," with a haunting high-pitched laugh. It occurred to me later that maybe he wanted me to ask him to change, he would conform and then expect or want the new format to fail. His genius was obvious and you couldn't help liking him.

Luckily, Howard didn't bet any money on his predictions as he'd made one a decade earlier about New York Yankees play-by-play man Phil Rizzuto that proved dead wrong. The legendary "Scooter" had gone directly from the field to the broadcast booth in the mid-1950s. Cosell, just beginning his distaste for jocks with a microphone, told Rizzuto, "You'll never last. You look like George Burns and you sound like Groucho Marx" (a hilarious comment from someone who looked and sounded like Howard). As with his prediction about the success of *Eyewitness News*, he would prove wrong about

Phil Rizzuto, who lasted forty years as the Yankees announcer and became one of the most beloved media people in New York.

Howard was right about one thing. Channel 7 had started in the basement and been there long enough to acquire squatter's rights. But while WABC may have been a loser when it came to news, the ABC network had developed a terrific reputation for sports coverage under Roone Arledge. Arledge had incredible vision and was solely responsible for making the Olympics an enormous hit on television. Roone recognized that the games transcended sports and had a deeper meaning than most people ever imagined. He turned the Olympics into an "us versus them" spectacle, wrapping the Unites States team in the American flag and creating a patriotic fan base that included millions of nonsports fans, a lot of them women who normally wouldn't be caught dead watching a ball game. And of course, Howard was a huge part of ABC's coverage, providing incredible exclusives. He'd work on the number one show, the *Wide World of Sports*, on Saturday and then come back to the last place local news department on Monday.

Howard needed a serious attitude adjustment even though his visit was nothing less than an entertaining performance. I still laugh thinking about it and we eventually became friends away from the workplace. However, since Howard had already checked out my management style, he knew instinctively he could no longer have his way in the newsroom. Under the previous news director, Howard had ruled the sports department like a dictator. As sports director, he would not allow any other sportscaster to appear on the station. Never, ever, not if hell were freezing over. Which meant that if Howard wasn't available for any reason, there wasn't a sportscaster on the newscast. But it was even worse than that. He may have been the only main sports anchor in the country that flat out refused to anchor the eleven o'clock newscast. While our competing stations provided viewers with scores in one of the most rabid sports towns in America, Howard, having left a prerecorded sports commentary, would be sipping martinis in a bar or out on the town rubbing elbows with Rona Barrett's *people*. In other words, he didn't want to anchor the eleven but didn't want anyone else to do it either.

It was high school all over again. *I'm not dating her anymore, but don't you dare ask her out.*

Weekend anchor Doug Johnson tells the story about Howard's evenings at the trendy 21 Club where he would hold court at the bar after the six o'clock newscast. Howard, who lived in the bedroom community of Pound Ridge, would pull a stunt at closing time. He'd tell five or six guys, "I'm going to get a limo. Do you want a ride home?" Of course, he had plenty of takers who wanted a ride with a network celebrity. Little did they know that once the limo left Manhattan, they would be asked to chip in for the cost of the ride.

We couldn't have a sports anchor who was bellied up to the bar every night at eleven, and we knew this situation had to be fixed immediately. "So, Howard," I asked, "why don't you anchor the eleven o'clock newscast?"

He leaned back in his chair. The mere suggestion seemed to be taken as an insult. "You don't need *me* to read *scores*. Grimsby can read the scores."

Incredibly, that had been the policy. With no sportscaster at eleven, the anchorman had been reading the scores every night. No highlights, no postgame locker-room interviews, no trade rumors, nothing. This in a city with the Yankees and Mets, two NFL franchises, two NBA teams, the NHL Rangers and a host of horse racing tracks. How he managed to get away with that still amazes me. His first visit was obviously setting me up to continue this country-club work schedule. It wasn't going to happen, but I didn't want to risk losing him.

Despite the baggage and the arrogant attitude, Howard Cosell was a special case. He got exclusive interviews no one else could snag, and he could gain access anywhere. The man was the most connected newsperson in the world of sports. Cosell, who also possessed a law degree, was a brilliant journalist who could speak eloquently on seemingly any subject. And of course, there was his enormous vocabulary that occasionally left you pulling out the dictionary after he'd left your office. Despite the fact that Howard fought my vision the entire way (basically because it was a concept that included a team of sports reporters rather than a one-man sports department), his point of view actually complimented the underlying concept of *Eyewitness News*.

Howard was always willing to dig deeply into any subject, always looking for a different angle, and had the ability to see the underlying bones in a sports story that many of his contemporaries glossed over. The problem was that Howard had no earthly concept about how to produce meaningful television; his content was superb, but his pieces looked like something from the 1950s. While I wanted him on the staff, he couldn't know I really didn't

Howard Casell's Greatest Interview with
The Greatest, Muhammad Ali

want him on the eleven o'clock news. Fortunately, my youthful confidence knew no bounds and I let him know that the first thing I had to do was get an eleven o'clock sportscaster. Grimsby's days of reading the scores were numbered. Howard looked at me gravely and I could see the wheels turning. He knew he could either give up the martinis and work the late shift or allow someone else to join the sports department. I gambled that he'd do anything rather than have to work nights, and I was right. I even offered a solution before he had too much time to think about it.

There was a radio sportscaster I had heard in New York, Lou Boda, who had the kind of straight delivery I wanted. I mentioned his name and Howard smiled broadly and thought he would be acceptable. I knew Boda was a solid radio reporter but soon discovered he had absolutely no television charisma. Boda was thrilled to make the jump to television, though his best work would eventually be done calling football games on radio.

Meanwhile, for every "personality" that was no longer part of the newscast, there was time to fill and not enough reporters to fill it. Unlike Philadelphia, I couldn't just fold my arms and bob my head like Barbara Eden in *I Dream of Jeannie* and *poof!* expect a roomful of reporters to magically appear. The New York unions were a lot more restrictive and had things really compartmentalized at WABC: writers could only write, editors could only edit, etc. And God forbid if any nonunion person actually touched the equipment. You had to treat every piece of gear like a hot stove. This would force me to look outside the station, but I preferred it that way. As a result, we would have a more seasoned staff of reporters. I could cherry-pick the best from around the country since just about everyone wanted to come to New York.

Even if we were the smallest fish in the world's biggest pond.

Chapter Fifteen

When you're basically building a newscast from scratch, it can take an awfully long time to get things done. Television executives who don't work in the news business often move at a glacial pace. In a perfect world, we could take a year to work on sets, graphics, find new staffers, and deal with unions. My goal was to get the new format on the air during the November ratings period (there are three each year: February, May, and November), which left me about ten weeks to hire a new on-air staff and get everyone comfortable with the style of reporting. We immediately put the word out that we were looking for the best and brightest reporters in the country, and as you can imagine, it didn't take long for the talent reels to start pouring in.

But the technical side was just as important. The content might change drastically, but if the newscast didn't *look* right, it would fail. Everything had to come together at the same time if we were to be successful. And New Yorkers are notoriously impatient; the viewers wouldn't be the type to sit around waiting for a newscast to hit its stride. We had to hit a home run right out of the gate. That meant we had to practice before putting such a groundbreaking venture on the air. In other words, dress rehearsals for both the on-camera people and those behind the scenes.

A plan was worked out with Big Julie Barnathan. We started rehearsals between newscasts a few weeks before the launch, which I'd penciled in for November 17th. That was far enough into the November sweep ratings to give us an excuse if we didn't score well. At first, we didn't need the on-air talent since we had to get the studio crew, directors, and producers comfortable with the new system. We could get any warm body to sit in the anchor chairs and pretend to be Grimsby and Cosell until we actually needed them.

When I arrived, the newscast had been using stationary camera shots that were set up before the beginning of the show. The camera operator would frame the shot and when the director gave him the okay, he'd lock it down and generally wouldn't have to move for thirty minutes. In those days, every local newscast in America pretty much looked the same. No fancy preproduced opens with music, no eye-catching graphics. You were pretty much going to hear a staff announcer introduce the anchor with some ticker tape sound effects in the background and then the anchor would read every story.

You didn't need to see an air check to know this. The wooden stools behind each camera were a great indicator.

Camera operators were told that they'd never need something to sit on again because they'd be constantly moving. You'd have thought from the looks on their faces that I'd handed each of them a bag of manure. They rolled their eyes and went through the motions while the directors and producers offered input from the booth. The union cameramen weren't happy being ordered around by management. At one point, one of them said to me, "If you have something to say to me, talk to my shop steward."

Luckily, Big Julie was in my corner and they grudgingly complied with the requests from the directors and producers. They knew Julie had an incredible reputation, having been a key player in some of the more innovative breakthroughs (like slow motion) during coverage of the Olympics. Playing ball with him was imperative if they wanted to get any future plum network assignments.

The people had been so set in their ways, so stationary during a stagnant newscast, it took three full days for everyone on the technical crew to get the new movements down pat. We'd keep the crews working overtime until everyone was comfortable with his or her job.

And though they weren't happy about the extra work and the physical demands of their new duties, their paychecks were getting fatter. All the overtime was adding up, so they began to think that maybe this new guy from Pennsylvania wasn't so bad after all. They started to become more cooperative, knowing I was putting money in their pockets.

On the fourth day, we started rehearsing with the directors, Merle Bredwell and Marty Morris, along with the anchors and reporters. But this time, we used real thirty-minute scripts, complete with film, graphics, and music. It was a visually intensive newscast and we needed to make sure every facet would work perfectly. The anchor would toss to the reporter on set, who would then introduce his or her own story. Graphics appeared, film rolled, and the people in the control room began to see the plan take shape. We started to see nods of approval and a glint of excitement.

These were true dress rehearsals except we had the ability to stop and go over things whenever we had a problem. We even practiced announcer Scott Vincent to get the introduction to the newscast just right. He became the voice of *Eyewitness News* for many years. Rehearsing a thirty-minute newscast could take more than an hour on some days, but the crew pressed on as we worked out every bug we could think of. I would stop in the middle of the script and ask for suggestions, ideas to make things look even better. People became eager to contribute and I found we had some very clever minds beneath the tough union exteriors.

The newscast needed one more whistle to go along with all the production bells: sound. We'd used an upbeat instrumental in Philadelphia, a cut lifted from the James Bond movie *From Russia With Love.* I wanted something along the same lines for New York, but something so different, so unique that anyone hearing it would instantly know they were watching a newscast, not a Sean Connery movie. As it turned out, we needed Paul Newman more than James Bond.

Marty Morris and I picked the music during a visit to the ABC's huge record library. The longtime librarian brought out a huge stack of albums that fell into the instrumental category, and I knew we might be there for a long time. We listened to cut after cut, dropping the needle on vinyl for hours. After a while, we didn't even look at the album covers. After going through dozens of records, we finally found what we were looking for as about seven seconds of music just popped. It had such incredible energy it jumped out at everyone in the room.

"That's it!" I said. A lot of people in the room had perked up at the same time and everyone nodded. But the snippet of music ended in a few seconds and I shook my head. "But it's too short."

"No problem," said an audio technician, gently pulling the record from the phonograph as if it were made of gold. "I can loop it and make it as long as you want."

We all agreed the music was perfect. The seven-second instrumental clip was from, of all places, the soundtrack of a Paul Newman movie, *Cool Hand Luke.* It was called the "Tar Sequence." The incredibly fast tempo, close to that of "Flight of the Bumblebee," couldn't help but drive up the excitement level of our viewers. As it turned out, the composer was none other than Lalo Schifrin, who had created the pulse-pounding beat of the *Mission Impossible* theme just two years earlier. The music would eventually be used at most of the ABC stations. And we didn't just use the sequence at the beginning of the newscast; it was also used as "bumper music" going into and returning from commercial breaks and at the end during the credit roll. Schifrin still likes to say he's more famous for the *Eyewitness News* theme than anything else in his long career.

Graphics would be used at a level never before attempted. Since there were so many people now on the set, it would give us the opportunity to "super" (short for *superimpose*) the on-air person's name along with our new logo, so the viewer would see an anchor and on the bottom third of the screen would read, *Roger Grimsby, Eyewitness News* or *Tex Antoine, Eyewitness News.* This continuous use of the newscast name and logo would, in time, burn into the brains of the regular viewers. On the occasions reporters were live in the field or not on the set, they would "tag out" their stories with their name, followed by "Channel 7, *Eyewitness News.*" By the end of each newscast, the viewer would have seen or heard the name of the newscast and the number of the channel they were watching about two dozen times. And they would have heard our theme music a dozen times.

Since all of these new elements required much more attention from the technical staff, some of the rehearsals were a bit rough at first. We were truly increasing the workload and the details tenfold. But things started coming together and more important, I could sense the staff truly beginning to believe in the product. It is one thing to march into a newsroom and tell people you have all the answers and "how you did it" somewhere else; new news directors do it every time they change jobs. But it is another for the members of the staff to get their hands dirty, put those answers into motion, and see the results. It helped that I was there by their side. I tried hard not to show any doubt; in reality, I had none anyway. Years later, Leonard Goldenson asked, "Did you ever doubt *Eyewitness News* would succeed?" It was the first time I ever thought about it and told him so. But if your staff ever senses that you don't totally believe in what you're doing, they won't either. My attitude began to trickle down. They began to work harder and get more excited as we got closer to the launch. Anytime I felt frustrated, I'd hold it in until I got back to my hotel room and then just pound the hell out of a pillow.

Even Roger Grimsby got on board as he could see the light at the end of the tunnel. I'd told him, "You're going to be sharing the stage, but the stage is going to be much bigger."

Every day of my first ten weeks was long. I was arriving at nine in the morning and getting back to my hotel at midnight. My family wouldn't arrive till January anyway, and I really had nothing better to do than throw myself into my work. There would be plenty of time to scale back a little after the launch, as New York and all that it offered would still be there.

The rehearsals went on for about ten days. Meanwhile, we still had two newscasts a day to put together. Despite the heavy workload that added rehearsal after rehearsal to everyone's regular duties, the content of our newscast was getting better. The reporters who had come on board were coming up with great stories. Everyone started to look forward to the end of the rehearsals, as they were eager to set sail on the new ship.

I dangled another carrot in front of the new reporters: the promise of additional face time. "You don't have to do just one story a day," I told them. "If you can knock out two good stories, I'll put you on both newscasts." I saw several pairs of eyes grow wide. The lure of doubling their amount of on-camera exposure was too great to resist, and they started bringing back exclusive after exclusive. They saw that a little more effort on their part would help their careers. In a market the size of the New York metropolitan area, there was never a shortage of stories. WABC had just never fielded a staff of reporters to find them.

Though I had a dream about where I wanted to go, I couldn't do it without the input from a competent staff. I gave them the destination but let them help figure out how we were going to get there. In many successful operations, the best ideas come from the rank and file; people who simply follow orders from the top of the mountain seldom take your ideas to the next level. I impressed upon the staff that we had an open door policy, that we all needed to share and discuss ideas if we were truly to realize our potential. I wanted to change the skeptics in the newsroom into contributors, and the suggestions started to pour into my office.

On November 3, three new reporters arrived: Bob Lape, Doug Johnson, and Bill Aylward. It happened to be Election Day, the television news equivalent of Super Bowl Sunday, not an easy assignment for a reporter on his first day. Thankfully, they were all seasoned journalists so we simply gave them a crash course on the new format. They hit the ground running, turning stories while jumping into the rehearsals that were already underway.

I had arrived the day after Labor Day. It was now the middle of November. The rehearsals were looking great; people had really gotten their new jobs down pat.

It was time to light the candle.

Chapter Sixteen

On November 17, 1968, I knew that what was about to hit the air in less than twelve hours would change television news forever.

As long as all the staffers did their jobs the way they were supposed to.

I'm not sure if the term *micromanage* existed back then, but the concept certainly did. I was determined to stay out of the way when the clock struck six. It wouldn't do me or the staff any good to be hovering around, making everyone nervous. There are many news directors who routinely call the control room during a newscast; this upsets everyone (since the reason for the call is never good) and generally starts the technical error snowball rolling downhill at breakneck speed. And sticking your nose into every little detail just conveys the message that you have no confidence in your staff. Creative people are wired differently and aren't very effective if they're walking on eggshells, though I'd spent just about every rehearsal sitting next to the producer and director in the control room or out in the studio, I would watch the first edition of the new *Eyewitness News* from the comforts of my office. I wanted the staff to know I trusted them, that even if I wasn't in the building, everything would go off like clockwork.

And it just about did.

Despite a few glitches that only someone in the industry would notice, the six o'clock newscast looked like a million bucks (especially in comparison with *Noisemakers*). The music, the movement, the graphics, and most importantly, the interaction between the anchors and reporters worked perfectly. Shortly after six-thirty, the newsroom was filled with an enthusiasm I hadn't seen since my arrival.

The executives at WABC and the network were in awe at what they'd seen.

R to L Bill Beutel, Roger Grimsby, Geraldo Rivera, Roger Sharp, Doug Johnson

The new blood gave the newscast a true shot in the arm. I'd managed to get those three new reporters in time for the launch, guys who would become key players down the road. Bob Lape, a solid, talented reporter, joined us from WBZ in Boston where he had cemented an excellent reputation as a political reporter. He would take care of the city hall beat but eventually gain fame for a unique feature segment. Doug Johnson came from Philly; I'd watched him on the competition there and knew he had the talent and style to fit into the format. He and his producer Norman Fine had managed to give KYW a run for its money, even though we had ten times the staff. I was so impressed I also hired Norman Fine to produce the 11:00 p.m. news. Bill Aylward arrived from WJZ in Baltimore where he had been an anchor. He'd been recommended by Executive Producer Bob Hoyt and would handle some of the anchoring duties while covering crime and politics. And we'd picked up a guy to do features named John Bartholomew Tucker, quite a character who had made a good living doing national voice-overs.

Meanwhile, our six o'clock news had an interesting lead-in. Before the days when people threw chairs on Jerry Springer or jumped on Oprah's couch, movies, game shows, and soap operas were the staple of daytime television. WABC ran a ninety-minute program simply called *The 4:30 Movie*. Sometimes we aired very good films, but mostly it was a B movie sci-fi cheesefest. Occasionally, we would break up a miniseries like *Roots* into several parts.

In the bigger markets like New York you'd receive daily ratings for every fifteen-minute period. I had noticed that when the movie at four thirty was a good one, we managed to hold on to the bigger audience from six o'clock until six fifteen and until the end of the newscast at six thirty. In less than six months, we were not only holding on to the audience, we were building on it.

On Good Friday in 1969, the afternoon movie was *The Robe,* starring Richard Burton, one of the great religious flicks of the 1950s. That afternoon, *The Robe* got a 17 rating and a 34 share, which meant more than a third of the New York area audience was tuned to WABC-TV during that time period.

Eyewitness News got a 19 rating that night, two full points higher than the movie. (And remember, the six o'clock newscast didn't even have a 1 rating for *Roger Grimsby and the Noisemakers* less than six months earlier.)

This told me that people were tuning into our newscast whether they liked the movie or not. And if they were watching another channel at 5:59 p.m., they were getting up from their chairs and tuning in WABC (or at least having the kids do it).

Since the occasional good movie was helping us at six, we started to look for a strong lead-in for the eleven o'clock newscast to use as a promotional vehicle. But while WABC controlled the hours outside of prime time, we couldn't do anything about the floundering network in the evening. At that time, ABC had very few decent shows in prime time as it truly had earned its nickname the Third Network. When the fall schedule for 1969 came out, the offerings at ten o'clock were not exactly inspiring. *Love, American Style* was bad enough, but who at ABC could possibly think a show called *Jimmy Durante Presents the Lennon Sisters* would pull decent ratings? I didn't see much help coming from the prime-time lineup. Fortunately, ABC would have one bona fide hit right out of the gate on Tuesday nights—*Marcus Welby, M.D.* The pilot had gotten good buzz when it aired as a movie of the week in March. It was an hourlong medical drama featuring Robert Young, who had endeared himself to millions as the perfect dad on *Father Knows Best*. His protégé was a handsome young motorcycle-riding doctor played by James Brolin, who is now married to Barbra Streisand. It became the first ABC offering to ever finish a season as the number one-rated prime-time show, as it reached the top in its second year.

While Tuesday was not the traditional day of the week to put your best news stories, it was a day when viewers were tuned in to ABC just before the late newscast. We decided to hitch our wagon to the brightest (and only) star on the network. We would run our strongest stories on Tuesdays and promote them by having the anchor tease them during *Marcus Welby*. If there was any kind of breaking news on that day of the week, we'd tell the viewers about it during *Marcus Welby*. Viewers who watched other stations at eleven started sticking around on Tuesday night.

We also started selectively breaking in to regular programming more often with weather bulletins. While New York is not exactly tornado alley, there is plenty to talk about during the winter. So anytime snow, sleet, or freezing rain was in the forecast, we'd break in. Since so many people in the New York area commute to work, we provided a great time-saving service by giving them advance warning that weather was going to affect their trip.

With all the in-house promotion and frequent break-ins for news and weather bulletins, we were giving the viewers the impression that we were always on top of things, that something interesting was happening at *Eyewitness News* no matter what the hour. Shots from the newsroom always featured a flurry of activity in the background, and it wasn't staged. In the city that never sleeps, we had to give the impression that the people in the newsroom never did. Because in reality, our staffers were working their tails off.

Incredibly, the one thing that was derailing our progress was something most newspeople live for. Major breaking news. In the early days of *Eyewitness News*, I must confess I actually dreaded any big stories that could bring the country to a halt. (And the sixties probably had more major news events than any other decade. During the span of two days in 1969, we had both the first moon landing and Ted Kennedy's Chappaquiddick incident.) Viewers were beginning to sample us and stick around, but they didn't quite trust us with the really important stuff. When major news events popped up, the viewers went back to their old standby anchors at WNBC and WCBS.

But on the average day, we were making significant progress. And the average day is when you breed loyalty among your viewers. These days, many stations only pull out the stops during sweeps months. But if you can break big stories on a daily basis, the ratings periods will take care of themselves. We kept plugging along every day, often coming up with small exclusives that would set us apart.

Meanwhile, the crews reported they were getting attention in the field. Viewers started yelling, "Hey, *Eyewitness!*" when they'd recognize one of our people or see a news vehicle.

While the audience for the six o'clock newscast was steadily growing, I wanted to double it by taking the newscast to a new level—expanding it to an hour. A lot of people who work in New York commute on a daily basis, and I knew many of them simply weren't home in time to catch our newscast. It was the opportunity to develop an entirely new audience.

Naturally, my superiors were a little apprehensive about this, having done a one-hour version before without any success. They wanted to see if we could compete with a thirty-minute broadcast before jumping into the deep end of the pool. I'd bring up the idea every month but was always told to be patient. They saw the ratings trend was going up but wanted to make sure we weren't just a flash in the pan. While most viewers across the country are very slow to change, New Yorkers will often go with the hot hand and jump on the nearest bandwagon.

As the ratings continued to grow and the staff became more comfortable with the format, I finally got the approval to expand the newscast to an hour. We would simply slide the ABC network newscast to seven o'clock. (In the eastern time zone, prime time begins at eight, so local affiliates have a lot of latitude in what they can air during the previous hour.)

Formats for half-hour newscasts were pretty standard at the time, usually consisting of three news segments (known as "blocks"), followed by weather and sports. So putting together a rundown for an hour was a definite challenge.

The first incarnation of our sixty-minute newscast was actually inspired by radio. At that time, there were two all-news radio stations in New York but I loved the slogan of WINS, an AM radio station with the slogan, "You give us twenty-two minutes, we'll give you the world." The station, which called itself "Ten-Ten WINS" since they resided at 1010 on the AM dial, would use a "news clock" by which the top story of the day would come up three times each hour. You could always count on news at a certain time, weather at a certain time, etc. If you just wanted a baseball score, you could rest assured that you could get it at fifteen or forty-five minutes after the hour. Just like clockwork. Commuters loved this station. Sports fans that had no interest in news knew exactly when to get the latest scores.

I thought we could use the same approach with an hourlong newscast, dividing the show into three segments. We'd start the newscast with the lead story at six, then go back to it at six-twenty and six-forty. We would simply rewrite all the stories twice to keep them fresh. Weather and sports would have three segments each hour. It seemed like a no-brainer.

But it was a big mistake, as the commuters who listened to WINS were done with traveling when they watched television. I quickly discovered that what worked on radio didn't necessarily translate to TV at all; it was truly a case of apples and oranges. Our ratings showed people were tuning out at twenty after six as they'd quickly figured out the same stories were coming up again. Twice. There was no reason to stick around for the entire hour as the last forty minutes would be a double rerun of the first twenty. Ironically, the

longer newscast resulted in viewers watching *less*. The people who had been tuning in for thirty minutes were now watching just twenty.

It took only two weeks for this experiment to die as I put a stake through its heart and cut my losses as quickly as possible. I didn't want to alienate the audience we'd built with a format they clearly didn't like. With an hourlong format, it

Sunday New York Times: L to R Roger Grimsby, Tom Dunn, 2nd Row: The author, Melba Tolliver, Milton Lewis, John Tucker, 3rd Row, John Schubeck, Bob Lape, Tex Antoine.

was obvious we needed sixty minutes worth of fresh news stories if viewers were going to invest an hour of their lives. So we simply pressed the reporters to come up with more stories and gave them the flexibility to let their pieces run longer if the situation warranted.

Nothing takes long in the Big Apple. Hence, the term *New York minute*. In a town that believes Hall of Famers are only as good as their last game, *Eyewitness News* blasted out of the starting gate like Secretariat. New Yorkers are quick to slap tags on everything, so when we got off to a terrific start, we became a watercooler newscast. And trust me, if we were bad, New Yorkers would not have been shy about telling us. Within the first year, we were getting lots of press and positive feedback from the viewers. The *New York Times* did a Sunday story in the arts and leisure section. TV editor Harry Waters wrote, "Eyewitness News is the catchy title WABC-TV has bestowed on its two evening wrap-ups of local events, but to, at least this eyewitness, the show might better be called, *Wiseguy News*." We got a nice picture of the whole news team and he captured the essence of the entire concept. The ratings showed a steady upward trend.

Now we had to fine-tune the product. Our reporting staff was developing nicely, and I was proud of the hires we'd made. But I needed to find more experienced help for the anchor desk to take things to the next level.

One thing that jumped out during every newscast was Roger Grimsby's sarcastic wit. While it could often be brilliant and his snappy repartee with Howard Cosell was a definite draw to the New York audience, it was getting to be a bit much with Roger in the solo anchor position. A few clever quips every hour was one thing, but we didn't need him to utter a snide comment after every single story. We all figured there was only one way to balance this curmudgeon, at least in the eyes of the viewers.

We all talked about it and decided to pair Grimsby with a coanchor who would be his opposite number. Sort of a television news version of a "straight man." I like to promote from within, but there was no one already on the staff who fit the bill.

The surest way to success in television is *box office*, a loose term encompassing glitz, pizzazz, energy, and glamour that translates into audience drawing power. Our new product was creating a buzz around town, but WABC-TV had literally nobody on the air that the audience knew. The station had to rectify that situation as quickly as possible while getting a compatible partner for Roger. And there was only one way to do it.

Raid the competition.

Since there had been no way to attract any anchor to *Roger Grimsby and the Noisemakers,* I hadn't even bothered to look for a coanchor before we launched the new format. We knew the strongest advertisement was to broadcast a newscast proving we were serious about competing in the market. We'd already gotten the new *Eyewitness News* look on the air, graphics, set, music, and format. And we were providing the viewers with solid content on a daily basis, along with a fair amount of exclusives. It was obvious to anyone in the business that we'd hired top-notch reporters. The format was new but the content was the result of old-fashioned hard work; our reporters and photographers were simply outhustling the competition. This gave prospective talent at the competing stations the feeling that the station was actually turning around. Thanks to people like Julian Barnathan and some solid news staffers, *Eyewitness News* had the appearance of strength from the very first day we debuted the format.

After the launch took a ton off my plate, we began looking for Roger's partner in earnest. We'd been watching the competition, looking at the ratings, and had some ideas about a possible coanchor. Once things began to settle down and we'd had some time to make our first impression, I picked up the phone and went to the top, approaching the most senior anchorman in New York, WCBS-TV's Jim Jensen. To illustrate the revolving door nature of television news at the time, Jensen had been at channel 2 just four years. He had gotten his big break as the "pool" reporter in Hyannisport, Massachusetts, during the days following the Kennedy assassination in 1963. Shortly thereafter, he was hired as an anchor at channel 2 and quickly became a force to be reckoned with. His connections to Camelot had come in handy as he had provided excellent coverage of Bobby Kennedy's New York senate campaign. He had a tough no-nonsense anchoring style; we all agreed he was our first choice and would complement Grimsby very well while putting a serious dent in channel 2's ratings.

We arranged for a meeting with Jensen through his agent, Ralph Mann, of International Creative Management. He didn't want to take a chance and meet at a restaurant so we hired a car. The station rolled out the red carpet, renting a limousine for the occasion, and I picked up Jensen after one of his newscasts at the West Fifty-seventh Street broadcast center of CBS. We drove around the city in style as I explained how *Eyewitness News* was going to change the world and how he would be one of the leaders of this exciting new concept. Jensen listened intently and said he was very interested. When the evening came to an end, I was certain we had a good shot at getting him to jump ship.

But I later found out he really wasn't warm to the idea of moving across the street. He'd told Ralph Mann, who was always looking for the best deals for his clients, that he really wanted to stay at CBS. Mann did a masterful job of letting me down easy. As it turned out, Jensen wasn't kidding about staying put; he ended up being channel 2's anchor for an incredible twenty-nine years.

So with Jensen off the table, it was on to plan B. Next up, CBS network correspondent Morton Dean. We shared something in common since he had also worked for Westinghouse in Boston at the same station that had employed reporter Bob Lape. I was told Dean had been a strong city hall reporter in New York before making the jump to the network, and an anchor with a nose for politics was very appealing even though I had that particular beat covered with Lape. Dean would prove to be a valuable asset on election coverage as an anchor's knowledge of politics is always painfully obvious to the viewers during those fly-by-the-seat-of-your-pants newscasts. I approached him about joining *Eyewitness News* at a lunch at Le Biarritz on West Fifty-seventh Street and broke the ice by recalling the glory of our days at Westinghouse.

Morton Dean had checked out *Eyewitness News*. He was polite but very candid about our product. He'd said he didn't think *Eyewitness News* was going to make it. He declined the offer before I even had the chance to make one. I understood his point of view as it is tough for many people who have made the jump to the network to go back to local, especially when the local station was currently residing in the ratings basement. But it wouldn't have been a good fit to bring someone aboard who didn't totally believe in the format.

A few years later, when our operation was the toast of the town, I was having lunch in the very same restaurant with Harry Reasoner and Mort, showing a ton of class, came up to say he had made a mistake. He was barely getting any airtime on the *CBS Evening News* with his reports.

But the tides, as they so often do in television news, turned for Mort. A few years later, he was appointed weekend anchor for the *CBS Evening News* and often filled in for Walter Cronkite. I saw him again at the same restaurant and it was my turn to return the favor. I walked over to his table and congratulated him on making it without *Eyewitness News*.

But since he and Jensen were out of the running, I still didn't have a coanchor for Grimsby. And we really wanted someone who already had a following in New York.

Then the gossip machine worked in our favor, and you have to understand that in an industry filled with people who make a living being nosy, nothing is more alluring than a story about someone within the business about to take a fall. It is a business that worships success, but roots for failure. (See *Couric, Katie*.) Television news gossip traveled with the speed of e-mail decades before the Internet even existed. In this case, a very popular head was about to roll.

The word around town was that WCBS-TV's news director, Lee Hanna, was not getting along well with Tom Dunn, his eleven o'clock anchorman. Dunn, who bore a resemblance to Connecticut Senator Christopher Dodd, had strong ratings at eleven o'clock. But Hanna was getting ready to dump him anyway. Sometimes personality conflicts can even trump talent that brings you good ratings. Hanna obviously knew he could simply plug Jim Jensen into the late newscast while keeping him on the six o'clock. Dunn was apparently walking on eggshells around Hanna and not at all happy. He was reportedly considering work in the political field. We'd heard he was having conversations with supporters of Richard Nixon when the former vice president was running for the Republican nomination against Nelson Rockefeller earlier in the year. Making a pitch for Tom Dunn looked like a no-brainer; it was a marvelous opportunity for us to hire one of the best-known anchors in New York. Dunn was right behind Jim Jensen in seniority, having joined WCBS just four months after Jensen in 1964.

Tom Dunn was represented by Bill Cooper, one of the top agents at the time who counted Mike Wallace, Roger Mudd, and a host of other network news superstars among his clients. We all agreed we had to move as quickly as possible to avoid the notion that we were hiring someone who was being let go by CBS. In television, especially New York, the appearance of someone being "damaged goods" is a very real thing with the audience. It would look like a coup if we had lured Dunn to *Eyewitness News*. If we'd waited until he was unemployed, it would appear as though we were bottom-feeding. But we also knew that Dunn was desperate to make a move immediately as he had no desire to be out of work. He would have absolutely no bargaining power if he was spending time at the unemployment office.

I called Bill Cooper and not surprisingly, he didn't waste any time scheduling a meeting. The agent, like most of the people who represent television anchors, started out playing hardball. He went through his entire presentation with demands for a huge salary and a laundry list of perks. He obviously didn't know that Dunn's problems at channel 2 were common knowledge. I listened politely to the entire sales pitch without saying a word. When he was through, I motioned him forward to my desk and slid a single piece of paper toward him. I said in a very low voice, "You've got one minute to take this offer. And we'll cut it in half after Hanna gets done with him." He swallowed hard, exhaled deeply and said, "You've got a deal." We shook hands and we had found the perfect balance for our anchor desk.

So now WABC had Roger Grimsby, whose on-air demeanor was not unlike taking sandpaper to fine china, and Tom Dunn to smooth him out. I explained to the affable Dunn the importance of being himself when coanchoring with Grimsby. We had noted that Grimsby's attitude was trickling down to the other reporters. Bill Aylward, one of our more credible newsmen who we had first selected to work with Grimsby, was making the same mistake as did another of our anchors, John Schubeck; both were trying to imitate Grimsby in style and delivery. In Aylward's case, it really didn't fit his personality; he was the sort of guy who'd stop to help people change tires on the way to work. And as New Yorkers would eventually come to learn, there was only one Roger Grimsby.

Dunn smiled and assured me he could hold his own with Roger, and we were on our way. Hiring the 11:00 p.m. number one anchor from WCBS was the first step toward credibility for *Eyewitness News*, and we knew he'd bring viewers with him. Dunn was, by his own admission, basically lazy and not really a competitive person. He did his very best to be his own man, but like the others before him, slowly began to deliver the news Grimsby style, which apparently affected anyone who came near it like some incurable sarcasm virus. We spent hours talking with Dunn about the problem to no avail. It didn't take long before all the viewers were getting were two Grimsbys: cold, snarling anchors.

Someone suggested that getting Dunn out in the field might improve things. We pushed him as hard as possible to go out and cover news as a reporter in addition to his anchoring as a device to increase his credibility with the audience. He always did an acceptable job, but his basic low-key approach prevented him from really breaking through to the level of superstar anchor.

Eventually, the problem would resolve itself. But not in a good way.

In 1971, I came to work one morning and learned our own anchorman was the subject of a major news story, and a scandal at that. Dunn, an avid pilot, had gotten himself involved with some shady real estate promoters who needed a well-known, credible partner. He had been set up as the front man for some partners who sold mortgages properties. There was one minor detail that landed them in court: they were selling property they did not own. Dunn loved flying his own plane. He got mixed up in a scheme to fly prospective buyers over the properties in his airplane while his partners pointed out the highlights of somebody else's land below. Only in New York.

Real estate speculators were sucked into the scheme, obviously figuring that anything involving a major market anchorman had to be on the up-and-up. Tom Dunn was indicted for participating in the fraudulent mortgage scheme. He cut a deal with the prosecutor and pleaded guilty to a misdemeanor in return for his cooperation with the authorities.

Credibility is everything in the news business, and no one at WABC could imagine viewers trusting someone who'd helped others commit fraud, inadvertently or not. It took only a few moments with ABC's corporate lawyers to work out exactly how we would dismiss Tom Dunn. By the time he got to the office after cutting his plea bargain deal, his termination papers were ready. He tried to offer an explanation for his actions, but no one wanted to hear about it. We simply told him it was over. Ironically, after just a few months, agent Cooper had some network offers in hand, along with a chance for Dunn to become the news director and anchor of a New York independent station, WOR-TV, which had no real news operation. Tom took the job at channel 9 and flourished for years. The public, it should also be noted, has a very short memory and will often forgive the transgressions of someone it likes.

Several years later I became a news advisor to WOR-TV, and my first meeting with Dunn was about as exciting as my last. He had the great voice and status around which to build a news team. He eventually ended a twenty-three-year career anchoring in New York on channels 2, 7, and 9; a genuinely "nice" guy retiring at fifty-seven years of age on his own terms to Florida where he had anchored for ten years before coming to New York.

Meanwhile, we were back to square one again, still without the coanchor needed to complement Roger Grimsby.

Chapter Seventeen

Ironically, the person who ended up being the perfect partner for Roger Grimsby was someone who used to anchor at WABC.

We'd been racking our brains for possible coanchors, but the cupboard was bare. After checking out all the talent at the competition, it was clear that the solution either didn't want to work for us or wasn't already on the air in New York. Finally, Don Dunphy came up with the name of Bill Beutel.

Beutel was an interesting story. An army veteran, he'd written a letter to Edward R. Murrow asking for advice on pursuing a career in the news business. Incredibly, Murrow wrote back and told him to enroll in Columbia University's Graduate School of Journalism. Beutel, with a warm soothing voice, started his career in radio, working first in Cleveland (small world)

before moving to CBS Radio in New York. When WABC started its newsroom in the early sixties, Beutel was the anchor of a newscast called *The Big News*. (Whoever had been coming up with the names for newscasts and promotional slogans at WABC certainly had unusual taste, though it was better than *Noisemakers*.)

Dunphy knew Beutel well, having worked with him closely for four years. Don had produced Bill's weekend interview programs as well as serving in the same capacity for out-of-town coverage of political events. He told me Bill Beutel was the consummate professional, an excellent writer and journalist, and a very nice man.

Beutel had grown frustrated with WABC and had left the station shortly before my arrival. And when he left town, he also left the country, taking a job as ABC's London

Anchorman Bill Beutel

bureau chief. When he took that job, he was succeeded by—you guessed it, Roger Grimsby.

Beutel was the anti-Grimsby. A lean polished man who simply exuded class, Bill no doubt fit in very well in London. He was, to put it simply, a very proper human being. If Ian Fleming had written James Bond as a news anchor, he would have looked and sounded like Bill Beutel.

Dunphy thought it would be a perfect match. In this case, opposites would definitely have to attract.

I called Beutel in London and invited him to New York but for more than just a job interview. Roger was about to go on vacation, and I suggested that Bill fill in to see how he liked the new format. He worked it out with the network and agreed to the trial run. Though it wouldn't tell me how he'd mesh with Grimsby, it would at least afford me the opportunity to get to know the man and see how he interacted with the staff.

When he arrived, we had a nice conversation in my office. But I needed to see if he had the resolve to handle Roger.

"Everyone who sits next to Grimsby becomes just like him," I said, telling him I didn't need another sarcastic anchor. "Are you man enough to be your own man?"

Bill Beutel looked at me sharply, and with his newly acquired transatlantic attitude responded, "Of course, my man, of course."

It didn't take long for him to provide me with a glimpse of the future. During Grimsby's two-week vacation, Beutel was definitely "his own man." He demonstrated a sense of humor and quick wit that were different, more straightforward than the sardonic, dry demeanor that characterized Roger. In our new format, Bill Beutel was a completely different anchor,

Roger Beutel, General Manager Kenneth McQueen

warm to the touch, easy to watch and listen to. Where Roger Grimsby was a hot dog and a beer, Beutel was champagne and caviar. The combination would provide something for every New Yorker. The society page set would love the refined Beutel and was used to dealing with New Yorkers like Grimsby. The blue-collar crowd already loved Roger and would appreciate the fact that Bill never talked down to them even though he wore pocket squares.

Now we had to get Beutel on board. Working with Bill in the newsroom was a breeze, but his agent was another story. Where I was dealing from strength with Tom Dunn, I didn't have much leverage when it came to Beutel. His agent, Ralph Mann, knew his client was talented and how badly I needed a coanchor. He simply would not budge off his asking price of $100,000. I told him we were only paying Grimsby $60,000.

"He won't come here for that," said Mann, adding that Beutel was quite content to continue working for the network in London. "You must be out of your mind. He won't come here for less than one hundred thousand." It was money-where-your-mouth-is time, so I went to the GM, who went to corporate. The answer was, "Hell, give it to him."

"We can't," I said, knowing Grimsby would hit the roof when he found out. (And I *knew* he'd find out. There are no secrets in TV.) "We can't hire a new guy for forty thousand more than Roger. We can't give money to Beutel and not to Grimsby."

ABC surprised me again when they told me to hire Beutel for six figures and give Grimsby a raise to match it.

So I got to have an enjoyable meeting with Roger in which I told him he would have a coanchor but get a forty-thousand-dollar raise. Even Grimsby didn't have a sarcastic comeback to that. Eventually he would return the favor to Bill as he got an offer from WNBC and we had to match it to keep him. Of course, we were then required to bump Beutel's salary up to Roger's new level.

The two seemed to blend well right off the bat though Bill, being more low-key, came off as a bit less compelling than Roger. So we decided to build on his strengths while promoting the two as a team. We'd hired a new advertising executive, Jerry Della Femina. It was the beginning of gorilla advertising for news. Amusing but right to the heart of the viewer. We directly attacked CBS and NBC with ads showing we were attracting audience from their stations.

The CBS eye with a tear flowing from it struck a bit too close to home, and Bill Paley called Leonard Goldenson personally and we pulled it after a few weeks. He also devised some very clever promotional spots that suggested both anchormen were equally important. In one, Roger and Bill are walking down a street, each holding a news script as they head for the WABC studio on Sixty-sixth Street. A typical New York couple loaded down with shopping bags is headed toward them. Roger gives Bill a gentle elbow and says, "They're looking at us. They probably recognize me." But then the couple passes and they actually pay fierce attention to Bill, who beams.

We had a series of these promos that showed the two to be friendly rivals and not above poking fun at each other. In a classic spot years later, Beutel describes Roger.

**400,000 NEW YORKERS HAVE ALREADY SWITCHED
TO CHANNEL 7 EYEWITNESS NEWS
SOME OF THEM MUST HAVE COME FROM CHANNEL 2**

EYEWITNESS NEWS ⑦
WHEN ARE YOU GOING TO SWITCH?

400,000 NEW YORKERS HAVE ALREADY SWITCHED
TO CHANNEL 7 EYEWITNESS NEWS
SOME OF THEM MUST HAVE COME FROM CHANNEL 2

EYEWITNESS NEWS ⑦
WHEN ARE YOU GOING TO SWITCH?

"People always ask me, 'What is Grimsby like? Brash and arrogant?' No, not really. I'd do anything for Roger. Except lend him money." Up until that time in the history of TV News advertising, viewers had seen nothing but highbrow ads featuring classical music and deep-voiced announcers intoning the virtues of CBS and NBC. ABC had nothing to boast about nor the budget to do anything if it had.

Despite the different exteriors, the two men were, at heart, solid journalists. They got along well and had great respect for each other. Within a few months, the new anchor team was a hit.

One of the few disputes between the big men was a tug-of-war over a device called an "eye light." Bill had happened to visit the ABC studios one day when he noticed Barbara Walters had a tiny light near her seat at the anchor desk. The eye light could magically erase any hollows or dark circles beneath the eyes. Beutel, a strikingly handsome man who really didn't need any help, became obsessed with getting eye lights added to the *Eyewitness News* set. Grimsby, who couldn't care less about his on-camera appearance, forbade anyone to install eye lights in the studio. Though this never became an argument, the eye light discussion kept popping up until Roger finally relented, but he warned the union electricians there would be hell to pay if anyone installed an eye light on his side of the set.

The eye light expense for Beutel was authorized and I thought that would be the end of it. But there was a surprise waiting the same day the thing was installed. When the two anchors arrived on the set at ten minutes till six, Roger discovered to his great horror that the electricians had installed the eye light on the wrong side of the desk—his. In a fit of anger, Roger marched into News Director Ron Tindiglia's office, threw his script into the air, and stormed out of the studio.

The crew went into a panic for something like this had never happened. One of the producers in the studio called Don Dunphy and told him, "Roger just walked out! The news goes on in ten minutes and we have to get somebody!"

Dunphy slammed down his phone and jumped into action. He ran out into the hallway where he spotted a young reporter who had just started working at the station.

Her name: Joan Lunden. (Her real name, Joan Blunden, a slight change we made for the better.)

Dunphy caught up with her, told her to run down to the studio as fast as she could and prepare to coanchor the six o'clock newscast with Bill Beutel. Petrified, Joan ran to the studio, was quickly made up, jumped into the anchor

The accidental anchor—Joan Lunden

chair next to Beutel. As a result of Grimsby's tirade she only had pages 1, 5, and 60 of the hourlong script, but she did as good a job as possible for a last-minute recruit. Of course, Joan was in her twenties and certainly didn't need any help in the looks department from an eye light, which unfortunately did strange things to her face that night.

By the next afternoon, the lights had been switched, Roger returned to work, and the anchor career of Joan Lunden, a new television personality, was born prematurely.

All because someone installed a light in the wrong place.

Joan became the accidental anchor of 1975. On another occasion, Saturday night anchor Gil Noble had a day off but someone forgot to tell anyone. A young writer named Alan Weiss was getting his first shot as a producer, but he began to worry when he still had no anchor with only thirty minutes until airtime. In a panic, Alan put on a jacket and tie and was about to do it himself when he remembered Joan lived across the street. He ran to her building and begged her for help. Still wearing a jogging outfit, Joan threw a blouse over the top of it, ran to the studio, and slid into the anchor chair just as Alan tossed her the script. She did the first few minutes out of breath with wet hair. Joan slapped on some makeup during the commercial break and saved the newscast. That exposure marked her as a true star and Joan went on to become the anchor of *Good Morning America*. And Alan Weiss? He won an Emmy for supervising the Eyewitness News coverage of the shooting death of John Lennon, December 9, 1980 outside his Dakota apartment building, by a crazed fan. He's now the producer of *Teen Kids News*, the children's program syndicated to 220 TV stations in America.

Beutel and Grimsby settled in nicely and worked together for sixteen years. Now that we had that coanchor situation fixed, we turned our attention to the most glaring problem at WABC.

We had almost nothing but white males on the air.

Chapter Eighteen

The first time I met Geraldo Rivera, he was making trouble for the station. And he wasn't even an employee.

He would continue the trend after we hired him.

He was a street leader representing a group of Puerto Ricans, the Young Lords, and he was working very hard at impressing me as their lawyer. He called himself Jerry, Jerry Rivers, and was strutting defiantly across my office, espousing the cause of the downtrodden masses.

I had earlier called Gloria Rojas, a Hispanic reporter at WCBS, and begged her to come by and talk to us about joining the *Eyewitness News* team. I told her, "You are just wallpaper at WCBS; at *Eyewitness News* you will be a star." But she was too comfortable with her position there to take such a chance, and at that time there were very few opportunities for minorities and women in the industry. She had the same reaction most of the established TV newspeople had in New York. Why go to a perennial loser, WABC? But while she turned me down, she told her friend Jerry Rivers that I was looking for a Hispanic reporter.

Jerry Rivers was working out of an office in Harlem, deeply entrenched in the issues of legal aid for the underprivileged. After his talk with Gloria Rojas, he came down for an interview.

He didn't show up in a business suit.

He sported the long hair that was still in fashion, an open shirt, jacket, and bell-bottomed slacks. His dress could only be described as urban chic. He sure didn't look like any reporter I'd ever seen on television.

He also hadn't gotten the memo that I was the employer and he was the job applicant. After working in television for more than a decade, I was fully aware of the power and arrogance of top management, but he felt the need to deliver a lecture on that subject. Eyes flashing, coupled with a nasty disposition, he still had enough in the smile and charm department to capture complete attention. Every sentence was filled with an underlying anger and deep, sincere passion. He wasn't just preaching; the man actually *cared* about the people he was trying to help. He possessed the similar kind of magnetic presence that I'd recognized in Tom Snyder; there was a constant turbulent emotion that was close to boiling over in the man's eyes. He had what is known in the television industry as "IT" with capital letters. There was no doubt; he could be a superstar in television news. He was ripe for the sort of television journalism that we were in the process of branding. The only problem was that Jerry Rivers was a lawyer and had no journalism experience whatsoever.

I knew the news world was changing, that women and minorities had to be

brought into the system, and there were almost no experienced ones to be found. I appealed to his sense of justice.

"Look," I said. "If you really want to help the people who need it, you'd better forget about small-time lawsuits and get on television." I told him he could help people one by one or he could learn journalism skills and report to the mass audience that television does with greater impact than any other medium.

The simmering pools of anger in his eyes calmed down as the lightbulb went on instantly. He wanted to know how he would acquire the skills to become a television reporter. I'd already done my homework and told him I would arrange for him to get into the Columbia Journalism School's minority training program. He would have preferred to start on the air that day, learning on the fly, but his lawyer's training and street smarts told him he just might need a little help first.

After coming to an agreement to start him at AFTRA minimum, $18,000 a year, we enrolled Geraldo at Columbia. The journalism course was three months long. About halfway through it, Rivera came into my office begging to go out on news stories. He'd been bitten by the journalism bug and was chomping at the bit to start his career. I resisted at first but eventually let him go out with the regular reporters to observe. I foolishly thought that being closer to the news business would put a dent in his hunger to get on camera. It only made things worse because he felt he could communicate the material even better than our staff reporters. Once he started hanging around during the filming of a news story, his arrogance took over. I made him wait until the classes were completely over and for good measure, gave him my own highly detailed lessons in exactly what I wanted from him. But he still had the look of a kid on Christmas morning who'd been told not to open his presents.

Then there was the issue of letting the viewers know he was a minority, which they might not pick up from a guy with the name of Jerry Rivers. I insisted that when he eventually went on the air, he use his proper name, Geraldo. He told me he had been known as Jerry Rivers since college as he was trying to become part of the established world around him. Incredibly, he didn't see the inroads he could make if everyone knew he was a minority. He protested the name change from every conceivable angle including, "Nobody will know how to spell it." It surprised me that he would want to downplay his true ethnicity, but that's the way things were in the sixties. This brash, arrogant young man still had the anxiety of losing his footing in the community if he didn't conform to the party line. I wanted him to not only step over the line but erase it altogether.

Because the line was quickly disappearing in America. Looking back, it is hard to believe people like Gloria Rojas and Geraldo Rivera once harbored a real dread of opportunities being taken from them solely because of their ethnicity. It seems unthinkable that I had to badger a man known as Jerry Rivers to take back and embrace his Hispanic birth name of Geraldo Rivera.

When Jerry finally became Geraldo and finished the Columbia course, we decided to throw him into the deep end of the pool. To protect my investment, I assigned a young apprentice film editor, Marty Berman, to work with Rivera. Berman was a sharp young man in the editors' union who was only allowed to work as an apprentice with limited editing capability. He once suggested that John Schubeck film a report on men's new high heel shoes atop the unfinished World Trade Center. Cameraman Bob Ailes somehow got to the top with Schubeck and filmed a dazzling report that Berman edited to music. With that aggressive, daring streak, he would make him a good complement to Geraldo. He was trying to get a break, and teaming him with Geraldo would give him a shot at getting a regular union job. Marty's eyes had the same fire as Geraldo's.

The two hit it off immediately and became a great team. Berman would not only edit Rivera's stories, he helped plan them before Rivera went out with the film crews. I was thankful Marty was working out because quite honestly, no one else wanted to work with Geraldo. The staff considered him too hot to handle. The veterans in the news department had been really putting the heat on me for hiring someone with no news experience.

We gave Geraldo some office space in the basement, and he immediately turned it into his kingdom. He hired his own "interns" without going through the proper channels and tried to "freelance" when it came to stories.

Assignment editor Al Ittleson gave him a long leash but had to give it a tug once in a while to let Geraldo know he wasn't running the place. Despite the fact that Geraldo was making his own rules as he went along, we knew we had something special.

L to R Marty Berman, Geraldo Rivera and the Author

If we could just manage him. We quickly found out that his talent was so special we had no choice.

Geraldo's first big coup came when he got a phone call from a doctor working at a mental hospital on Staten Island. The facility was called Willowbrook, which housed many mentally retarded children and adults who had been abandoned by their families. Despite its pleasant name, Willowbrook was a cesspool of human misery and criminal neglect. Geraldo sensed this was a good story and quickly jumped in a car to check it out.

A few hours later, Geraldo realized he had an exclusive on something that could turn the community on its ear. This story wasn't just about the usual groups of poor people Geraldo fought to help; these were retarded people who had been thrown away like trash. They had no one to stand up for them and couldn't fight for themselves. Geraldo immediately called in and talked with Lou Pinkster, who was working the assignment desk.

"Look," he said, "we have this great story. I'm at this diner with a doctor who is describing horrendous conditions at a hospital. Let me skip the early show to check it out." Geraldo's limitless energy and ambition helped him turn stories at an amazing rate, as he was routinely doing pieces for both the six and eleven o'clock newscasts.

Pinkster heard the excitement in Geraldo's voice, sensed he was on to something good and agreed to give Rivera the time to dig. Geraldo then said, "I'll need a camera crew out here to film this."

Pinkster, who had already gotten used to Rivera's pushy demeanor, didn't want to commit until Geraldo had hard evidence. "Oh no," he said. "I send a crew only if you can get inside the facility." Geraldo, knowing he had no story without film, went back to the doctor and begged the guy to get him inside. The doctor, who was already apprehensive about his disclosure, finally agreed. He quietly slipped Geraldo a key that would let him and the film crew in through a back door.

The next day, Geraldo arrived with cameraman Bob Alis and soundman Dave Weingold at four in the morning. Alis said Geraldo put the key in the door and hesitated a moment. Alis told him that you couldn't hesitate in a situation like this one and pushed him through the door. The three men walked into a wall of stench as the smell of human waste was overwhelming. But once our crew was inside, it was anything but quiet as Geraldo became the bull in the china shop. He began interviewing staff members and patients who related the deplorable conditions of the facility. He even got access to files, finding incriminating documents. Incredibly, the three men moved through the hospital and shot the entire story without once being stopped. Quickly realizing he'd uncovered an enormous multifaceted groundbreaking story, Geraldo came back to the station and immediately came to my office. After hearing what he'd found, we decided this story was simply too big and too emotional for one report. It was like pulling up a weed that pulled up other weeds attached to it.

We expanded his investigations into a multipart series that would air at the same time over consecutive days. At that time, there was some real concern among the top brass at WABC as to whether or not a story broadcast serially could command ratings. But if this story couldn't hold viewers' interest, nothing could.

Not only did we all agree the story was worth several parts but that each part should run longer than two minutes, which was pretty much the standard rule of thumb for stories in those days. The film was simply too compelling; no viewer could possibly get bored or look away at what had become a human warehouse devoid of hope. These disenfranchised patients in Willowbrook were so neglected, so horribly treated, that we owed it to them to give their story proper treatment, ratings and time limits be damned.

The response and the community outrage were overwhelming. Geraldo's story was picked up by newspapers and radio stations all over the country. And the concerns about running a series of reports vanished instantly. Our already high ratings increased each day. Marty Berman had done a wonderful job editing the segments, with every new segment building on the previous one. It was like a serial, but it was real life and an incredibly compelling story. Geraldo had so much material that Marty reedited everything into a documentary called *Willowbrook: The Last Great Disgrace.* ABC broadcast it on the network to thunderous acclaim. We all won a George Foster Peabody Award for the work. But more important, we had saved lives.

It created a great deal of human empathy and hit home with a lot of people who had the power to change things. Hugh Carey, a New York gubernatorial candidate, saw the stories and made mental hospital reform part of his platform. He told voters that if he were elected, he'd change the laws to protect retarded people. He visited Willowbrook, and when he was elected, actually followed through on his campaign promise.

Geraldo wasn't done after the documentary, for his heart is as big as his ego. In the wake of the documentary's stunning success, Geraldo and Marty wanted to do more, so they started a charity in their basement office called One to One. Running a nonprofit organization from a television station was hardly professional, but we all looked the other way because we were so proud of the change our coverage was bringing about. The charity took a quantum leap when John Lennon and Yoko Ono attached their names to it and actually visited the newsroom. Geraldo managed to get them to perform a fund-raising concert at Madison Square Garden to benefit children with mental challenges. (The concert was later released as an album in 1986 titled *John Lennon: Live in New York City.*) We eventually aired a telethon to raise money for the charity. The Willowbrook story changed the American consciousness about retarded people who are no longer labeled with such a demeaning term. *Mentally challenged* isn't merely politically correct, it is simply accurate.

It started out on a simple tip called into the station, but it mushroomed far beyond what any of us expected and distinguished Rivera for his fearless reporting. It was helping me realize my dream of combining news reporting with news making. We were not only doing our jobs, but we were doing them well and making the world a better place.

The reporting style and excitement Rivera brought to *Eyewitness News* was worth it, but we had to pay the price with his growing ego and influence. The change from young street lawyer to superstar was rapid. I'd told him he could make more of a difference on television, and the realization simply fed his ego. He was now a crusading Gotham City news superhero, with everything but a cape and magical powers.

All this with less than a year's experience.

Naturally, this didn't sit well with the veterans in the newsroom who had paid their dues for years before coming to New York. Though they wouldn't fault his ability as a journalist (yet), they felt that after Willowbrook Geraldo became bigger than any story he covered.

Others on the staff complained that he was given special treatment, as he was allowed to wear chic variations of his channel 7 blazer without a white shirt and tie. They were right. I finally said in desperation that we treat all reporters equally, but that some were more equal than others. We wanted Geraldo to be different, to stick out. The long hair and groovy clothes were unlike those of any other news reporter. And to be honest, sending the man out to interview hookers and visit heroin dens dressed in a blazer and necktie would have looked ridiculous.

The rough neighborhoods he covered weren't exclusively in New York City. One series on migrant workers called *Migrants Dirt Cheap* took Geraldo out to some rural areas. In this case, the foreman in charge of the migrant workers took exception to a news crew near his property and stuck a shotgun into the news car. Geraldo, who was driving, simply floored it and moved on to another farm.

Meanwhile, his name recognition took another step when he was regularly discussed on the radio by Don Imus. The I-Man, already a major force on

WNBC's AM radio station, would, according to soundman Dave Weingold, refer to Geraldo as the "Puerto Rican hubcap thief." (This was long before the term "politically correct" even existed.) Weingold, often a member of Geraldo's crew and in the middle of many a practical joke, tells the story of their response to Imus. One day the crew pried one of the hubcaps from a news car, cleaned it up, and stuck an *Eyewitness News* logo in the middle. They then marched down the street to the NBC Studios and walked through the building carrying the hubcap. No one stopped them so they continued on to the radio booth. While Don Imus was on the air, and without so much as a second look from security, they walked into his studio and placed the hubcap on his desk.

Bob Alis shot for Geraldo on many occasions and likened his popularity to that of a rock star. On any given shoot, women were either throwing clothes at Rivera or trying to rip the ones he was already wearing from his body.

Rivera brought together a mix of reporting and helping people in a way that presented a constant challenge to management. I had to set guidelines for the staff, yet I still had to be flexible. I used my basic news judgment and instincts to keep Geraldo honest and maintain journalistic integrity, but it took many hours of my long day. My job description was expanded and now included the duty of "Geraldo's handler."

Though he brought back some incredibly compelling stories, he always tried to push the envelope and was constantly in trouble. We had many confrontations, but I remember one of his responses quite well. He'd made an expeditious but foolish decision to reshoot the opening to a story in a staged settin, rather than having to travel all the way across town to the proper location. He was caught when an elderly woman called WABC and complained she had seen herself in the background of Rivera's stand-up and the reporter was nowhere near the story. It was a serious breach of ethics, and he was getting out of control. I promptly called him in and announced he was being suspended without pay.

In the middle of our discussion, I was summoned upstairs to the ABC law office, where Attorney Everett Erlicht (nicknamed the ticket man) and ABC News president Elmer Lower nervously awaited. Both insisted that I fire Rivera immediately. Erlicht kept saying, "I'll be dammed if we're going to lose our ticket (FCC license) over that guy."

I knew that I'd slammed into a serious bulkhead and the thought crossed my mind that this might be the most difficult moment in my WABC career. While a suspension was in order, I didn't think that firing a guy who had become our star reporter was a good idea. But then divine inspiration struck. Fortunately, I maintained my composure long enough to remember that an

ABC News correspondent had recently shot film inside a Las Vegas casino and used it on the network news. Showing gambling of any kind was a FCC taboo at the time. I insisted if Rivera had to be fired, the ABC News correspondent should be fired as well. After some more verbal haggling, we agreed to simply suspend Geraldo.

When I returned to my office and told him I'd waged a battle on his behalf and saved his job, Geraldo didn't show the slightest bit of appreciation. He was hardly contrite and drew a line in the sand.

"If you suspend me," he said, "I will have ten thousand Puerto Ricans lying elbow to elbow, side by side, all the way down Sixty-sixth Street, and the news cars would have to drive over them before anybody could get to work."

When he said this, I sadly thought to myself that in just under two years we'd traveled such a long way. From the moment we'd announced the hiring of Geraldo Rivera, we'd rolled out the red carpet to make him feel at home. Jerry Della Femina, our advertising guy and his group, dreamed up a promotional spot to let the viewers know he was part of the team. We'd actually gone to Spanish Harlem and filmed a Puerto Rican wedding. During the wedding, Geraldo walked in as a guest, flanked by Roger Grimsby and Bill Beutel. Geraldo then took care of the introductions by saying, "My friends, let me introduce you to my friends." As the spot continued, viewers were treated to the sight of Grimsby, sans jacket, burning up the dance floor with an attractive Hispanic woman.

So Geraldo's threat was not the kind of reaction one would hope for after fighting and winning such a front-office battle. I'd just saved the man's job, and he was threatening to turn the episode into a public relations nightmare.

As it turned out, Geraldo calmed down and took the punishment gracefully. I even slipped him extra expense money for two weeks to keep the peace. But it still was full-time work keeping Rivera out of trouble, and I found that the best way to accomplish it was to keeping him working night and day on stories and series. His appearances each night on *Eyewitness News* were always a special event. Strong reactions to his reporting were routine as he covered social issues in New York with great passion. And he no longer had to dig for good stories, as New Yorkers now knew that if you needed to right a wrong, Geraldo Rivera could help you get results. He was constantly being tipped to scandals by viewers and he followed up on each of them. Truth, justice, and the American way happened to wear long hair and bell-bottoms in the Big Apple.

Since he really put his heart and soul into coverage of social issues in New York, strong reactions to Geraldo's reporting were pretty routine. He did another famous series called *The Littlest Junkie*, which was an expose of the heroin epidemic in New York City. At its heart, the segment showed a remarkable piece of harrowing, unforgettable footage: a baby being born to a heroin-addicted woman and then immediately going into drug withdrawal. Viewers couldn't help but be touched and outraged by the film of the twitching newborn. We aired the segments on consecutive nights. One actually ran uninterrupted for an unheard of eleven minutes. Since a thirty minutes newscast has twenty-two minutes to fill after you allow for the commercials, the piece took up half our newscast that night.

I was promoted to vice president of News for the ABC-owned television stations in May 1972. But that didn't mean I had to stop managing Geraldo. I had succeeded in getting Al Ittleson appointed to succeed me as news director. Al had been a news writer at channel 7 and had worked his way up to assignment editor when I arrived in 1968. He had been working in radio for years. He'd learned television well and was among the first to strongly support the efforts to develop the *Eyewitness* format. While I was out establishing the format at other ABC stations across the country, Al was keeping things humming in New York. But now he had to deal with Geraldo as well.

In October, I got word that Geraldo was supporting Democrat George McGovern in his race against Richard Nixon for president of the United States. That in itself did not surprise me, but apparently in his passion for everything he does, Geraldo was offering to make speeches at colleges and universities as well as to endorse McGovern and lend his name to be used in newspaper ads and campaign publicity. Reporters often talk politics in the newsroom, but it is a standing rule to remain apolitical in public. You can't maintain any objectivity with the viewers if they know you support a certain candidate or political party. (You may have heard the term *liberal news media* a time or two.) But Geraldo didn't seem to care if anyone knew he was supporting a Democrat.

The newspapers were unanimous in their condemnation of Rivera's actions. So too were most rival television people who rarely missed the opportunity to take a shot at anyone connected with *Eyewitness News*. Mike Wallace, *60 Minutes* star reporter, said, "I think it's dead wrong." NBC's John Chancellor said simply, "People involved in news should not endorse." Though newspapers have been doing this since the invention of the printing press and William Randolph Hearst was famous for manipulating elections, it was just not done in television. Our own ABC anchorman, Howard K. Smith, said that Rivera had abused the privileges that went with his job.

This was now more than a local problem, it was a network problem, so I called Geraldo in for a meeting. I explained that he was compromising

ABC's standards as well as his own ethics and neutrality. It took a long time to explain these basic journalistic principles to a young man who was still new to the profession, but he finally got the message. He promised to stop his political activism. But his ego wouldn't let him drop the issue entirely. He kept biting the hand that fed him.

Meanwhile, I thought that demanding that one of our reporters remain objective would be seen as something positive. But nooooo. The first blast came from the American Civil Liberties Union. The executive director, Ira Glasser, sent me a letter with copies to the four ABC-owned television stations and ABC President Leonard Goldenson, charging that my rebuke of Rivera was "an unconstitutional violation of Geraldo Rivera's right to free speech and association."

Then sportscaster Jim Bouton, who was also a McGovern supporter, decided to join the festivities and announced he would take an unpaid leave to continue his campaigning. Bouton had been given time off earlier in the year to run for a delegate's seat to the Democratic Convention, causing a small headache. This apparently encouraged Geraldo, and he began talking directly to newspaper columnists. He told one that he had "agonized" over his agreement with me to stop his involvement with McGovern's campaign activities. He told anyone in the press who would listen, "I'm not a political reporter, my assignments are to report the plight of people less fortunate than others in society. I can't understand why this should disqualify me from speaking out as a citizen on national politics."

Eventually, Geraldo Rivera followed Jim Bouton's lead and took a leave of absence despite his promise to get back to covering news. He thus opened the first crack in his ABC career.

But Geraldo was so damn talented he was basically the Rasputin of the broadcast industry. He rebounded from that incident and continued his strong reporting for *Eyewitness News*.

But of course, not without causing me to keep the Excedrin bottle on my desk topped off.

In October 1973, the station sent Geraldo to Israel to cover the Yom Kippur War. In one of his first reports, Geraldo was crouched on the side of the road in the Golan Heights. He was reporting on the shelling by the Syrians. In a dramatic manner he announced that the bombs were getting too close and said, on camera, he had to get out of there. All of this was captured on film and looked great on television. The shelling was at least a mile away but that didn't stop Geraldo from creating the drama. To the average viewer, nothing seemed amiss.

But to anyone who'd seen action in a war, this bit of theatrics was not only painfully obvious but an insult to any soldier who had put his or her life on the line.

After he got back, anchorman Roger Grimsby, a combat veteran, knew something was amiss and made no secret of his feeling that Geraldo had faked the story. Roger implied that Geraldo wouldn't have been able to tell the difference between incoming and outgoing fire. One night, Grimsby received a call from Geraldo. He asked Roger to come down to his office in the basement.

Marty Berman, Geraldo's partner, remembers getting a knock on his door at ten o'clock that night. He found Geraldo, whom he'd never seen looking so rattled before.

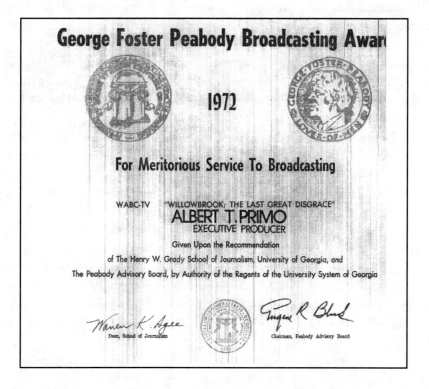

Geraldo said, "I just got into an argument with Roger Grimsby. I punched him. He fell down and he didn't get up. I think I might have killed him."

"You mean, you just left him there?" asked Berman, incredulous.

"Well, I wasn't thinking straight," said Geraldo.

"Oh Christ!" snapped Berman.

"I didn't know what to do," said Geraldo.

"Well, you'd better come inside," said Berman. "We'll just have to wait until the eleven o'clock news to see if he comes on or not, and then we'll figure out what to do."

Grimsby had gotten up, went to make up, and had his two black eyes covered though no amount of makeup could hide the shiners. He anchored the news at eleven o'clock very uncomfortably. Luckily for Geraldo, Grimsby refused to speak about what happened. But Roger later told me he never messed with Geraldo again.

Despite the theatrics and questionable ethics, Geraldo was in the right place at the right time. Since his stories were broadcast in New York, they were seen by just about every network executive because they all lived in the area. ABC decided that Geraldo was too talented to just work on a local station, so they brought him over to the network's news division.

He distinguished himself with brilliant reporting all over the world, ultimately becoming a star correspondent with *20/20*, the first ABC News magazine. I was thrilled that some part of *Eyewitness News* was moving to the network. But Geraldo's ego and troublesome ways continued to plague him.

As he documented in his book *Exposing Myself* (yet another wonderful book title from a former WABC employee), he lost his job in a dispute with Roone Arledge over ABC's coverage of the death of Marilyn Monroe. Managing Geraldo proved even too much of a headache for Roone Arledge, who is one of the masters of the care and feeding of television superstars.

Despite the headaches, despite the ego, Geraldo was a huge part of my success and that of *Eyewitness News*. When the Willowbrook story was first broadcast, I could only think, *If I do nothing else in my life, this story has made it all worth it.* Rivera's passion for his work was exceeded only by his caring for his fellow man. The work on Willowbrook made a difference, saved lives, and changed the world into a fair place for some special people who couldn't fight for themselves.

If you can have that kind of impact on society, ratings are secondary. For that, I thank Geraldo Rivera from the bottom of my heart.

Chapter Nineteen

Television makes it own stars.

Getting Geraldo Rivera on board gave us some badly needed diversity, and he literally stuck out like a sore thumb in a sea of white males. But while minorities were hard to find in broadcasting, women of all colors were practically nonexistent during the 1960s in any sort of prominent role. Most of the females were tokens, being relegated to light features, weather (during which they were known as "weather bunnies"), or live commercials.

We needed to let our newscast reflect the world in which we lived. It seemed ridiculous that half the viewers were female yet women made up less than 10 percent of all television newspeople. At one point during my time at KYW in Philadelphia we actually had to go to Detroit to find a woman in the broadcasting business. Our find, Trudy Haynes, was working in radio but took to television very well and with some careful training and work became a real star. I knew we could do it again. So we began to search for women, keeping a sharp eye out for females with an ethnic background. A journalism background was another story. During that time period, it was nearly impossible to find anyone with television news experience to fit the bill.

Being Italian, I was truly enjoying my ancestors' influence in New York. Little Italy was a city unto itself, with its outdoor restaurants and imported foods you couldn't find anywhere else. (It was also well known as the site for many a Mafia rubout, but that's another story.) It seemed that just about every other person I'd meet on the street was a *paesan*. At that time, Italians made up about 40 percent of the population in the Big Apple. But I didn't have a single news reporter or anchor that had a vowel at the end of his name. And raiding the competition wasn't the answer; with the exception of WCBS weekend sports anchor Sal Marchiano, no one else had any staffers of the Italian persuasion. I was determined to find a woman whose personality and reporting would speak to the Italian population and hopefully attract more viewers to *Eyewitness News*.

But I didn't know many people in town, so I started asking for help. We had a crackerjack producer named Howard Weinberg who jumped into the project and started checking into the records of major universities in the area, including NYU and the prestigious Columbia. Howard felt certain he'd find several recent graduates from which to choose. He was flabbergasted to find that there was not a single person of Italian descent who had majored in journalism at any of the nearby universities. He did find two Italian Columbia grads that hadn't majored in journalism, but English was a second language for them.

My hope of finding an Italian with television experience or a news background died quickly, so we started to broadly canvas for candidates with a different set of prerequisites: a college degree, a sharp mind, and a set of street smarts. We put out the word, and the first response brought a lot of applicants. Unfortunately, most of them were models or actresses that were sent by local talent agencies. You'd have thought I was casting a mob movie as the parade of Italians began filing through my office, with each young lady going through a sales pitch usually reserved for Broadway or Hollywood directors. As I patiently listened to these people unravel their life stories, I began to see a pattern. Though they were all very attractive and telegenic, the pressure to assimilate and become regular Americans had made their natural ethnicity disappear. None seemed truly authentic. I conveyed this to Howard, who instinctively swung in the other direction. No actresses this time, just educated Italians.

The next group of candidates seemed like smart homemakers you'd find in the supermarket line in Bay Ridge. They were all good, kind people but their personalities were predominately maternal. I couldn't imagine any of them shoving through a crowd of reporters with a microphone. It was relatively wide of the mark we were trying to hit. We wanted someone with good gut instincts and a New York attitude who would be daring and not take shit from anyone. Someone who could use her personal background to look for new angles on old stories.

Finally, after countless interviews, we got a tip from a woman named Mary Sansone about a young Italian woman who was working in Mayor John Lindsay's office. She was the youngest member of the Mayor's Commission on Human Rights and not only had a bachelor's degree but a master's as well. Her first and last names were unmistakably Italian: Rose Ann Scamardella. It would barely fit across the bottom of the screen.

Howard Weinberg gave her a call. Rose Ann was under the impression he was interested in doing a story about her. Howard spent three hours with her and told me our search had ended.

I gave her a call, heard a voice that couldn't be from anywhere *but* New York, and invited her to come down to my office for a chat. She recalls that the first person she saw when she entered the building was Geraldo and that kind of blew her away.

The woman who strolled into my office would have been right at home at one of my mother's Sunday dinners but looked like she'd be as comfortable making meatballs as playing stickball. The dark hair and eyes combined with a Brooklyn sidewalk accent and a spunky personality told me within minutes we found the person we were looking for. She was a typical New Yorker, a little rough around the edges with a soft heart and a wicked sense of humor. Rose Ann had a wide-eyed innocent look that belied a very sophisticated political mind.

She liked our plan to add diversity to the newscast, especially with women and minorities. When I expressed an interest in hiring her, she was interested but felt it was her duty to remind me that she had absolutely no background in journalism. But she'd been on the other side of the fence, her job having brought her into contact with reporters on a regular basis. She'd had plenty of conversations with the newspaper, radio, and television beat reporters who hung out at city hall. Working for the mayor of New York, you couldn't help but deal with the media at some point.

We scheduled an audition for the following week. I sat in the control room, giving her guidance through the intercom. But I could see she had the raw talent to succeed.

Rose Ann Scamardella

She'd already given her notice to Mayor Lindsay as she had been accepted to law school. I had to convince her that television offered much more. In typical New York fashion, she decided to give it a try for the three months before law school started. Of course, she kept that very much to herself.

I told her that I simply needed smart New Yorkers who knew their way around and could get by with a few raw rookies since we had so many veterans. Finally, I appealed to her sense of pride.

"You think these people have something you don't, outside of some experience?" I asked.

She smiled. "Okay, I'll do it," she said. "I'll join your news team."

Rose Ann took her schooling very seriously and worked hard to absorb as much as she could. When she was ready to report, Howard Weinberg took a proprietary interest in producing her material, much like Marty Berman had done for Geraldo Rivera. She chose her stories well and was doing a great job for a rookie reporter, but the staff was getting a bit annoyed at having people who hadn't paid any dues working in the number one market. No one was cutting her any slack, especially Roger Grimsby. He would often lead into her reports with his now legendary skepticism.

And while she was getting flack from her coworkers, I was hearing it from the higher-ups. The suits at ABC corporate headquarters remained uneasy about the woman with the strange Italian name who spoke Brooklynese on their flagship station. Shortly after Rose Ann hit the air, I was attending a management cocktail party. Leonard Goldenson's personal secretary came up to me and said, "That Italian woman. She still on the show?" She was clearly telegraphing the fact that her boss was not at all happy with this particular hire.

It occurred to me that perhaps it was Rose Ann's voice that might be grating on some nerves and keeping some people at ABC from taking her seriously. Her Brooklyn accent was sharp enough to slice a stale bagel, so I set her up with a voice coach named Lillian Wilder.

Lillian was well-known for her work with actors and had just started taking on newspeople as clients. She was tough on Rose Ann, who left many a voice lesson demoralized over the harsh treatment and ended up whipping through the Kleenex in my office. She was basically a Big Apple version of Liza Doolittle; her "rain in Spain" was "Noo Yawk." But she was a trooper, working to eliminate the nasal twang until one day the ray of light filtered through the clouds and she just "got it." With that weight lifted from her shoulders, nothing stopped her and she became enormously popular while her journalism skills grew. She was so beloved that even Roger Grimsby was forced to rethink his attitude and finally show Rose Ann the respect she deserved.

Rose Ann eventually moved into anchoring and was very comfortable as well. Her sharp sense of humor let her hold her own with Grimsby, and she could connect with the viewers by just raising an eyebrow.

I began to hear about her popularity from Howard Weinberg. He and Rose Ann would go out to eat but it would take them a good part of their lunch hour to walk two blocks. Howard told me she would literally be stopped a dozen times by fans and well-wishers, knowing she was "one of their own."

But her impact didn't hit me until I was in bed watching television one weekend. My wife and I were tuned to WNBC, watching the new hit comedy program *Saturday Night Live*. During this particular episode, Gilda Radner appeared as a wild Italian whose hair looked as though she'd stuck her finger in a light socket. She introduced her character as Roseanne Roseannadanna, and after a few seconds, I made the connection.

"Oh my god, she's supposed to be our Rose Ann!" I said to my wife. It was at that moment, in bed late on a weekend, that I realized we'd created something that now had national attention. As far as I was concerned, the fact that Rose Ann had a caricature on a network television show (and one on NBC, no less) could only mean that she had achieved superstar status.

The bit was hilarious and the character would eventually become a regular fixture on *Saturday Night Live*'s "Weekend Update" for four years, featuring Radner's catchphrase, "It's always something." Radner would also talk about her relatives, Nana Roseannadanna, Polyanna Roseannadanna, and her "musically happenin' cousin" Carlos Santana Roseannadanna. Years later, a Roseanne Roseannadanna doll was actually produced for *SNL*'s twenty-fifth anniversary. Bob Schieffer may have a bobblehead, but I'm not sure how many local newscasters have ever had an action figure on store shelves.

On the Monday after Roseanne Roseannadanna's first appearance, I arrived at work and found a carnival atmosphere in the newsroom as several people were recapping the satire for anyone who hadn't seen it. Rose Ann Scamardella was delighted at the recognition and didn't mind the parody in the least.

Despite her national attention and the fact that she had turned into a solid journalist, the top brass at ABC never seemed to totally accept her. Too ethnic, too *Noo Yawk*, not polished enough. They kept telling me to get her to change her surname, which by now was probably the most memorable in New York television news history. But I refused their request; why should Rose Ann, or anyone for that matter, deny her heritage by changing her last name? I pointed out that sports fans certainly didn't have any trouble pronouncing Joe Garagiola's name when he burst on the scene as a color announcer. And

NBC didn't turn him into Joe Smith when they hired him to work on *The Today Show*. In my opinion, Rose Ann had become just as great a television personality as Garagiola, evolving from news correspondent to anchor of the main *Eyewitness News* programs and finally becoming one of the top-rated personalities at WABC. And we didn't need research or ratings to know she was immensely popular. I wished some of our executives would trail her on her way to lunch just to see the public's embrace.

Rose Ann Scamardella from reporter to 5 PM Co-Anchor with Ernie Anastos Eyewitness News

As her reputation grew, Rose Ann changed into a different woman. It often happens to those who have fame suddenly thrust upon them. Like the rest of our reporters and anchors, she found herself working for the most popular news program in New York and struggled with the powerful effects of celebrity. By now she was an anchorwoman working alongside Ernie Anastos, who the station hired from Syracuse as it began expanding the *Eyewitness News* team. Her popularity put a lot of strain on her marriage to a New York legislator, now a judge. They had a baby daughter, but after a while, the relationship began to crumble and sadly ended in divorce. She later fell in love with an ABC cameraman and a quick courtship turned into an engagement. When Rose Ann got married a second time, her wedding was filmed and aired on WABC to mark the height of her celebrity. Still a Brooklyn gal at heart, she had mixed emotions about her nuptials being broadcast and afterward seemed to regret bringing such an important personal moment into the public eye.

Then, an experience in the field changed her dramatically. Shortly after her wedding, she was sent to Italy to cover a catastrophic earthquake in Udine.

It was an event that killed many citizens but showed the incredible courage of the people whose lives were undone by the terrible damage. Having to witness and report on such devastation within her ancestral country struck a strange chord of sadness and longing in Rose Ann. Reading about tragedy from the anchor desk is one thing, but seeing it in person can be emotionally devastating. In the same way that the coal mine story had changed me back in the fifties, Rose Ann would look at things differently from that point on. It happens to many people in the news business when dealing with an emotional story on a personal basis. She eventually came to the conclusion that she could in no way accurately report on what she saw or faithfully render the magnitude of the disaster. There was no way for her to transfer her personal raw emotion to the viewer.

Family concerns led to her departure in 1984. She'd asked WABC for a few months off to take care of personal things. After she'd been away, the station asked her to return in July instead of the agreed-upon date in September. Management told her she had to come back early or not come back at all. So she announced her decision to give up television journalism. With the same determination she'd shown as a reporter, Rose Ann opted for a premature retirement from the business at the height of her popularity. Everyone thought she was crazy to throw away what seemed like such a charmed life, but no one could convince her to stay. By now, her AFTRA minimum salary of $18,000 a year had grown to almost $800,000 a year. She still walked and moved to Connecticut with her new husband. Seventeen years later, they were divorced and she now lives alone in a waterfront home, filled with *Eyewitness News* memorabilia, including an autographed picture from Gilda Radner. She is now poised to enter the Internet business.

Chapter Twenty

I'm not really telling you anything you don't already know here, but there is a definite double standard when it comes to men and women in television news. And it is one of the few things that sadly hasn't changed in the fifty years women have been reporting and anchoring. You never hear anyone talk about the hairstyles or clothes of Brian Williams or Charles Gibson, but Katie Couric wears white after Labor Day and the fashion police descended on the poor woman as if she'd committed a horrible crime. Jane Pauley practically invented the term *bad hair day*. Deborah Norville was deemed "too sexy" when she followed Pauley on *The Today Show*. Regardless of your opinion of these women, it is unfair to judge them journalistically in this manner.

But Jane's coiffure perils were nothing compared to what we went through in the early days of *Eyewitness News*. Once Howard Cosell resigned himself to wearing his toupee at all times, I thought we were done with hair issues.

Ha. An extremely bad hair day was headed toward *Eyewitness News* like a runaway freight train. And it didn't belong to a woman.

It was mine.

While my search for an Italian reporter forced me to turn over every rock in the New York metropolitan area, we already had a wonderfully talented African American woman on staff at WABC. Her big break is the stuff of Hollywood discoveries, for she was truly in the right place at the right time. It didn't hurt that she was smart and attractive and possessed a wonderful sense of humor.

Melba Tolliver began her television career working in the secretarial pool at the ABC network in the mid-1960s. She'd moved to New York from Akron, Ohio, to study nursing at NYU. She soon decided that while a job in medicine wasn't for her, New York *was*. Scouring the newspapers for interesting classified ads, she discovered that ABC was looking for secretaries. She thought a career as a researcher might be interesting, and this was a foot in the door at a network.

Though she didn't know shorthand, she could type, so she applied and got a job working for Donald Coe, an operations manager. Shortly into her career, AFTRA (the American Federation of Television and Radio Artists) had gotten into a bitter dispute and called for a national strike on March 29, 1967. The picket lines were populated by the union's 18,000 members in more than one hundred locations across the country.

The streets of New York's broadcast row were lined with famous newscasters and actors, causing an unlikely scene of people carrying picket signs while signing autographs. The strike would last thirteen days and end just in time for regular staffers to broadcast the Academy Awards that year.

But having to operate for nearly two weeks without any trained air talent is an eternity to a television station. With all the regular on-camera people carrying signs in midtown Manhattan, it left a huge void to be filled by . . . somebody. Managers scrambled to find anyone who fulfilled two criteria: a *telegenic* personality and the willingness to cross a picket line in New York City, a heavily unionized town. That last part was the killer, as defying a union line could send you to a permanent blacklist.

Managers were frantically looking for someone, anyone, to pinch hit for one of the anchors of a daytime newscast. Marlene Sanders was the anchor of a five-minute midafternoon newscast called *News With a Woman's Touch* that aired at five minutes till three, just before ABC's hit soap opera *General Hospital*. But Marlene was on the picket line with everyone else. ABC was about to put a man on the anchor desk when Purex, the sponsor of the newscast, stepped in. Purex, a laundry soap manufacturer, thought it didn't make sense for a man to anchor something called *News With a Woman's Touch*.

So Elmer Lower, president of ABC News, quickly called a meeting and asked, "Does anybody know any woman around here who could sit in for Marlene?" Coe, who had put together the contingency plan for the strike, mentioned that he had a smart secretary with a good personality and thought she could do it. He also knew Melba had some public speaking experience as she had entered a beauty contest to become a spokesperson for New York tourism (called "Miss New York is a Summer Festival"). She had also taken some acting classes. Lower agreed to let Melba take care of it for the day but wanted his staff to search for someone more qualified to take over later.

Coe asked Melba if she'd like to take a shot on the anchor desk and of course, she agreed. She didn't realize that the crew for the newscast was made up of managers who had little or no experience running the technical end of things. She got one piece of advice from the director. "No mater what happens, keep smiling."

Melba had never even seen the studio and was surprised to see a chintzy set that looked like it was made out of cardboard. The crew gave her a crash course on reading the teleprompter.

The newscast was a technical disaster as it went to black at one point. Melba kept smiling and apparently made an impression despite the glitches. When she returned to Donald Coe's office, she found her boss was happy with her performance. He told her the other managers thought she did just fine and should continue to fill in for the duration of the strike.

Of course, now that she was on-air talent, crossing the picket line was a whole 'nother story. The next day when she arrived for work, someone on the line yelled, "If you think you're gonna be a reporter, you'll never be a member of AFTRA!" But this was the only incident of harassment.

Blessed with striking good looks, she met the challenge with poise and charm yet managed to bring something edgy and different during her few days filling in.

Then the turbulent sixties took over and opened the door a little wider for Melba.

President Lyndon Johnson had established the Kerner Commission to look into the race riots of 1967. The findings placed some of the blame squarely on the backs of the media. This passage pulled no punches:

> *Our second and fundamental criticism is that the news media have failed to analyze and report adequately on racial problems in the United States and, as a related matter, to meet the Negro's legitimate expectations in journalism. By and large, news organizations have failed to communicate to both their black and white audiences a sense of the problems America faces and the sources of potential solutions. The media report and write from the standpoint of a white man's world. The ills of the ghetto, the difficulties of life there, the Negro's burning sense of grievance, are seldom conveyed. Slights and indignities are part of the Negro's daily life, and many of them come from what he now calls "the white press"—a press that repeatedly, if unconsciously, reflects the biases, the paternalism, the indifference of white America. This may be understandable, but it is not excusable in an institution that has the mission to inform and educate the whole of our society.*

Someone at ABC obviously read this and realized it was time to add some diversity to the newsroom, so an in-house training program was created. Melba, having displayed a natural talent, was an obvious choice for the program. In fact, she was the only choice. In the space of a few weeks, she'd gone from secretary to being the lone trainee in a program designed just for her.

When the strike was over, she was sent down to "local," figuring she could polish her skills at channel 7. (Looking back, it is amazing how many "gifts" we received from the network in the form of really talented people they thought they were sending down to the minor leagues.) Thrilled to be typing scripts instead of memos, Melba threw herself into her new career. She started out shadowing everyone in the news department; one day she'd go out with a crew, another she would look over the shoulder of the assignment editor. She started to get bitten by the bug, so she enrolled in a few journalism courses at NYU. Eventually she found her way onto the reporting staff.

I spotted her one afternoon and knew she would be perfect for *Eyewitness News*. She was smart, attractive, comfortable on camera, and would add more diversity to the white-bread staff. Unlike Geraldo, she did not have an urban look. Her personal appearance was more along the lines of Diahann Carroll, a woman who had become the first black actress to star in a network show in the fall of 1968. The sitcom was called *Julia*, with Carroll playing a single mother. It was considered groundbreaking for a network, and Carroll was nominated for an Emmy in 1969. The character of Julia was pure middle-class, and Melba seemed to fit into that mold. The two women even had similar straight hairstyles and their fashions were clearly influenced by the white establishment. At that time, fashions within the black community were rapidly changing to reflect the sense of political and social ascendancy. Melba was at first unfazed by these changes; after all, she was finding great acceptance among the high ranks of mostly white journalists. She had proven to be a tough, dogged reporter. She had a personality that was accessible to famous people, and she managed to get interviews with all sorts of celebrities. They seemed naturally at ease with Melba, so much so that they often said and did quirky and revealing things that made wonderful copy. At one point, she had been interviewing Stevie Wonder when the singer ended up performing an impromptu song about *Eyewitness News*.

Her most famous interview resulted when she was assigned to meet Mick Jagger at Kennedy Airport. He was finishing up his successful American tour and was headed back to London. We thought it would provide a different look at the Rolling Stones lead singer and sent her out to JFK to intercept him. When she arrived, she was blown away at the number of media people crammed into a room that was reserved for a news conference. Photographers were standing on tables to get their shots. With great pluck and confidence, she asked the writer of "(I Can't Get No) Satisfaction," "So, Mick, are you satisfied yet?"

Jagger did a double take, then turned to her with his famous snarling grin and said, "Do you mean sexually?"

It was the sound bite of the year and had the media horde roaring. Jagger loved the exchange with Melba so much he asked for a copy of the piece and eventually included it in a Rolling Stones film. It was also chronicled in a book in which Melba is described as a "girl reporter."

Melba was developing a reputation of being unpredictable, but in a good way, for the viewers. She was always searching for the edge in any story and would put herself through great effort to avoid taking the usual path. She described her mind-set of going out on a story as looking for an opening that nobody else might see, something that suddenly reveals the complexity of what she had been trying to uncover. Her stories made the viewer feel she had gone as deeply as possible, turning over every rock to find the truth. Where other reporters might present the two sides to every story, Melba would find the third.

She covered a wide variety of topics, and her versatility became apparent. I liked to put people in nontraditional positions, so we eventually got Melba to cohost a local *Monday Night Football* pre-game show with none other than Frank Gifford and Don Meredith. It was a casual, unorthodox show that showcased her talents and willingness to do things most women wouldn't try at the time. Melba would do all sorts of maverick reporting for that show, even going so far as to try her hand dressing up in a football uniform and kicking field goals after a Giants practice.

By her own admission, Melba felt that because she was black, people had an easier time trusting her and would tend to open up. She developed a trademark style in which she would have the photographer get footage of the faces in the crowd at whatever event she was covering. She always felt the audience reaction was as powerful and important as whatever and whoever was the subject of her piece. Melba's instinctive use of

Melba Tolliber in the community and on the air

the audience played right into my hand about putting the subject of a report into a wider context to show how it might be digested and reacted to by those who were also eyewitnesses. As her journalistic talents grew, she managed to narrow the gap between reporter and viewer, to bring them even closer together.

And yet, being a woman, Melba was subjected to the usual criticisms females endure to this day. Though in her case, it was because of the color of her skin, not her clothes. She'd get an occasional comment about her hair from the black community; some may have felt that her personal "Diahann Carroll" style was telegraphing a retro idea of a black woman that was no longer relevant.

In other words, her hairstyle was too "white."

But that wasn't the real problem with the hairstyle. In her mind, it was becoming too much of a pain to constantly spend time straightening her naturally curly hair. Eventually, she opted for a radical change. Now, normally if anyone wants to make a drastic makeover to his or her appearance, such as shaving a moustache or dying hair another color, that person generally gives the news director a heads-up. For example, if your brunette anchor wanted to go platinum blonde, it affects more than just the next newscast. Billboards, promos, and all sorts of things would have to be changed.

But in Melba's case, she didn't tell anyone, probably because we would have told her that what she had in mind didn't seem like a good idea. And though she didn't really think about the timing, she made the change before one of the biggest stories of her career in 1971. She would be covering the wedding of President Richard Nixon's daughter Tricia in Washington DC.

She'd been looking around for the right hairstylist to make the change and had gotten several recommendations from her friends. She had admired the hairstyle of actress Cicely Tyson, who at the time had a short but natural look. The morning before the event, she visited a hair salon in Harlem (where she lived), and the straight hair along with its high maintenance was history. That evening, she showed up at the Waldorf Astoria early in the evening to do some interviewing in preparation for the wedding. She would be heading to Washington DC the next day. A national venue was a rare and unusual event for a local reporter to cover, but those were some of the bold steps we'd begun taking.

One of our producers spotted her slipping into the hotel and couldn't help but notice that she was sporting a new hairstyle. He called me at home to give me the details. Knowing that Melba was due to appear that night on the eleven o'clock newscast, I waited until she was back in the studio before placing a call to her.

"I hear you've changed your hair," I said, by way of an opening line.

"Yes, I did," she confirmed.

"Am I going to like it?"

"I don't know, Al," she said, exhaling a bit of exasperation. "Why don't you watch the show and see."

And so I paced around the house, counting the minutes until eleven o'clock. I didn't have to wait long until Melba appeared and saw that any resemblance to Diahann Carroll was long gone. She was now sporting an Afro that, in my mind, made her look closer to Angela Davis, the socialist organizer who was associated with the Black Panthers. (In reality, it *was* closer to Cecily Tyson's style.) My first reaction wasn't good, and I was extremely upset that she had changed her appearance so radically without talking to me about it first. At that time, I didn't have the understanding or the vision to realize that this particular hairstyle would soon be very popular among black people and that Melba was merely reflecting in a very superficial way the tidal changes in America. Of course, looking back, it was just a hairstyle. She was still the same person, the same solid journalist. And bottom line, it was her natural hair. (I wouldn't want to spend an hour every day straightening my hair either.)

As soon as the newscast was over, I called her again. "Well," I said. "I don't like your hair."

"Why not?" she asked.

"You no longer look feminine." (I regret that comment to this day.)

"Well, Al, there's nothing I can do about that. I like it. And I guess you're going to have to live with it."

I played the "big story" card, hoping she'd take the hint. (Not that I had any intention of replacing her.) "Tomorrow's the wedding," I reminded her.

"I realize that."

I knew the change in Melba's appearance would overshadow any story she might do. "Then you do realize that your hair is going to be talked about."

"Al, like I said, the hair is what it is. There's nothing I can do about it now."

"I just wish you could have thought this through" was the last thing I said before politely excusing myself.

I knew the fallout from my superiors wouldn't take long. They didn't miss a newscast either.

The next morning, my bad hair day began the moment I walked in the door. I received a call in my office immediately after my arrival. It was WABC General Manager Ken McQueen, and I could tell from his tone that he wasn't

Melba Tolliver with
film editor John Cook,
who saved the stories of many
Eyewitness News Reporters

happy. He didn't beat around the bush. "What the hell happened to Melba's hair?" he snapped.

I'd given this a lot of thought on my commute to work and knew that in reality Melba's hair wasn't any different than Geraldo Rivera's real name. The outward appearance doesn't change the reporter inside. I'd gone to bat for Geraldo and I had to do the same for Melba. Regardless of my personal opinion, I always fiercely protected my team.

I tried to diffuse McQueen's anger, acting like it was no big deal. "What do you mean? She's allowed the change her hairstyle." Then I subtly let him know I was on her side. "Why, do you think it's wrong?"

"*Do I think it's wrong?*" McQueen's voice went up and cracked. "When I saw her on the news last night it scared the hell out of me. I wanted to jump and hide behind my couch."

I wasn't wild about Melba's look either, but I found it hard to believe McQueen's reaction. "You're kidding me, right?" I asked.

"No, I'm not kidding, Primo. It is awful. You've got to take her off the air right now. She cannot go to Washington looking like that."

I knew there was no way I could take Melba off the air even if I wanted to. For one, it would be admitting that a reporter's appearance was more important than ability. And we would have been opening ourselves up to a major lawsuit, not to mention ridicule from our competitors. Tricia Nixon would have been pushed to page 2.

But bottom line, keeping her on the air was the right thing to do, and I was determined not to budge.

Up until this day, I'd had an excellent rapport with Ken McQueen; he'd never objected to anything I did. He'd been a hands-off general manager; as a man with a sales background, he'd always had the good sense to let the news department alone since it was now far and away the most popular local news program in America. But it occurred to me that McQueen was more than likely being pressured by his superiors. He quickly proved me right when he said, "*Everybody's* upset about this. I have to do something."

He was drawing a line in the sand, but I had to stand my ground or I would lose the trust and respect of the entire newsroom. "I'm not taking her off. *We're* not taking her off. Do you realize what it would imply if we took her off? For one thing, the black community would skewer us. And then so would the rest of our competitors. We could lose everything over this. You tell them, those guys up there. Or I'll tell them."

I knew the moment I finished that sentence that it could be a turning point in my career and wondered if it could possibly come to an end because of a trip to a hair salon. But somehow, my argument wasn't getting through to Ken McQueen. He relayed my response to his superiors, who apparently didn't agree either and didn't want Melba to appear on camera. She was told she could do the Tricia Nixon story without a stand-up. But her producer ignored the order and put her on camera anyway, sent the film back, and her new look hit the air. Then the shit hit the fan.

Melba did her wedding piece from Washington as originally planned, though not surprisingly, her hairstyle became bigger than the story she covered. Her new look, considered daring for a television news reporter, was reported in all the Washington and New York newspapers. Her Afro was almost as big a story as the wedding itself. *Tricia Nixon's wedding upstaged by reporter's new hairdo. Film at eleven.*

When Melba returned she was, as she remembers, "called into the principal's office" and told by McQueen she would be covering landfill stories and have to use a scarf to cover her hair while on camera. Or wear a wig. She wouldn't do either, so for the next few days, viewers only heard Melba Tolliver and didn't see her.

Meanwhile, the reaction from other media outlets was predictable. Melba was one of our stars, and suddenly her face was nowhere to be found. I knew we were going to get hammered by our competitors who would see this as a legitimate reason to take a shot at the number one newscast in town. They would see Melba out on stories, so they knew she was still working. I continued to work on my superiors but wasn't having much luck.

After a few days, a reporter from the *New York Post* called Melba and flat out asked her if she was being kept off the air. She declined to comment but was now starting to worry. She had a contract but wondered what management could do to her legally if she didn't comply with their wishes. The reporter then called me, and I knew it was time to take my argument up a notch before we incurred the wrath of our viewers. Finally the higher-ups caved, and Melba was back on the air, new hairstyle and all (and thankfully without a scarf or wig).

By the time Melba returned on camera, her reputation as an independent woman had grown by leaps and bounds. And the response to her new look was very positive. Even the viewers who didn't care for her hairstyle defended her right to wear it. Looking back, it is sad that she is often remembered for her hairstyle change as much as for her fine work as a reporter and anchor.

After I was moved to the network as vice president of ABC News, Melba did a few pieces for the network. She even made an appearance on a late show pilot that I developed and produced to run head-to-head against Johnny Carson. Her high visibility on the station and within the black community made her a frequent news item. But no matter how famous and recognizable she had become, Melba always took a few moments to talk with her admirers and donated quite a bit of her time to give speeches at high schools.

Eventually, *Eyewitness News* became a victim of its success, and the competition started raiding *us*. Melba was hired away by WNBC, who after years of trying to emulate *Eyewitness News*, poached one of our most popular stars with the oldest trick in the book: a bigger salary. It was seen as their desperate attempt to finally master the elusive format.

Melba had a very successful career and like many of the people from the old *Eyewitness News* team, is working on a book. At least her working title is something classy and considering the way she got her first break, highly appropriate.

The Accidental Anchor.

Chapter Twenty-One

Not all of our new hires were raw rookies. Don't get the wrong idea; my first preference was to hire people with at least ten years of major market experience. So we considered ourselves very fortunate to add Bob Lape to the *Eyewitness News* team.

Lape, who used his full name Robert in his reports, came to us from WBZ-TV in Boston where he had been working as a political reporter. We had met once at a Westinghouse function when he was serving as the news director of WBZ Radio. He'd heard I'd gotten the job in New York and called me to see if there were any opportunities. I told him there were many, invited him down for an interview, and quickly hired him.

Robert Lape

He was truly a terrific, painstaking investigative reporter, which was a tremendous asset in a city with so much dirt to dig up. Lape also had a very commanding presence on camera. Unlike Melba, Rose Ann, and Geraldo, he didn't need any on the job training. Bob was able to hit the ground running on his first day. He adapted very quickly to the *Eyewitness News* format; for him, it was just a matter of refining his techniques.

In the late sixties and early seventies, Lape was our city hall correspondent. He had the task of covering John Lindsay, who was perhaps the most glamorous, highly visible mayor in the history of the city until Rudy Giuliani. Lindsay was blessed with perfect hair and a chiseled jaw, and it could be argued that his good looks had a lot to do with his election to Gracie Mansion. His news conferences would be mobbed with reporters from international magazines and newspapers, people who would hang on Lindsay's every word.

Lindsay's political affiliations were fodder for plenty of stories. Elected as a Republican in 1965 with the endorsement of the Liberal Party (yes, you read that correctly) Lindsay would become a Democrat in 1971. During his first term as mayor, he turned down an offer to be appointed to the United States Senate when New York Governor Nelson Rockefeller needed someone to fill Robert Kennedy's seat. (Second choice was a man named Charles Goodell, father of the current NFL commissioner.)

Since so many journalists basically showed up every time John Lindsay took a leak, Bob Lape thought it would be interesting to show the viewers the mayor's point of view. He had the resourcefulness to position one camera behind Hizzoner to film the journalists asking questions and fielding answers. For the first time, viewers had the opportunity to see the incredible horde that recorded the mayor's every move. This was the kind of innovation that really made *Eyewitness News*. The audience was given treats like this virtually every week.

Despite his fabulous body of work as a hard news reporter, Lape developed a unique following because of a weekly feature we started on Friday nights. Lape was from a small town, Akron, Ohio, where the choices of restaurant food were limited to diners, steakhouses, and the local Chinese joints. Though he was pretty much a meat-and-potatoes kind of guy, he was fascinated by the incredible dining choices offered by New York. The city is a theme park of restaurant offerings, and anyone earning a reasonable salary can easily make dining out a cultural activity. You could live in Manhattan for years, eat out every night, and never visit the same place twice.

So one Friday, assignment editor Al Ittelson told Bob Lape to take a break from city hall. (It is generally accepted that most politicians are impossible to find on Fridays anyway since they usually take the day off.) We launched a weekly series called *The Eyewitness Gourmet*. The segment would begin with an interview of a New York area restaurant owner, who would then take the film crew to the kitchen. They would get footage of the restaurant's chef preparing the establishment's signature dish, and then the reporter would wrap up the piece by tasting it at the end.

Lape did a few pieces, which turned out to be highly entertaining. He enjoyed doing the segment, and the crew enjoyed the free meals at quality restaurants. (As one photographer put it, "If you worked with Lape, you got a guy who knew what he was doing . . . and you ate good!") Then he came up with an idea that would send most offices into a meltdown situation. Bob thought that we'd never know if the audience truly liked the segment unless we offered the recipes. I told him we couldn't tie up secretaries to deal with the project, so he arranged to have any mail forwarded to the restaurants. It was a great idea, wouldn't cost anything, and I was curious to find out what kind of response we'd get.

The first segment that offered a free recipe was shot at a French restaurant. Bob was told the dish he would be sampling was *rognons a la moutarde*. He didn't speak French but thought it sounded very classy and expensive. He was right about the second part.

But in the case of this particular restaurant, the specialty of the house was something he probably would have fed to the cat.

Kidneys with mustard sauce.

Though he would later develop a very refined palate thanks to this series, this wasn't his idea of typical French restaurant fare. But he saw the potential humor in doing the piece and directed the cameraman to get a close-up of the raw, bloody kidneys as he said, "Kidney lovers, attention. This one is for you." That had to be one of the all-time great teases ever aired on *Eyewitness News*. Viewers, teased by the fact they would have the chance to see a hard news reporter eat something that looked and sounded disgusting, wouldn't dare change the channel.

At the end of each segment, he would sample the dish. In this case, he dined on kidneys smothered in what he called "a delicious Dijon mustard sauce" and then offered the recipe to any viewer who wrote to him or the restaurant. I thought the feature ended the week on a lighthearted note, and in this case it was downright hilarious. (Viewers had to be wondering if he really liked the dish or was just being polite because I was wondering the same thing.) However, I wished we'd started the "write in for the recipe" concept with a different dish as I couldn't imagine anyone would possibly want a recipe for this particular meal.

Then the mailman showed up will a full sack on Monday. And Tuesday. And Wednesday. We were all shocked to receive five hundred requests for that highly offbeat meal. But then, as the segment grew in popularity, the station would receive upward of 20,000 requests for recipes. The all-time record was 26,000 for Junior's cheesecake recipe. (This was before email existed, so just dealing with recipes could tie up a restaurant staff for a while, but the owners didn't care since one segment on our newscast brought them more business than they could deal with.) *The Eyewitness Gourmet* became such a hit we started airing two and then three segments during the week. The ratings spiked on newscasts that featured *The Gourmet*, and the sales department quickly seized on the opportunity. Commercials that ran next to *The Gourmet* segment eventually sold for an incredible amount of money at that time.

Not too shabby for something that started out with kidneys and mustard sauce.

The beauty of the segment was that Lape knew he'd never run out of places to eat. *The Eyewitness Gourmet* capitalized on New York's abundance of great restaurants, and it once again branded a television format that no one had ever considered. The television restaurant review caught fire in record time and left the competitors scratching their heads as they wondered why no one had thought of it before.

Meanwhile, Lape still had to take care of hard news four days a week, but despite his excellent coverage, found he was now typecast as the food expert. He could turn the biggest exclusive of the month, but people only wanted to talk about food. Once, when showing up to cover a fire, one of New York's Bravest asked him, "Here to sample the Red Cross donuts?" On another occasion, he was doing a piece on pollution with Governor Hugh Carey when Carey suddenly went off on a tangent, saying, "I don't think that lemon sole was nearly as good as you said." One of his favorite comments came from a viewer who spotted him and yelled, "Hey, it's the guy who eats!"

Lape obviously looked forward to Fridays in those early days, as did the viewers. The segment stimulated the restaurant business in New York, so much so that restaurant owners whose establishments were not featured by *The Gourmet* actually began to allege that our selection process was influenced by bribes. I never would have guessed something as light as a cooking feature would cause legal problems, but the complaint took on a life of its own.

The minute it became obvious that *The Gourmet* segment was a hit, Lape had been besieged by public relations people who were trying to get their restaurant clients on the air. A local tavern had been lobbying hard for a segment, but Bob simply didn't think their food was very good and didn't want to compromise his standards. (Besides, recommending an eatery with less than fabulous food wouldn't sit too well with the viewers either.) The story goes that a patron asked someone in the tavern why the place hadn't been featured on *The Eyewitness Gourmet*, and the response was "You have to pay to get on there." Apparently this comment was overheard by a government official and the game was on.

The Federal Communications Commission actually launched an immediate investigation into our selection process. Incredible as it may seem, this government agency actually spent tax dollars researching the inner workings of restaurant reviews. We had been totally scrupulous in our method of choosing the restaurants to be featured and were frankly a bit demoralized by having to submit to a full-blown FCC investigation. Anyone who works in television will tell you that visits from "Uncle Charlie," as the FCC is known, are about as pleasant as getting a prostate exam with an umbrella.

On the other hand, it occurred to us that because the allegations were made and taken so seriously, it only proved the powerful influence of our newscast. Eventually it got back to us that the other local stations were jealous of the feature. Nothing ever came of the investigation since we had done nothing wrong. That didn't stop the complaints, as we had to undergo two more investigations which, of course, turned up nothing. Eventually Bob got tired of having to defend the segment, so he asked every restaurant owner that he featured to sign an affidavit stating no money had changed hands. *I solemnly swear that I have not bribed Robert Lape to do a segment in my restaurant.*

So *The Eyewitness Gourmet* lived on and grew in popularity. Since the FCC couldn't do anything to us, the competition decided to come up with its own versions of the feature that wouldn't seem to be too much of a rip-off of Bob Lape's concept. But by then Bob had developed such a reputation as a connoisseur of fine food that those wannabes never managed to put a dent into *The Gourmet's* ratings.

The segment continued for many years, during which time more than a million and a half recipe requests were received. *The Gourmet* became a fixture on all the ABC-owned stations and of course was the legitimate forerunner of a number of cooking shows and the Food Network. When Lape eventually left the station in 1982, he went on to become a food critic, writer, and host of his own radio show that he does to this day. He'd come a long way from kidneys with mustard sauce. And despite his now consuming interest in food and cuisine, he loves to remind me that he can still fit into his old *Eyewitness News* blazer with the Circle 7. (Though recently Bob said he doesn't know what happened to the blue jacket. How convenient!)

Fate sometimes works in funny ways, as food found its way into every facet of his life. A few years ago, Bob reviewed a cookbook by a woman named Joanna Pruess. It was apparently a match made both in heaven and the kitchen as they eventually married. And you've gotta love the title of the cookbook Bob and his wife have written since they met.

Seduced by Bacon.

Chapter Twenty-Two

Growing up Italian, you learn how to make meatballs and sauce at an early age. You start with ground beef and pork (the latter gives everything great flavor), eggs, spices, cheese, breadcrumbs, and whatever else your grandmother threw into the mix. Then after you've fried the meatballs part of the way, you add them to some nice tomato puree and let the concoction simmer for hours until the sauce picks up the flavor of the meat.

Without all the extras, you're just eating hamburgers and ketchup. Which is basically what New Yorkers were getting from their newscasts before *Eyewitness News*. A bland, tasteless product.

Creating a successful newsroom is a lot like cooking sauce. You need a lot of different ingredients to spice things up and make people take notice. And by 1970, our human melting pot was attracting attention like the smell of sauce pouring from a Little Italy kitchen.

I'd been very lucky in attracting some people to the team, and when you think about it, the stars really had to align for everything to work. What were the odds of finding three star reporters from Akron, Ohio, to work in New York City? Who could have predicted a rookie reporter with a long name would have inspired a bit on *Saturday Night Live*? And what made Roone Arledge create *Monday Night Football* at the very moment we needed someone to replace Howard Cosell while Howard needed something else to do?

Perhaps none of the paths to *Eyewitness News* were as bizarre as the one taken by reporter Robert Miller. In fact, if the man hadn't taken up smoking in his younger days, he might never have become one of New York's most solid reporters.

Miller was on a career path to become an auto mechanic when he was drafted into the army and sent off to Korea. When he returned

Robert Miller

home in one piece, he knew two things: he didn't want a career as a grease monkey and the GI Bill would fund his education. Problem was, he didn't know what he wanted to study.

Miller got his answer courtesy of his nicotine habit. One day after lighting up, his world changed as the advertisement on the book of matches caught his eye. The ad touted a career in broadcasting and a school in New York City. Already blessed with a great voice, Miller enrolled in a six-month program and discovered he really enjoyed broadcasting. He then took his newly learned talents to the airwaves as a disc jockey in Easton, Pennsylvania. He started to move up the ladder and continued to spin records in Youngstown, Ohio, but wondered about the other side of the radio industry—news. Miller started scouring the want ads and eventually got a job as a writer and editor for ABC Radio in New York. After a while, the folks on the radio side sent him over to the television network where he became a copy editor for Peter Jennings.

Miller liked what he saw of the new format right off the bat and approached me about the opportunities that might exist for him. I also liked what I had seen of Miller in front of the camera since he did some weekend reporting along with his writing duties. While he was not looking for a career on camera, I knew he was a smart guy, a fabulous writer, and the kind of solid reporter you need on a daily basis. The great voice didn't hurt either. Miller was bowled over when I offered him a full time gig as a reporter, which at that time would triple his salary.

Miller was a versatile guy who handled breaking news and soft features equally well. As our staff began to stabilize, we realized we needed to venture outside of the city since so many people who commute to New York watched our station. So Bob Miller was handed the title of *suburban reporter*. On the first day of his new beat, he ventured out to New Providence, New Jersey, to do a feature on a high school football kicker who had no arms. On another occasion, Miller went to cover a bloody Ku Klux Klan march in, of all places, Connecticut. Eventually, as *Eyewitness News* began to generate a huge amount of revenue, the station gave me access to toys like helicopters and planes so we could send Bob out quicker and farther.

Bear in mind that this was taking place before the days of microwave and satellite trucks, so Bob Miller had to hustle to get his film back to the station for processing. On once occasion, his news car was pulled over for going eighty-five miles per hour in New Jersey. The cop, apparently an *Eyewitness News* fan, let our crew go with a warning.

Geraldo Rivera wasn't the only reporter on our staff to expose medical fraud. Miller found a Willowbrook of his own. Bob did some digging and with the use of hidden cameras and microphones, exposed several medical practitioners who were cheating their patients. Things got so dicey that Miller actually had some bodyguards standing by while conducting his investigations. The series of reports landed one man behind bars for six years, thanks in part to Miller's testimony in court. Luckily, we kept good "follow-up files" in those days because when the man was released from prison, he started his fraudulent practice again, only to be nailed by Geraldo this time.

Miller also developed a relationship with the hard-to-get-to-know Grimsby. Both were Korean War vets who had actually been in the same frontline area. Bob's combat experience came in handy when he had to dodge bullets and rocks during his coverage of the rioting in Newark. On the other hand, he was sensitive enough to cover the Karen Ann Quinlan right-to-die story, a gut-wrenching tale of a brain-dead woman which rivaled that of Terri Schiavo.

Another guy who was already on board was a diminutive reporter named Milton Lewis who had two decades of newspaper experience and the contacts that go with it. Milt was a terrier of a reporter, not afraid of anything, but his stories were more print than television. WABC paid Lewis as a tipster in city hall. His job was to call the assignment desk whenever a story was breaking and we needed to send a camera crew and reporter. One day I called him in and along with Al Ittleson, we discussed different ways to do stand-ups in front of the camera. I told him that his involvement in the story made it unique and that he had to add his own personality, which was memorable for anyone who'd met him. Al and I came up with the catchphrase, "Now listen to this!" Every time viewers would see Milt on camera, they'd know something juicy would follow his signature line. He used old-fashioned phrases like "hanky-panky" or "playing footsie" to describe political backroom deals. That, combined with a nasal voice that sounded like comedian Gilbert Gottfried, made Milton Lewis a character, but a character who knew how to dig up dirt. Cosmetically, he was everything a television reporter shouldn't be, which made him totally credible with the audience. The *New York Times* once referred to him as the "Little Guy versus the Establishment." That was a damn good description.

While on a shoot with Milton Lewis, soundman Dave Weingold spotted a urinal just sitting on the side of the street. Only in New York. For reasons known only to the crew, they stopped the news vehicle and actually loaded the thing into the back. (I can only assume the car smelled bad enough that the urinal didn't cause enough of a problem.) When they returned to the newsroom, they waited for the assignment editor to walk out of the room, then placed the urinal next to his desk with a note that read, "Our story is a real pisser." The urinal later ended up next to Milt's desk, no doubt from an assignment editor who didn't care for his new office decoration. Milt, apparently not big on traditional tchotchkes, kept the urinal in his office. Right next to the parking meter he already had. He also kept a record player with one record and he would fire it up if he wanted to chase anyone out of his office. The record was by the Philippine Bamboo Orchestra.

Milton was responsible for perhaps the biggest on-air breakup in the history of *Eyewitness News*. During the Christmas season, he had to do a story at the federal courthouse and discovered a homeless Chinese man living in a cardboard box. Milton decided to do a story on the man braving the cold. The viewers could see the man's face periodically peering out from under a mountain of blankets as Milton vividly described his plight. "Well, there he is," said Milton, "living in this box. I don't know why he doesn't go on welfare." At the mention of the word *welfare*, the homeless man got very indignant, jumped out of the box, and reamed Milton a new one.

In Chinese.

When the man was done venting (Lord only knows what he said), he jumped back into the box and pulled the blankets over his head. Milton turned to the camera and said, "Well, he must be cold, 'cause I'm freezing to death. Milton Lewis, Channel 7, *Eyewitness News*."

When the director punched up Grimsby and Beutel at the end of the piece, the two were laughing so hard they couldn't continue. Beutel managed to say, "We'll be back," and they broke for a commercial. But two minutes later when they returned they were still laughing uncontrollably so they had to break for another commercial. The people in the studio weren't helping matters as they were laughing as hard as Grimsby and Beutel. They burned three of four commercial breaks back-to-back until they finally regained their composure.

If you wanted someone to negotiate a hostage situation at a prison, you probably wouldn't enlist the services of an art professor.

Unless he worked for *Eyewitness News*.

If you want more bizarre proof that the stars aligned to form the most perfect news team in the history of television, look no further than John Johnson. A sharp contrast to Milton Lewis, Johnson was a cultured, elegant man with a soothing voice that exuded class. And like many others, his path to the news business was something you couldn't make up.

Art was, and still is, John's passion. He studied the medium while painting and rose to the level of professor. He was quite content teaching art history in college while wielding a brush in his spare time. But there was something else on his palette besides oil paint.

The desire to write.

John penned a piece entitled "Super Black Man" for a collection of essays in a book called *Black Power Revolt,* which also featured Malcolm X as a contributor. Someone at ABC noticed the piece and set up an interview with Johnson. He apparently came across so well that the network thought he'd be a fine addition to the staff. ABC offered him a job as a writer and associate producer within its documentaries division and John seized the opportunity. He could always go back to the art world if things didn't work out.

But they did, and when ABC's Frank Reynolds was sick one day, John was asked to do some interviews. He did so well the network turned him into a correspondent. And in 1971, the network sent this man who had been surrounded by the beauty of the art world into one of the ugliest and bloodiest situations in New York history.

The Attica Prison riots.

John Johnson

Prisoners had taken over the facility and were holding hostages within the facility. John was one of the first to go inside for a negotiating session, as the inmates probably realized the power of the media. They begged John to "get the story right for us." At one point, things exploded and John actually had an officer hold a gun to his head while yelling the "N" word repeatedly. John begged the man for his life, and thankfully, the cop didn't pull the trigger. When state police stormed the prison and killed twenty-nine inmates and ten hostages, many reporters wrote that the inmates had killed the hostages. John was an eyewitness and maintained it wasn't true. Still ABC refused to air his report, which was later proven to be accurate.

I'd noticed John's coverage for ABC and was stunned to find out that this incredibly brave reporter was a mild-mannered artist. He'd been frustrated with ABC's refusal to air his piece on Attica and jumped at the chance to join *Eyewitness News.*

John's love of democracy made him a true "voice of the people," and his work at Attica showed he was a reasonable and honest man. During another hostage situation in Spanish Harlem, police used John as a negotiator. He managed to disarm the gunman and save lives though the cops naturally took all the credit.

All this from a guy who actually called his mother after every newscast.

John slid into reporting and anchoring easily and proved to be one of our more versatile staffers. He was also one of the few people to become close with Roger Grimsby and discovered that during the Korean War most of Roger's unit had been killed. John felt this left a permanent scar on Roger's soul. His friendship with Roger was really put to the test when Grimsby was let go in the mideighties and John was chosen to be his replacement.

John's greatest value was that everyone, from prisoners to celebrities, trusted him. On one occasion, he traveled to Arkansas during Bill Clinton's first campaign, seeking an interview with the candidate's mother. He knocked on the door, chatted with Clinton's mom, and was invited inside. Clinton's mom made popcorn while the two watched Gennifer Flowers spill her guts about her alleged affair with the candidate.

John, like many others from *Eyewitness News*, was eventually stolen away by the competition and worked in New York for thirty years. He retired to spend more time with his ailing father and wrote a book about their relationship called *Only Son: A Memoir*. After his father passed away, he decided to go back to his first love, painting, and spend much of his time making the world a more beautiful place with oils and canvas. He lives in upstate New York and maintains an apartment in New York City.

Sometimes our reporters made names for themselves by simply using common sense. In the case of Bill Aylward, he once did something so obvious during a high-profile court case that I was amazed no one else had ever thought of it. Even more amazed were the lawyers involved.

Aylward had been covering the Alice Crimmins murder trial. Crimmins was an attractive redhead accused of murdering her own children, and her story gripped the city. The trial was tailor-made for New York's tabloids, including allegations of extramarital affairs. The Crimmins case stayed on the front pages for quite sometime.

During the trial, Bill Aylward picked up on something that both the prosecution and defense had missed; something so basic and so obvious it would seem to be part of Police Investigations 101. Bill used simple common sense to take the story in an entirely different direction.

During the trial, Crimmins's lawyers tried to point the finger at someone else, maintaining that someone could have easily climbed into the children's bedroom window and kidnapped them. The prosecution maintained this was impossible as they claimed the window was inaccessible, which meant that the children could only be taken away by Crimmins and an accomplice through the front door.

Bill Aylward reporting from Alice Crimmins Trial

So basically, the defense contended that a person could climb in the window while the prosecution said it was impossible. Yet neither side offered proof. Aylward knew there was only one way to find out; so during a recess, he and a *New York Post* reporter, George Carpozi Jr., took a ride to Crimmins's apartment. Incredibly, they found it open and empty, as the super was busy painting the place. He let Aylward and Carpozi inside.

As soon as our photographer was rolling, Bill Aylward easily climbed through the window! Incredibly, neither the prosecution nor the defense had checked this out. We ran the story that night, and the *Post* carried it as well.

When the trial resumed the next day, the prosecution team wiped the omelets from their faces and had to take their case in a different direction. The judge was concerned about Aylward's report but kept the trial going. Crimmins was eventually convicted but not on the evidence of accessibility.

Stories like that one showed our viewers that we were regular people. Teams of high-priced lawyers had missed something obvious, and Aylward was there to pick up after them.

Roger Sharp was yet another reporter who hailed from Akron, Ohio, and if it weren't for my love of music and TV watching, I probably would have missed this talented man. I first saw Roger on, of all places, *American Bandstand*. He was the anchor of the network cut-ins during Dick Clark's show.

When I arrived in New York, ABC had pretty much buried the guy on radio. I'd remembered what a captivating presence he had, so I called him and offered him a job on the spot. I knew that anyone who could anchor for the network, even

L to R Ron Tindiglia—Assignment Editor—
News Director, Doug Johnson, Roger Grimsby,
Bob Lape, John Johnson

during a rock and roll show, didn't need to audition to join the *Eyewitness News* team. But it was still difficult to get anyone to come to WABC because of its lackluster news efforts. Roger had started working in the business at eighteen and already had a ton of experience.

Roger sometimes referred to his reporting career as playing "airport roulette" as his assignments had taken him all over the globe and usually put him into harm's way. Bullets actually whizzed by his head during one story.

Sharp proved to be an excellent anchor and reporter, though he managed to raise a few eyebrows while doing a story on the water shortage in my new hometown of Greenwich, Connecticut. Known for its old money wealth, the city was down to a fourteen-day supply in the reservoir. Roger did a story, detailing the fact that even rich people had to conserve because "You can't flush with a bank account."

Roger's wife, Gun, tells a great story about the news team's frequent trips to Chips bar. Between newscasts, many staffers would head to Chips, which was across the street from the station, and actually get something to eat. Bill Beutel would wander in and begin "grazing." He'd stop by one table to chat and ask, "You gonna eat those french fries?" Then he'd have his next course at someone else's table, asking, "Are you going to have the bread with your meal?" Gun says that Beutel could often eat a very filling meal without sitting down or opening his wallet.

Doug Johnson grew up in Western Canada and started at a tiny television station there in the 1950s, then moved up the ladder until he landed in Toronto. There, like Roger Grimsby, he wore two hats, serving as news director and anchor at that city's largest station. But those two jobs didn't pay as much as the one offered in Philadelphia, so Johnson headed south to take an anchor position. Unfortunately for Doug (but not for us), the station went under and left him out of work. I saw it as a great opportunity to hire someone I'd admired in Philly while at KYW, but someone at WCBS had the same idea. Channel 2 had already offered him a job when I'd first contacted Doug. Though Johnson knew CBS was the Tiffany network and this was a chance to work at its flagship station, he realized there were limitless opportunities at WABC. He saw it as a station that was such a mess it had nowhere to go but up, and of course he was familiar with the concept from watching KYW. He turned down the offer at WCBS, and said they called him four times in an effort to get him to change his mind.

Doug was another reporter who, like Geraldo, truly cared about people and at one point kept thirty families from becoming homeless. A cruel landlord was about to demolish a building in the Bronx with no concern about those he was about to evict. Doug discovered he was breaking the law and did several stories. Eventually the city got involved and saved the building—and the homes of those people.

Celebrity was taken to a new level in the heyday of *Eyewitness News*. On one occasion, a man climbed the Brooklyn Bridge and threatened to jump into the river. Doug Johnson arrived at the scene, at which point the man told the police he wanted to talk

Eyewitness News Team growing into the legend of Broadcast Journalism

to the media. A cop handed Doug a walkie-talkie, and just like that, he was Dr. Phil. Johnson who will tell you he was not equipped to handle such a situation but nonetheless managed to talk the guy down.

As the newscast became more and more popular, Grimsby was becoming more accepting of his coworkers. Doug, who lived in the same building as Roger for a time, got along very well with the curmudgeon. About two weeks after Johnson joined us, he did a story and was surprised at the comment from Grimsby.

Doug Johnson

"Well," said Roger, "that was pretty good." Coming from a guy who seemed to have little tolerance for anyone, it spoke volumes.

Doug will tell you that today you couldn't get away with the stuff that went on back then, especially the drinking. Frank Gifford will tell you that he loved working with Roger Grimsby, got along great with the guy, and that he always knew where to find him if he wasn't in the newsroom (*Chips* bar). Many would agree that ABC employed some of the hardest drinking news anchors at its owned and operated stations. Tex Antoine came back from dinner one night after hoisting a few and actually gave the weather report for Russia and Africa. (One was cold, the other hot.)

It also didn't help that one of the ABC studios was located in a building that also housed a bar. (This would later be the location of the ill-fated Harry Reasoner-Barbara Walters newscast. It was ill-fated because, as it was once put, Reasoner liked martinis and hated Walters.) There was also a subterranean tunnel that actually ran under the building, offering staffers in other buildings an opportunity to "go underground" and grab a quick one. Had *Eyewitness News* launched during prohibition, the product would have been pretty dull.

This all came to a head at the legendary Christmas party of 1972, which was held on a weeknight. Naturally, the booze flowed freely for the number one-news team, as we were all being rewarded for a job well done. Around nine thirty, someone pointed out that it might be nice for those appearing on the eleven o'clock newscast to get back to the studio. Even though they really were in no condition to appear on camera.

The newscast that followed would be a staple of YouTube if a copy existed. (I'm sure one does, but it disappeared very quickly after the newscast before upper management could grab it and use it as evidence.) Roger could hold his liquor like a man with a hollow leg, but on this night, he got to the middle of a story and just stopped reading. No smart-ass comment, no sarcastic toss to another reporter, nothing. He just stopped cold and looked straight into the camera. Luckily, the director sensed what was happening and punched up Bill Beutel, who finished the script in what must have appeared to the viewer as a dual-anchor story. Those who weren't on the air and watched that night wondered if we'd all have jobs the next day.

But when you're number one, you're cut a lot of slack. No one said a word.

The newscast became so popular with celebrities it even had a "green room," which is a waiting area for celebrities on shows like *The Tonight Show*. Considering the fact that people like John Lennon and Yoko Ono wandered through from time to time, it wasn't that unusual. We were not only the hottest news team in town but a star magnet as well. Had Rona Barrett still been around, she would have been in heaven.

What viewers couldn't know was that the stuff behind the scenes was even more entertaining than our newscast. The station was a busy but happy place, with no shortage of jokes and cutting remarks to keep things loose. The staff worked hard and played harder. And practical jokes were becoming the norm. On one occasion, a crew was sent out to get a film of an old folks home and brought back footage of a cemetery. Cute.

Doug Johnson tells the story of a freelance photographer named Nate Cohen who, on one occasion, tried to "help the story along." Bess Myerson, the former Miss America who had become the consumer affairs commissioner in New York, held a news conference at a poultry plant in Long Island City. Doug covered it, asked the requisite questions, and headed back to the station. When he sat down to review the film, he saw Bess Myerson and heard something in the background.

"Cluck, cluck, cluck. CLUCK, cluck, cluck, cluck."

Johnson, knowing there hadn't been any live chickens at the location of the news conference, tracked down Cohen. The photographer admitted he'd been doing his best chicken impression during the entire news conference. He was simply trying to provide Johnson with some "natural sound" for the piece.

Eyewitness News 1969

Nothing was sacred. One night when Grimsby and a few staffers were walking to the studio, a woman tried to stab Roger with an ice pick. Doug Johnson, Geraldo Rivera, and a security guard managed to subdue the woman and the story made the local newspapers. Roger was later presented with a new jacket—complete with a brightly painted bull's-eye on the back.

Grimsby's comments, though still dripping with sarcasm, were becoming lighter without Rona Barrett to kick around. Just before Tiny Tim, the *Laugh-In* singer with the falsetto voice, was scheduled to get married on *The Tonight Show*, Roger came up with this politically incorrect classic. "Tiny Tim gets married on network television on December 18. If on December 19 he starts to sing bass, we'll know."

On two famous Hollywood stars who remarried and got divorced for the second time, he said, "Maybe this time it will work."

On the state of scandals that plagued a New Jersey city, he said, "If Diogenes were to visit Newark these days, he'd put out his lamp."

He also poked fun at the technical difficulties that inevitably occur during a live newscast. To the viewer, this seemed like self-deprecating humor. On one occasion, Roger read an intro to a sound bite, only to have some politician flap his gums with no audio. Roger, not missing a beat, said, "He was whispering."

When the reverse happened, audio without a picture, Grimsby was ready for that one as well. "You'll have to take our word that really was Mayor Lindsay you just heard."

It only took a little over a year for the other stations to realize we were becoming a major player in the market. I'd heard through the grapevine that the competition was concerned. On December 10, 1970, I picked up a copy of the *New York Times* and discovered what I'd been hearing was fact.

The headline read, EYEWITNESS NEWS CAUSING CHANGE AT OTHER STATIONS. The article talked about what was happening at

Winning our first Emmy L to R Steve Skinner, Al Ittelson, Larry Goodman, John Tucker, Norman Fein

WCBS and WNBC, and I couldn't help but smile when I read the phrase, "At WABC-TV, Channel 7, they're chuckling with satisfaction because they're the cause of it all." The piece told readers that there was now a three-way race in New York. What was about to happen at channel 2 was called a "major overhaul." Meanwhile, channel 4 had started its new concept by stealing one of ours, showing news staffers talking casually as the newscast began. It was obvious that our more relaxed and open concept had taken root in the other newsrooms. And it was a signal to me that the days of the single male anchor pontificating from an ivory tower were finally dead and buried forever.

Years later, a man named Ed Joyce was the news director at WCBS-TV and was pretty much the leader of the pack when it came to bashing the *Eyewitness News* concept. At one point, he had to attend a meeting of CBS news executives and was forced to watch a few of our newscasts. Afterwards a corporate exec wondered aloud, "Why can't we do it like that?" Would have loved to be there for that one.

Chapter Twenty-Three

When Howard Cosell died of a heart embolism on April 23, 1995, he was still regarded by most of America as the preeminent sportscaster in the business even though he had been completely retired for almost a decade. Howard loved to say, "I tell it like it is," dozens of times a day. It was true, as he really pulled no punches for the audience.

Howard could be a giant pain in the ass, but he still provided both incredible access and the ability to launch a watercooler comment without warning. Bob Lape tells the story of the time Howard had a world champion boxer as a live guest seated next to him. Bob had been introduced to the boxer before the newscast and couldn't possibly know what was coming as he sat at the desk on the set that was directly behind Howard's. Unbeknownst to Lape, the boxer had been involved in a rather sensitive and embarrassing marital dispute. Cosell, after introducing the boxer to the viewers, turned to the man and asked, "So how is it that your wife came to shoot you in the groin?" Needless to say, it was all Lape could do to recover his composure a few minutes later when it was his turn.

Of course, viewers loved the barbs between Grimsby and Cosell that occurred on an almost nightly basis. Once, Howard launched into one of his thesaurus, grabbing dissertations as he tossed back to Roger. Grimsby countered, "Howard, if words were birds you'd be covered in white."

Bill Aylward tells of another zinger from Grimsby that was "borrowed" by Johnny Carson and later used on *The Tonight Show*, which was still based in New York at the time. Roger, as he introduced Howard, mentioned he had seen Cosell earlier in the day, "walking his pet rat."

Still, I knew Howard's days at channel 7 were numbered. Though he was still pouting over all the news format changes, he continued to impress on me that he was all WABC-TV needed. We were building the *Eyewitness News* team and he wasn't making an effort to get with the program. He still kept nagging about the little things, often making a big scene about wearing the new blazers. One day he flat out refused to wear one. I simply said, "Howard, don't walk on that set tonight without it." I was petrified, but when Roger

Grimsby introduced him that night, he was wearing the blazer. Still, Howard had too many irons in the fire between radio and the network, and I knew local news was not, and never would be, his top priority. I needed every staff member to put his heart and soul into the station. Everyone was committed except Howard. It wasn't fair to the rest of the staff to let Howard continue to just phone it in.

Howard also grated on people's nerves. He loved to throw his salary around to impress (and usually annoy) other members of the staff. On one occasion, soundman Dave Weingold was riding in the backseat of a news vehicle driven by photographer Elliott Butler while Cosell occupied the front passenger seat. Butler and Cosell had gotten into an argument over something, when finally Howard played the money card.

"Elliott, do you know why I'm right and you're wrong?" Cosell asked.

"No, Howard," said Butler. "Why?"

"Because I make a quarter of a million dollars a year."

"Howard," said Butler, "save your money."

Howard had been working on Roone Arledge to get more network assignments and began missing our newscasts. I told him we really wanted him to be part of the *Eyewitness News* team. He finally said something that truly pushed me over the edge. "Primo, I am *my own* team."

I gambled on Howard's ego to not make trouble and it paid off. In his mind, *Eyewitness News* was small potatoes compared to working for the network and Roone Arledge. With no regular outlet during the week, he turned up the heat on Arledge and his network career took off. We remained friends and he always talked up our efforts even as he made the covers of national news magazines as America's preeminent sportscaster.

I wanted to have the most spectacular sportscaster I could find to bring to the station. I wanted a celebrity, an athlete who was a household name with a personality that just jumped through the screen. Don Meredith, who had just retired from the Dallas Cowboys and played in the famous "Ice Bowl" game in Green Bay, was the first guy I called, well before he became a huge star on *Monday Night Football*. (Of course, he ended up with that slightly better gig, ironically sitting next to the guy I wanted him to replace.)

But we didn't just want any ex-jock, we were looking for athletes who had intelligence and a quick wit. We wanted our sportscaster to "match" the personalities of the existing staff, as viewers had come to expect a certain kind of attitude from our reporters and anchors. Perhaps none of those under consideration had a higher IQ than Bill Bradley, a Princeton basketball hero and Rhodes scholar. Bradley was still playing for the New

York Knicks when I interviewed him. I was surprised that someone who played professional sports in New York and was used to dealing with the media could be so painfully shy. In reality, he had absolutely no interest in a broadcasting career but only came to the station to get an inside look at television and learn more about the medium. He was a complete gentleman and both of us knew in an instant that a career in television news was not for him. (If you've ever seen Bill Bradley on the political campaign trail, you know he doesn't have the personality to be a sportscaster.) Bradley, though dry as burnt toast, would eventually win election to the U.S. Senate, representing the state of New Jersey. He would later mount an unsuccessful run for the presidency.

Continuing my theme of chasing sports stars in the twilight of their careers, I moved on to the recently benched Buffalo Bills quarterback Jack Kemp, the onetime idol of Joe Namath. Smart, good-looking, and personable, he was another perfect candidate. We really wanted him on the *Eyewitness News* team. His playing days were pretty much over and he was just sitting on the bench collecting a six-figure salary. He had not played in a regular season game for more than a year. I simply assumed that Kemp, like most fading stars, had too much pride to keep riding the pines. So I invited him to New York and tried to talk him into retiring from the Bills and becoming a sportscaster.

I told him that we needed a sports anchor, and we needed one fast. But Kemp's timetable wasn't the same as ours. During the interview in my office, I heard something I never in my life expected to hear from a pro football player. Kemp confessed he wasn't really interested in sports and hadn't been for years. This revelation blew me away; how could a man who played quarterback in the NFL *not* be interested in sports? He said the really important game in life was getting involved in the real world—politics. I couldn't quite understand it at the time but Jack Kemp had a game plan. He had a keen interest in economics even then, saying he couldn't really afford to walk away from that much money until the end of the year when his contract was up. As it turned out, he'd soon make a successful run for Congress in 1970 and eventually run for president. (You see the pattern here?)

So I continued to beat the bushes for jocks who didn't want to live in the White House and finally discovered the best one had no political aspirations whatsoever. Unfortunately, he already worked for somebody else and his contract wouldn't expire for a while. As it turned out, I didn't have to do much of the negotiating this time. Someone else literally gift wrapped him and dropped him into our news team.

Frank Gifford, an All American at the University of Southern California and an All American in life

The sports anchor on WCBS-TV was Frank Gifford, the all-American from USC and New York Giants football star. Gifford was an icon in the city, an incredibly popular, handsome man who was known around town as a class guy. I'd done some checking and couldn't find a single person who had a bad word to say about Frank. And it would be really nice to have a member of the Giants on the staff. His teammate, Kyle Rote, had been enjoying success at WNBC-TV and was getting a lot of network sports assignments, including one at Super Bowl III in which the Jets and Joe Namath beat the Baltimore Colts. Gifford, however, was far more talented than very-dry Rote, who was truly "old school" when it came to sportscasting. Rote didn't fit the *Eyewitness News* style at all while Gifford did.

Frank had begun dabbling in broadcasting in the late 1950s and started out by filling in for Yankee great Phil Rizzuto on his radio show in 1957. At that time, Gifford was also becoming friendly with the general manager of WCBS-TV. Then in the late fifties, a New York newspaper strike gave news honchos the idea to expand local news on television, so WCBS had more time to fill and used Frank to help fill it. It was a brilliant move as fans really got to know the hero under the helmet. WCBS hired him while he was still an active player with the Giants, and by the time he retired after the 1964 season, he was a seasoned sportscaster. CBS Sports began to use him as well on NFL games, teaming him with great play-by-play men like Jack Whitaker and Ray Scott. Eventually Gifford would host the network's pre-game show that was the forerunner of the *NFL Today*.

That would seem to be enough for Frank Gifford, or anyone for that matter. But there was something even better on the horizon. ABC was so far ahead of the other networks when it came to sports that it was irresistibly attractive. After hiring Tom Dunn away from channel 2, I felt confident enough to contact Frank about making a move, but he would only do so if he could get a deal like Howard Cosell's: one that offered work with ABC Sports. Luckily, Frank had a golfing buddy with a lot of clout who also wanted him to move across the street.

Roone Arledge.

Frank, like everyone connected with sports, was in awe of ABC Sports for its Olympic coverage developed by Arledge. But Roone wasn't going to be satisfied with something that happened every four years and had bigger fish to fry. He started negotiating with NFL Commissioner Pete

L to R Joe Namath, Roone Arledge, Frank Gifford, Monday Night Footbal

Rozelle about carrying a weekly game on Monday night. Rozelle had actually conceived the idea back in 1964, scheduling a game on Monday night without even televising it. The game was a sellout, and Rozelle let CBS televise a Monday night game a few times during the late 1960s. NBC picked up on the idea and broadcast a few AFL games on Monday. It was clear that the television audience and the ticket-buying fans loved the idea.

As the deal grew closer to reality, Arledge knew he wanted Gifford on the broadcasting team and approached Frank about jumping to ABC as the play-by-play man. Up until this time, Frank had served as either a host or color commentator but knew he'd be comfortable with play-by-play duties. Frank told him he was very interested but still had another year on his contract with WCBS, and Gifford was not the type to break a deal. Since this left Arledge without his number one-draft choice for the booth, Frank recommended Don Meredith. He'd interviewed the Cowboys quarterback years earlier and knew he was a natural on camera. How he'd gotten to know Dandy Don on a personal level is a story in itself.

Toward the end of Meredith's career, Dallas coach Tom Landry benched him during a game that Frank Gifford was broadcasting. After the game, Frank ran into him and saw that he was really despondent about being pulled.

"You goin' back to New York?" asked Meredith.

"Yeah," said Gifford.

"Mind if I go with you?"

Frank offered his guest room and Meredith spent a few days relaxing and reading books for a few days. Gifford called the Cowboys and told them that Meredith was fine. During that time, the two men had great fun and bonded as friends. On Gifford's recommendation, Arledge met Meredith at Toots Shor's restaurant and offered him the gig on *Monday Night Football.* Meredith became a huge star in his own right.

Gifford liked Arledge and considered him both talented and brilliant. Roone could also deliver work with the 1972 Olympics and *Wide World of Sports* in addition to the plum role on *Monday Night Football.* But with the contract issue, Arledge knew he'd have to wait for Frank, so he hired Keith Jackson to do the first year of play-by-play for *Monday Night Football,* knowing full well Jackson was keeping the seat warm for Gifford. Roone didn't want to wait an extra year to launch *Monday Night Football.*

I'd been talking to Roone about the possibility of hiring Gifford, and he wanted Frank as much as I did. ABC realized it had a unique opportunity to not only raid the competition but to hire a true New York living legend in Gifford. The network was also determined to break up the solid news team at WCBS, of which Gifford was a major part. (It also didn't hurt that they had a guy named Walter Cronkite taking care of the network news.) It was a rare opportunity to take care of several problems at once; Gifford would be a huge loss to CBS Sports and channel 2, and a high-profile addition to Roone's team and *Eyewitness News.* It was a true no-brainer. Local and network executives worked together in an unprecedented manner to accomplish the goal of moving Frank across the street. It was a real coup; the Giants can bring New York to a standstill on Sunday afternoons, and before Gifford's arrival, we were the only station in town without a "Big Blue" hero on staff. Frank made the jump and it served to launch his career into the stratosphere. His deal was actually with the network, but part of it required him to work on the early newscasts for *Eyewitness News.* If not for Roone Arledge, I never would have had a chance to add such a wonderful sportscaster and person to our team.

Frank replaced Howard Cosell and appeared on the early *Eyewitness News* program each evening. The response was overwhelmingly positive, and one can only guess how many die-hard channel 2 viewers we stole from WCBS in a matter of days. While viewers are generally loyal to stations, they'll follow an anchor they really like, and Frank Gifford certainly fit into that category. His class and connection to the Giants far outweighed the attraction of the Cosell-Grimsby on-air barbs. The nice thing about Frank was that he put just as much effort into *Eyewitness News* as he did for *Monday Night Football* and the Olympics. And unlike Howard, Frank was never a problem, always conducting himself in the newsroom and in public with class. When he ended up sharing a booth the next year with Howard on *Monday Night Football*, he became the target of Cosell's unrelenting criticism, but Frank never brought any of it to the newsroom.

Cosell absolutely detested the trend of athletes becoming sports announcers, which was one reason he never wanted anyone else in the sports department. And since Gifford had replaced him at *Eyewitness News*, Cosell basically painted a bull's-eye on Frank's back. If you ever watched the early days of *Monday Night Football*, you heard the constant digs from Howard, which were well chronicled in the movie *Monday Night Mayhem*.

Frank always took the high road on the broadcasts, leaving Don Meredith to launch zingers back at Cosell. Perhaps one of the best comebacks came during a Giants-Cowboys game in which neither side was playing well. Cosell had been droning on about "your respective teams" when Dandy Don quipped, "At least we *have* respective teams, Howard."

As it turned out, Howard Cosell didn't need *Eyewitness News* at all. He secured his place in history with *Monday Night Football*, but when he wrote his biography, Howard was not kind toward his partners in the booth.

On Don Meredith, he wrote, "I was tempted to tell him on the air, 'Look, Don you don't know what you're talking about.'"

On Frank Gifford, Cosell said, "Like President Reagan, he is a Teflon man; no matter how many mistakes he makes during a telecast, no matter how glaring his weaknesses as a performer, nothing sticks to him."

To illustrate the level of class Frank Gifford exhibited, consider this: Two weeks before Cosell died, Frank Gifford visited Howard to let him know he cared about him. Despite the years of on-air barbs, Frank considered Howard Cosell a friend and will tell you that to this day.

While Frank was doing a great job on our six o'clock newscasts, he also turned out to be a great help in my search for a weekend sports anchor. We had hired Rick Barry, a terrific basketball player who was still a star for the New York Nets. We worked around his schedule in much the same way as we had done when Gifford was still playing with the Giants. Everything was going fine until I learned about the one big problem with having a sports anchor who was still an active player.

He can get traded. And when Barry was sent to San Francisco, it wasn't the same kind of deal I'd made for Tom Snyder. No "sports anchor to be named later" would be arriving to take his place.

Quickly, we had an immediate opening for a weekend sports anchor, as Barry had hopped the first plane out of town and couldn't exactly give me a two-week notice. Gifford rode to the rescue. The guy holding the position at Frank's old station, WCBS, was Sal Marchiano. Frank had worked with him for a few years and liked him a lot, describing him as hardworking and honest, two qualities often hard to find in television news. He suggested I invite Sal for an interview. Frank's reference was good enough for me, so we continued our raid on channel 2 and brought Sal over to join the team. My only request of Sal was that he drop a few pounds. He laid off the pasta for a few weeks and even he admitted he looked a lot better after knocking fifteen pounds off the bathroom scale.

Marchiano, who wasn't an ex-jock but just a regular guy from Brooklyn, had started behind the scenes at WCBS in the mid-1960s, which at the time was using a staff announcer to voiceover highlights on the weekends. Gifford liked him and suggested that Sal take a shot in front of the camera. Marchiano auditioned, did a credible job, and was chosen to anchor the weekends.

I'd thought I was the first person to promote diversity in New York newsrooms, but according to Sal it was actually Frank Gifford.

On Sal's first day on the air for channel 2, he'd done a report that would be part of Gifford's sportscast. Frank looked at the script before the newscast and noted the reporter on the story was named Sam March. "Who's Sam March?" asked Gifford.

"That's me," said Sal, explaining that he thought it was a good idea to downplay his ethnicity.

Gifford wouldn't have it. "No," he said, shaking his head. "You're going to use your real name. Things are changing."

And so Sal remained Sal, as he has during his remarkable forty years of anchoring sports in New York. Gifford's insistence that he use his real name would provide him with a great thrill years later.

Sal Marchiano and Frank Gifford
starting out in sports

Meanwhile, I wasn't finished building the sports team, wanting someone for the eleven o'clock newscast. I turned my attention to the rolls of recently retired baseball players. Cosell actually came up with a suggestion that former New York Yankee pitcher and recently turned author, Jim Bouton, would be perfect for the eleven o'clock sports job. Bouton had just written the seminal baseball book *Ball Four*, a wickedly funny expose that told the painful truth about all our childhood heroes. Bouton had basically kept a day-by-day diary of the 1969 season. But he'd broken the long-standing clubhouse rule of keeping quiet about what actually happens behind the scenes. The skirt-chasing and drinking incidents in his book were eye-opening to baseball fans who thought all players simply drank *Yoo-Hoo* like Yogi Berra and said "golly, shucks" when they struck out.

In other words, *Ball Four* portrayed baseball players as human beings. The book was funny without being mean-spirited though I'm sure those who were portrayed in a negative light wouldn't agree. By today's standards, *Ball Four* would probably be rated PG. But Bouton's irreverent style was something I thought would suit *Eyewitness News* and give a different look to television sports. He was incredibly popular, except with the players.

Bouton's stories about Mickey Mantle, whose fans never knew was an alcoholic, did serious damage to the image of the Hall of Famer. Several other iconic stars took shots as well. In one anecdote, Bouton wrote that during one game a badly hungover Mantle staggered out of the Yankee dugout to win a game with a pinch-hit home run. With the crowd screaming, he then shuffled back to the bench and said to his teammates, "Those people have no idea how difficult that really was." It was a funny story, but it cost Bouton lots of friends and made him somewhat of a clubhouse pariah. I knew that most of his duties would be at the anchor desk since few players were likely to grant him an interview.

Bouton, who thankfully had no desire to run for president, took the job as the eleven o'clock anchor shortly after he retired from the Houston Astros. He was absolutely red-hot after *Ball Four*, and the book was a huge promotional tool. He turned out to be an exciting sportscaster and very clever, although controversial. He was constantly in trouble with the people in the newsroom and the general public. His comments, though most of the time hilarious, were often taken the wrong way. He only lasted a couple of years, and during that time, we had to watch him like a hawk. Behind the scenes he was a practical joker, at one point buying a huge logging chain and securing Doug Johnson's bicycle to his desk. Jim was always looking for the "angle" when all he needed to do was report the scores and give his own personal insight. But his angles didn't have anything to do with news, like seeking out a different side to a story. Bouton was always searching for a new way to perform; he wanted to bring a fresh new approach to television. One of them truly crossed the line.

Sal Marchiano

Sal Marchiano happened to be covering the New York Giants on that particular day. Head coach Alex Webster had called a news conference to explain yet another losing season. Sal had a good relationship with the coach, known as Big Red, as well as Wellington Mara, the longtime Giants owner who exuded the same kind of class as Frank Gifford. Sal brought back some sound bites and assumed Bouton would choose one for his evening segment.

Bouton had what he thought was a novel idea, a great "angle." He came on the set that night and began the story about Webster's news conference. He ended by saying, "When you lose that many games you sometimes sound like you're talking Russian." He proceeded to run the film of Webster's news conference backward. The garbled voice track did indeed sound Russian. The Giants did not find that very funny nor did much of the audience.

Sal Marchiano was furious that Bouton had used his hard work for a cheap laugh and hustled over to Yankee Stadium, where the Giants played at the time. He knew he had to do some serious damage control if we were to continue getting access to the team; being shut out of the Giants locker room would be devastating to the sports department. I could only imagine the fallout; the station that employed Frank Gifford would not be allowed to cover his team. Bouton already had limited access to clubhouses due to his book and this would only make things worse for everyone else at *Eyewitness News*.

Sal arrived at the stadium to find Webster and Mara in testy moods, but the team's owner absolved Sal of any wrongdoing. "We know you had nothing to do with that, but we're going to file a slander suit," Mara said. Then Webster, a former bruiser of a running back who stood six foot three and weighed in at 225 pounds, added, "If Bouton sees me walking down the street, he'd better walk the other way."

Wellington Mara wasn't kidding. The team actually sued Jim Bouton and WABC-TV.

We were getting tired of our on-camera talent having legal problems. While most news directors spend a good part of their days dealing with the next newscast, I had to waste time working with lawyers who were trying to diffuse the situation between WABC and the New York Giants. We had our hands full for many weeks defending Jim. When a process server came to the station to hand him a subpoena, a receptionist tipped off Bouton. Jim ran to get a film crew so he could record the event. The process server walked into the sports department and asked Sal Marchiano if he knew where he could find Bouton. "I don't know," said Marchiano. "It's not my turn to watch him today." Bouton was waiting at the far end of the newsroom so that the photographer could get a nice long shot of the man carrying the subpoena.

The case was finally thrown out of court after five years but not before many executives, including myself, had to testify in court depositions. The judge ruled that what Bouton had done was not slander because newscasters were also entertainers. He added that if public television could parody Richard Nixon, a local sportscaster could do the same to a football coach.

The Giants players did eventually get a bit of revenge on Bouton. On one occasion, he'd gone to the stadium to shoot some promotional pictures and actually climbed up on one of the goal posts. As he was sitting there, some players noticed him and began throwing footballs at him.

When Bouton's contract came up for renewal, I had already been moved up to vice president of News. Bouton's agent Bill Cooper asked for a meeting with the general manager. But there was more at stake than just our eleven o'clock sportscast.

Jim Bouton clowning around, one of his favorite things which cost him his job

At that time, ABC was making a series of bids for

the rights to carry major league baseball. While no one said it would help our case if Jim Bouton was gone from WABC, the signal was pretty clear from Roone Arledge. He was creating the most innovative sports programming in the history of television and didn't need another loose cannon to go along with Howard Cosell. While Howard told it like it is, Bouton held nothing back and often crossed the line. Everyone got the message. Agent Cooper started negotiating with GM, Ken McQueen, and the man who had succeeded me as news director, Al Ittleson. MacQueen, knowing there was no way we were going to keep Bouton, interrupted the agent's sales pitch and said, "Bill, we're not going to renew Mr. Bouton's contract."

Cooper just kept talking. "We're not going to ask for much money," he said.

"No, Bill, you don't understand, we do not want to renew on *any* basis," said MacQueen.

Cooper begged that Bouton be brought up to the office to personally plead his case. MacQueen and Ittleson reluctantly agreed though both knew there was nothing that could change their minds. Bouton, with all his verve and bravado, broke down at the news. It was a very sad ending to what could have been a great career at WABC. He had a lot of the natural moves, a sense of humor, and a good eye for a story. But Bouton had a fatal flaw: he always thought he needed to make things funny every single time. He crossed the line of good taste more often than was acceptable. He worked for a short time at WCBS and then his television career was over.

Jim kept pitching, both literally and figuratively. He mounted a baseball comeback that landed him briefly with the Atlanta Braves. He's written several books and the mouth that got him in trouble made him tons of money when he filled it with chewing gum. Bouton was one of the inventors of Big League Chew, shredded bubblegum that was sold in pouches just like chewing tobacco. It was a safe way for kids to emulate their heroes without getting hooked on nicotine, and it is still being sold today.

In 1997, an event changed Bouton's life and ironically led to forgiveness by the Yankees. His daughter Laurie was killed in a car accident. A few months later, Jim's son Michael wrote an impassioned letter to the *New York Times*, asking the Yankees to bury the hatchet and invite his dad to the annual Old-Timers' Game. After nearly thirty years as a clubhouse pariah, Jim was welcomed back to the House that Ruth Built and warmly received by the crowd. He told a New York newspaper that his invitation was "Laurie's gift."

With Bouton out of the picture, Sal Marchiano grew in stature and popularity. Frank Gifford had taken Sal under his wing, stressing the importance of acting polite and professional in public. Sal says Gifford was "a prince" and an incredibly nice mentor.

Another mentor turned out to be Roger Grimsby. Like most staffers, Sal was in awe of Grimsby's ability to come up with an incredibly witty line in a nanosecond. But Grimsby told him the reason all his lines were so damn funny was that he only used the good ones. "If you have a great line, go with it," said Roger, stressing that your "A" material is the only stuff that should ever hit the air. "If not, keep your mouth shut."

Sal was doing a solid job and literally "made a big splash" on the set in 1973. He'd been covering the Mets during their "You Gotta Believe" pennant drive inspired by their star relief pitcher, the late Tug McGraw. On the day the Mets clinched, he returned from the alcohol-soaked clubhouse with a leftover bottle of champagne. Geraldo Rivera was filling in on the anchor desk that night, and at the end of the newscast Sal popped the cork and squirted the bubbly over Geraldo, just like they do in the locker room.

The viewers already suspected the news team liked one another, but that proved it. This wasn't a preproduced promo but something that was live. It was this kind of stuff that kept viewers tuning in and watching carefully. You literally never knew when something bizarre would happen on *Eyewitness News*.

Sal, meanwhile, was making a name for himself covering boxing and got a huge break when Cosell refused to go to the Philippines for a heavyweight title fight because the place was under martial law.

The fight turned out to be the Thrilla in Manila and is often regarded as one of the greatest ring battles of all time.

Frank Gifford's insistence that Sal use his given name gave Marchiano one of the great thrills of his life, one he never would have enjoyed if he'd changed his name to Sam March. Sal had an acquaintance that knew Frank Sinatra. During the 1977 World Series, Sinatra was in town to watch his buddy Tommy Lasorda, who was managing the Dodgers as they took on the Yankees. Old Blue Eyes was watching *Eyewitness News* and when Sal's sports segment began, he told Sal's friend, "I like this kid. I watch him whenever I'm in New York. I'd like to meet him."

Marchiano, of course, was blown away when told that Frank Sinatra not only knew who he was but wanted to meet him. For a *paesan*, this was even better than being granted an audience with the pope.

Sinatra was shooting a movie in New York with some scenes set at the legendary disco, Studio 54, and a meeting was arranged. When Sal arrived, Sinatra came up to him, stuck out his hand, and said, "I'm from Hoboken. Where are you from?" The chairman of the original Rat Pack then complimented Marchiano on keeping his given name. "When I started out," said Sinatra, "they wanted to call me Frankie Satin. I told them my name is Frank fucking Sinatra."

Marchiano went on to work at just about every station in New York and is currently celebrating his fortieth year. He's just published a book, the title of which recalls a very funny line that once cost him his job.

Sal was working at ESPN at the time which is located in Bristol, Connecticut, a middle-of-nowhere place that wasn't exactly a hotbed of activity compared to New York City. One night, Sal closed the show with, "Happiness is Bristol in my rear view mirror." His superiors didn't think it was funny, and Sal never enjoyed that particular view again.

His book is titled *In My Rear View Mirror*, proving that some great lines never die.

Dangling the possibility of work with ABC Sports was a great recruiting tool, a plum assignment no sportscaster could resist. It was the ace up our sleeve whenever we needed someone for the sports department. In 1976, Don Curran, our general manager in San Francisco, spotted a wild, enthusiastic sportscaster named Warner Wolf in Washington. Don called me, told me about the guy, and suggested he'd be a great asset to the company.

Wolf was a screamer, a truly over-the-top super sports fan with a great eye for highlight footage. He absolutely packed his sportscast with wall-to-wall highlights. He'd introduce each highlight by pointing at the camera and yelling, "Let's go to the video tape!" He also collected great plays and bloopers, editing them into a feature he called *Plays of the Week*. I knew he'd been a great addition to our team but contacting him was a sensitive matter for me. He was under contract to Post-Newsweek and News VP, Jim Snyder, the man who had helped me at KDKA but never allowed me on the air. I begged for years to work the overnight shift, anything. Snyder liked to say this is no peanut whistle station, our 50,000 watts can be heard all over the country. He also liked to tell people that if he had put me on the air, there would be no *Eyewitness News* concept.

I flew to Washington to meet Warner Wolf and he came to the airport to pick me up. He is about the size of a Kentucky Derby jockey and for all of his shouting on television, a rather quiet, shy guy off camera. It was almost as if our roles were reversed, as he was giving me the tour of the area. He took me around to all the local sports hangouts, including the famous Gaslight

Warner Wolf

Club. He was happy working in the nation's capital, but what a surprise, longed to work at ABC Sports. It was clear he would never go to California for Don Curran but I thought we had a shot at getting him to work in local news if we could arrange some network appearances. I talked to Roone Arledge, who by now had dangled more carrots than Bugs Bunny, and once again he agreed to help. Warner came to New York and he went through an exhausting day with my boss, Dick O'Leary, who was the greatest ABC salesman. O'Leary took him through the station and then we all headed to a meeting with Roone Arledge.

Arledge kept us waiting for an hour. When we finally got to see him, Roone told Warner he had heard of him and then played the network card. He said there might be a place for Warner Wolf at ABC Sports. Arledge, unlike Dick O'Leary, didn't try to close the sale. He didn't have to. Roone was a guy who never returned phone calls and worked in casual clothes, keeping a dark suit in the closet for those important visits upstairs. It might have appeared to Warner Wolf that the meeting wasn't very important to Arledge, but that was the way Roone operated. I was in a panic and started talking about various assignments that might be available to Warner. Roone just nodded his head and smiled. I'm sure he was wondering how many local sports guys I was going to drag into his office.

We were successful in attracting Warner Wolf to WABC-TV and were able to deliver on our promise of getting him some work on ABC Sports. He had no agent but was able to negotiate a great deal. Roone kept his end of the bargain in a very big way, as he named Warner one of the first announcers on *Monday Night Baseball*. Unfortunately for Wolf, it turned out to be a ratings disaster for ABC. It was one of the few times ABC Sports did not make an impact with its coverage.

In true network style, he was pulled off the games after some bad reviews. It was a public humiliation, one of the first times in his life that Warner Wolf ever failed. But he had great courage and continued working at WABC-TV, still shouting, "Let's go to the video tape!" He became a huge star on *Eyewitness News* as fans loved his enthusiasm and knew they could always count on him for a ton of highlights. Anytime his highlights contained a bizarre-looking fan, Warner would use it to throw a zinger at a member of the news team. A shirtless fat guy in a rainbow wig might pop up at the end of the highlights, and Warner would say, "And Roger Grimsby was at the game!"

We'd come a long way from the days when Howard Cosell's sportscast consisted of just a commentary and maybe a toupee. Our sportscasters were all legitimate stars. But payback is hell, and *Eyewitness News* had become so popular that the competition continued its raid on our talent, this time going after the sports department. Channel 2 made Warner Wolf an offer to move across the street, he took it, and managed to get his quarter of a million dollar salary doubled. He flourished at WCBS-TV for years but his addition did not dent the ratings dominance of *Eyewitness News*. Channel 2 had assumed that hiring one of our biggest stars would steal our thunder, but our team was too strong and the viewers knew we were the only team that could pull off the format. Later, when CBS started downsizing and wanted to save money on the big salaried stars, Warner spotted it coming long before anyone else. He quietly maneuvered a return to his old station in Washington for even more money than he was making at WCBS. He may as well have changed his signature line to, "Let's go to the bank!"

PS Warner never gives up. He's fully employed on ESPN Radio and back on Imus in the Morning after being bumped there a few times by not ready for prime time sportscasters.

As with all great teams, nothing lasts forever. We were a victim of our own talent and success and started to lose even more people because they were simply too good at their jobs. It would turn out to be a trend. Geraldo Rivera moved to the ABC network. Bill Beutel was lured to *Good Morning America* but would return. Joan Lunden did the same but stayed.

New people replaced them, but it was never the same Camelot that we enjoyed in those early years.

Chapter Twenty-Four

The television news industry, like just about everything else, is a copycat business. If something works, we move at warp speed to duplicate it. Imitation may be the most sincere form of flattery, but in broadcasting, it is a matter of survival.

And sometimes, they try to clone you.

After seeing the smashing success of *Eyewitness News* in New York, the corporate execs at ABC were using me to help improve the news ratings in the four other major markets where the network owned stations. But this was in addition to my duties as news director at WABC and left me with so much on my plate I couldn't see the china pattern. I couldn't handle the day-to-day operations of one station while trying to fix four others so I pushed my superiors hard to make me vice president of News. They were concerned that our flagship station might have problems without my full attention, but I pointed out that as long as I was working with four other stations, it didn't have my full attention anyway. I told them there was only one way for me to work with all the ABC-owned stations: I had to be relieved of my duties as news director of WABC. I explained that my assistant, Al Ittleson, was quite capable of taking over the reins without missing a beat as he and I were on the same page as far as news coverage was concerned. And with all the extra duties I'd been assigned, Ittleson was taking care of a lot of my news director duties anyway. In my mind, there wasn't anything left to fix at WABC, but there were plenty of problems at the other four stations.

Finally, they relented. They gave Ittleson a well-deserved promotion to news director and I put my time and energy into working with the other stations, helping them implement the format that had been so successful in Philly and New York. Ittleson didn't miss a beat and our newscast continued to dominate the market. In less than two years, all five ABC stations were number one in the ratings and contributing an incredible 25 percent of the company's annual profits.

As *Eyewitness News* continued to grow into a major force in the bigger markets, the format was becoming a topic of conversation around the country, not just in New York. News directors of low-rated stations took notice of the speed at which *Eyewitness News* was catching on. Generally, it can take years to change viewing habits, but at the time the country was hungry for something new and it didn't take long for viewers to change their loyalties when they found something they liked.

I started getting calls from news directors at ABC affiliates around the country. They wanted the secret to our success but wanted more than an air check of a newscast. They needed more than just the playbook. They wanted to come to New York. They needed to learn our format and techniques in person, to see the minute-by-minute machinations that produced the product. So we started inviting them to New York. I was thrilled to meet with each of them and explain the concept of taking journalism to the next level. I showed them how they could turn their stations around just as we had done in New York and Philadelphia. I always got a lot of raised eyebrows and smiles when I told each news director it wouldn't cost anything to implement the change. While I didn't know it at the time, this practice would turn out to be the basis for another venture I would start in the future.

Meanwhile, the corporate organization continued to grow at 1330 Avenue of the Americas and so did the office politics. I needed a scorecard to keep everything straight. Ted Shaker was very busy worrying about the new executive on the corporate block, Elton Rule. Rule had been general manager of KABC-TV in Los Angeles and was brought in by Goldenson to run the network and as Shaker feared, take over the operation of the entire company.

Rule had a key assistant, a lawyer named I. Martin Pompadur, who was his main troubleshooter and a no-nonsense executive. A young man, Marty did not feel bound by the old corporate rules, and he liked to encourage innovation. He personally liked *Eyewitness News* and knew it was lifting ABC's fortunes. While we had very little contact, I knew he was a key player in the corporate hierarchy.

John Campbell, another Elton Rule protégé, was given the responsibility of bringing together the five network-owned television stations as a special division within the company. Shaker had run each of the stations independently. Due to the success of *Eyewitness News*, I started to get more exposure with Campbell and the brass downtown.

The first piece of advice I gave John was to start using the title *Eyewitness News* in all the ABC markets before any other stations or groups could lay claim to first usage and prevent us from having it. I suggested he make an immediate preemptive strike, using the name with the sign-off news and the sign-on news as I did on my first day in New York then legally registering it in each market.

We were able to get the job done quickly in Los Angeles and Chicago. Unfortunately, we were too late in San Francisco. The City by the Bay had a Westinghouse station, KPIX, which was already using the title thus preventing our using it there. As for our station in Detroit, well, that was a story in itself.

Thanks to our old friends, the consultants from McHugh and Hoffman.

After my early encounters with these guys, I thought I'd be rid of them forever. They didn't like me, didn't care for the format, thought Roger Grimsby was hopeless, and hated reporters on the set. I never dreamed they would actually use my ideas for their own benefit. But like unwelcome relatives who stay too long at Christmas, they continued to hang around ABC and stank up the place (and collect a big check for recommendations we never ever implemented). They could see early on that the audience was enthusiastic for *Eyewitness News* even though they were still of the opinion that the format was not as effective as I would have everyone believe. Even after it became apparent that Roger Grimsby was becoming an icon in New York, they had continued to recommend that he be fired. They said he was "too cold" and in their interpretation of the research, "incapable of succeeding" in the New York market. They further added that the *Eyewitness News* format, particularly the trooping of reporters into the studio to deliver their stories "live" on the set, took away from the anchors and should be discontinued. Looking back, they turned out to be wrong about everything.

I had been able to fight them off their positions by sheer personal commitment to my plan. Instead of just taking their recommendations at face value, I had put on my old reporter's hat and began digging. I carefully reviewed their research records and, lo and behold, discovered that their figures did not support their conclusions. They were so determined to prove their point that they did not take any of their own research into account when making their recommendations. I confronted them with their own research, and they were finally forced to admit that their recommendations were based on their personal interpretation rather than the research. They'd insisted on predicting that, in their opinion, the *Eyewitness News* format would fail because they personally didn't like the format. Their weak position was enough to allow it (and me) to survive.

Despite their "pride," they took the format they so detested and recommended it to their other clients! McHugh and Hoffman also worked for the Storer Broadcasting Incorporated, which operated stations in Cleveland,

Atlanta, Toledo, San Diego, and unfortunately for us, Detroit. For a company that had fought tooth and nail against the *Eyewitness News* concept, they sure jumped aboard the bandwagon once they worked for the competition. They secretly went to the Storer Detroit station and got them to install the title *Eyewitness News* on their programs before I could get ABC to make the move in that market. While imitation is the most sincere form of flattery, this ticked off everyone.

At this point in time, Dick Beesemyer was promoted to head of affiliate relations and WABC-TV needed a new general manager. This kind of opening at the flagship station brought out all the power brokers in the company, each of whom had his own favorite. The infighting was so vicious they had to settle on a compromise candidate, Ken MacQueen, who was the sales manager of WXYZ-TV in Detroit.

At about the same time, Elton Rule was crushing Ted Shaker and reorganizing the company. Then he moved Campbell up and brought in a new president of the owned-and-operated stations, his old friend Dick O'Leary, the general manager of WLS-TV Chicago. O'Leary had dutifully installed the *Eyewitness News* title at WLS but knew absolutely nothing about the journalistic format. He had also raided the CBS-owned WBBM-TV and hired Fahey Flynn, the most popular anchorman in Chicago, whom most thought was over the hill, including CBS. It turned out to be a stroke of genius. O'Leary teamed Flynn with a younger anchorman, Joel Daley, and added a colorful weatherman, John Coleman. He coupled that with a new sports package and a new set. It clicked and created a sensation in Chicago.

They would start something that O'Leary personally orchestrated through *Variety Chicago* reporter Morry Roth called "Happy Talk News." Roth, looking for hot copy to increase his space in *Variety* while promoting O'Leary's career, trivialized one of the greatest concepts ever devised in journalism. Unfortunately, the term found its way back to New York and stuck to *Eyewitness News* like superglue. It is a tag that has plagued every serious journalist at WABC since. Bill Beutel hated the term, saying that the staff members simply didn't take themselves too seriously. Frank Gifford said it wasn't really "happy talk" but just people being comfortable with one another. The term *happy talk* did not apply to what we were doing at *Eyewitness News* though a lot of people still refer to the format that way. By definition, "happy talk" occurs when an anchor might ask someone else on set "what did you do today?" The other person might launch into some time filling story about golf or shopping or anything. Happy talk is almost always personal in nature.

In our case, the unscripted parts of the newscast were simply remarks and those were usually made by Roger Grimsby in the form of one-liners. They were usually so sarcastic that they couldn't even remotely be construed as "happy." On one occasion, a new medical reporter was live on the set and did a report on why people have to wait in doctor's offices for such a long time. The film showed him sitting there, reading a magazine, with no sound. It made no sense. In tossing back to Roger, the reporter said, "Well, that's what I did today. And I'll be back in that doctor's office again tomorrow." To which Roger retorted, "Good. I certainly hope they find out what's wrong with you."

Happy talk? Not even close.

Still, competitors couldn't resist hanging that unflattering tag on our format, even dancing on the grave of one of our stars. When Roger Grimsby passed away in 1995, the headline for his obituary in the *New York Times* read, ROGER GRIMSBY, 66, ANCHOR AND INITIATOR OF "HAPPY TALK." I hate to use a cliché, but Roger surely turned over in his grave when that newspaper hit the stands.

Even before I got the job, I was asked by ABC to work on a number of news problems at the stations the company owned. In San Francisco, the ABC station, KGO-TV, consistently lost to the powerful KPIX. Roger Grimsby had been the news director/anchor at KGO but was only able to create enough excitement in the market to get himself promoted to New York as anchorman.

I suggested the station hire Pat Polillo, with whom I had worked at KDKA in Pittsburgh. Polillo had dropped out of the world for a year or so to write a book and bum around Cape Cod but had returned to the business as news director of WPVI in Philadelphia. He'd been successful in beginning the downfall of (my old station) KYW-TV as the dominant news station. Polillo laid the foundation for the "Action News" format and then moved on to become the news director for the RKO station in Boston. He ran into some difficulty there, working for general manager John McCrory, whom most regarded as a bit odd; John nonetheless went on to become head of all the Times-Mirror television stations.

My theory was that newspaper companies in those days would make strange choices when hiring executives to run their television stations. Many who didn't work in the industry thought everyone in television was insane and they would be better served hiring the most bizarre people they could dig up.

When Pat called me, I put him in touch with Don Curran, general manager of KGO and put the word in with John Campbell. He got the job and made a major contribution to the station. Through his efforts, KGO was able to become the dominant station in the market, due largely to placing major emphasis on the eleven o'clock newscast. KGO's competitors never bothered much with their late newscasts, believing the audience was too small to warrant the effort. It was true, but the problem wasn't the lateness of the hour. Polillo proved the audience wasn't watching at eleven o'clock because the television stations did not give them a reason to stay up late. He implemented the format and put some meat into the late newscast and the audience noticed. It was the beginning of the end for the opposition.

While I was being used to coordinate news activities throughout the network group, there was still no national news director position. When I pushed Campbell, he was really not interested because of a personal belief that the stations should operate independently. He was not an empire builder. And I'm sure he figured I was doing the job anyway.

I saw it as an opportunity to expand *Eyewitness News* and advance my career. I began a subtle campaign to extend my influence in that area. I generated groupwide ideas and sent them along to Campbell. I was quick to respond to his call for personnel at the stations, adding my people everywhere. I also made sure I kept Pompadur aware of *Eyewitness News* developments and the need to expand. He was the man Campbell talked with first before meeting with Rule.

At the proper moment, I called Pompadur to let him know that I was being courted by NBC, which by this time was being demolished by the *Eyewitness News* format in every market. Their top executives had finally stopped talking about how this format would never work and had apparently decided to fight fire with fire. When they finally made the move to cover news in *Eyewitness* fashion, it was too late. We had changed the rules of the game and the audience knew it. The minute our competition began to emulate our style, it validated our format and propelled us even more solidly into first place.

As is often the case in television news, nothing really happens unless you threaten to leave. I saw it in Philadelphia, and lo and behold, it happened again in New York. In May 1972, they sent me word from 1330 Avenue of the Americas to "Hold on, big things are going to happen soon!" I had lost patience with that version of "the check is in the mail" by this time, and I called Pompadur to lay the pressure on as forcefully and politely as I could. He went into action, and before twenty-four hours had passed, I was named the new vice president of News for the ABC-owned television stations. Campbell was moving up the ladder and O'Leary was walking in the door as president of the group.

Working with Dick O'Leary was an experience. He had the gift of the Irish, loquacious on every subject in the world, a spellbinder when it came to presentations and sales ranging from absolutely charming to dangerously cunning. At a meeting in Puerto Rico with all the station managers gathered around a conference table, O'Leary got so carried away making a point he smashed his fist down so hard my heart jumped. Everyone was just stunned, as grown men sat in silence with their heads down when O'Leary said impishly, "I think I just shit my pants." The break in the tension put everyone on the floor roaring with laughter.

O'Leary had stopped drinking after the Chicago success, but you couldn't tell. All of the alcoholic rage and anger were still part of his and our life. He was one of the smartest TV executives I have ever met. I learned a great deal from him.

One of the first assignments I got from him was to go to Los Angeles and fire News Director Bill Fyffe. Bill was one of those deep-voiced radio announcers who got into television and managed to work his way up to management. He carried a lot of baggage with him and had managed to lose the support of his staff and his superiors. The *Eyewitness News* format demanded that management be part of the team, not be seen as an outsider.

O'Leary agreed it would be poor judgment to start my new job by firing a news director. News directors needed recognition and status in the company to get each of them to fully implement *Eyewitness News*. He agreed to let me go to California to work out something with Fyffe and the general manager.

Fyffe picked me up at Los Angeles International Airport. When we got into the car, the first thing I said was "I'm here to fire you, Bill." He was stunned. His general manager, Don Curran, wanted him out because of the low morale. Fyffe's newsroom was filled with fearful people who were simply frightened of him. His anchorman, Joseph Benti, who had come to KABC from CBS, was morose. I soon found out the reason. While I was visiting with him in his office, he opened his cabinet and offered me some marijuana. I couldn't believe it. Joe knew he was dealing with a new corporate VP but just didn't care. I told him I was going to pretend I didn't see what had just happened and walked out of the office.

Fyffe was given a long list of objectives, which included counseling. If he promised to change his life, I would save his job. He agreed and I got the company to give him another chance, but it turned out to be a mistake. Fyffe did manage to turn things around, but he caused great trouble for many, many newspeople and the *Eyewitness News* format.

Fyffe managed to hang in long enough to succeed Ittleson as vice president of News when Al was promoted to ABC Network News as executive producer of *20/20*. Fyffe was responsible for the firing of Ron Tindiglia, whom I called *Super Ron*, a man who had who helped enormously in the early days of *Eyewitness News*. Ron went to CBS as VP of News for Owned Television Stations and became general manager of WCBS-TV. He started a consulting business working with the CBS stations and was instrumental in guiding *Entertainment Tonight* and *Hard Copy*, among other big-time syndicated shows. He died very early from lung cancer. Fyffe also played the major role of bringing Tom Snyder to WABC after his dismissal from *The Tomorrow Show*. He set up the promotion incorrectly and caused ABC to lose a true American classic when he eventually fired Snyder.

I always liked to say the day you are hired by the networks, someone up there puts a silver bullet away for you. Bill Fyffe finally got his and went on to work with an old ABC sales executive, Peter Desnoes, who started buying television stations and hired many *Eyewitness News* trained executives as general managers. He retired to Green Bay, Wisconsin, and fell to his death helping a neighbor repair a gutter on the roof of his house.

In the early days of network television, ABC had such consistently bad ratings that it had to develop desperate ways to get the attention of advertising agency time buyers. The "presentation party" each fall (now known as the network "upfronts") was created to get Madison Avenue to pay at least some attention to the new ABC season schedule.

The idea behind the whole affair was to wine and dine the young and impressionable buyers of TV time on both the network and local level and hope they'd throw a little business ABC's way, no matter the ratings. The event was usually successful as it loosened up the buyers and got them in a good mood. But it always seemed to carry with it a certain amount of guilt on the part of upper management. They were increasingly uneasy about having to grovel for business while CBS and NBC always generated tremendous revenues on the strength of their schedules alone.

Improving ABC's programming was a long and difficult job, but improve it did. As Leonard Goldenson and Elton Rule slowly gained confidence in ABC's schedule and growing share of audience, they began to grumble and question the value of the "presentation party." Everyone seemed to get the message except my boss, Dick O'Leary, now president of the Owned Television Stations division. O'Leary convinced his old friend Rule, a fellow salesman from KABC-TV in Los Angeles, that he should do it one more time. For the

Richard O'Leary the brilliant President
of ABC Television Stations

occasion, ABC rented out the entire Lincoln Center complex for the night. It was an elaborate event. Count Basie and his orchestra played jazz at one end of the building while at the other, a hot rock band played for the younger buyers. The finest food and drink flowed continuously to the guests who were then herded into the theater to view the new ABC network schedule and station programs. It was a great success.

The general manager of each network affiliate would come to New York to attend the party. They'd have the chance to meet the top ABC brass and many of the network stars featured in the fall series. The next day, the president of the division would take the presentation on the road to Chicago, Detroit, San Francisco, and Los Angeles and stage a similar event for buyers in each of those important television markets.

The day after the successful New York presentation, Dick O'Leary brought his managers together for a special lunch on the fortieth floor of the ABC building. It was an opportunity to show his key men to the senior management of the company. O'Leary, a tough hard-drinking salesman who had battled his way to the top, was being the perfect gentleman.

It was a rather quiet, sedate lunch over which Rule was presiding. Among the senior staff was a new corporate treasurer who had been recently hired and was seeking to win favor with Rule. He made a slightly negative comment about presentation parties kissing up to Rule and Goldenson. It was a tease, questioning the money spent and wondering aloud if it were something whose "time had come and gone." O'Leary turned purple with anger. He stood up and glared, his body reportedly seeming to tremble as his rage mounted. Then in one of the wildest displays ever seen since Win Baker's flying cocktail incident, he turned and walked behind the chair he had just vacated, lifted it, and hurled it across the room with every ounce of energy he had. It smashed to pieces. The managers said the tension was so great it was unbearable. The whole room was in shocked silence, and one could almost hear their hearts pounding. At last, Rule broke the tension with a calm smile, saving his old friend by saying, "Gee, Dick, I didn't know you cared so much."

The room erupted in howls of laughter, not so much for the wit of the comment but for relief that the ice had been broken. The lunch was quickly ended as O'Leary and the GMs headed for the airport. He wasn't fired, but it was the beginning of the end for a brilliant TV executive.

Chapter Twenty-Five

When it became crystal clear I was not going to get *Eyewitness News* on the ABC Network, I decided I would do it station by station. The future was upon me.

As the *Eyewitness News* concept was racking up ratings in all the ABC affiliates, my drive to put my format on the whole network grew in intensity and I turned up the heat again.

O'Leary called me to his office one day and said "upstairs" wanted me at the network. He was frustrated in his own attempts to move up the corporate ladder after the fantastic success he'd achieved in the Owned Stations Division and this was at least some slight reward for what we had accomplished.

Harry Reasoner, ABC NEWS, 1974
with Executive Producer Primo

Then he ruined my day. He said they wanted me to become executive producer for the *Reasoner Report*. I was very disappointed and told him I wouldn't go over unless I had a real mandate to change things. Without the *Eyewitness News* format, I didn't see how ABC was going to make any inroads.

I thought that was the end of it since I knew ABC would not let me use the format for the network newscast. Then I got a personal call from Harry Reasoner. He was told I didn't want the job and he did a great selling job on how they needed new blood at the network. He liked the success of *Eyewitness News* and was ready for some of his own since. He'd left the powerful CBS News and wasn't used to life in third place. I told him I would not come over unless I could make real change. He said he couldn't get involved in the politics but really wanted me there. It was nice that Harry wanted me on his team but it still didn't change the fact that I'd be using the tired old format, one that hadn't been able to deliver ratings. It didn't make any sense to me to keep the same format that couldn't get the network news out of last place.

I told O'Leary to tell Elton Rule I wasn't going. He could see himself in the same position and agreed. The next day he called me back into his office and said, "Rule told him, 'Primo didn't understand. I want him over there, period.'" I went over to meet with Bill Sheehan, VP of News now succeeding Elmer Lower as president of ABC News.

He knew what I wanted but said only that I was to become part of his new network team. Then he asked who my agent was. I was stunned, not realizing top management could even have outside representation. When he offered me an $8,000 raise, I said I would get back to him. I quickly called Ralph Mann, who represented Reasoner, Peter Jennings, Bill Beutel, and many of the top network newspeople, and asked him to get into it. In a single phone call, Ralph got an additional $20,000 and never charged me. Thanks, Ralph.

I was forced to accept the position and throw myself into the work. Since I couldn't bring the *Eyewitness News* format to the network, I decided to implement some changes through the back door by improving the quality of the stories and getting coverage from all over the world. I called general managers of ABC affiliates to get them to carry the program. Many had never heard from a network news executive.

Timing was in my favor when it came to news content. During this period, Watergate dominated the news with one revelation of wrongdoing after another and network news was appointment television. Vice President Spiro Agnew had resigned in October of 1973, and Richard Nixon would follow him out of Washington the following August. When Gerald Ford succeeded the disgraced president in 1974, he was obviously anxious to build his presidential standing with the American public, as trust in government had hit an all-time low. As executive producer of the *Reasoner Report*, I saw an opportunity to make a preemptive strike with the Ford people. The media had been ruthless in going after the Nixon administration, and I knew anything that even resembled an olive branch would be quickly grabbed by the new president's team.

So I put in a request to have Harry get an exclusive interview with the new president. I was surprised at the manner in which I received the response.

Ron Nessen, the former NBC correspondent, actually called me from Air Force One. His code name was "Sunbeam." My phone rang and an operator came on the line when I answered.

"Mr. Primo, the White House is calling, so please speak up. It is a radio call." Then I heard her contact the president's plane. "Ground to Sunbeam, come in. Can you hear me, Mr. Primo? Please speak up, this is an unmonitored call. Come in, Sunbeam." Nessen got on the line and told me Ford would be glad to give us the interview. The he asked if we would like to come to Camp David to do it. I almost jumped through the phone. No news crew had ever gone beyond the front gate and helicopter pad at the exclusive presidential retreat named after Dwight Eisenhower's grandson. I confirmed it with Nessen and set up the visit with Reasoner.

Camp David is part of a recreational park area in Frederick County, Maryland, about an hour north of Washington. When we arrived, the Secret Service carefully searched each of us. We had a full network crew, and the agents proceeded to ask for the camera gear. They actually wanted to take everything completely apart before letting us in. Most times agents will simply ask you to turn on the camera so they'll know it really is a camera. But I couldn't allow them to dismantle very sensitive equipment. I raised an objection and said we might as well go back home since the search would ruin our ability to shoot the footage. Ron Nessen stepped in and came to our rescue.

There is a large security force and heavy barbed wire surrounding the entrance. All of the buildings are painted olive green to make them difficult to see from the air and remain that color to this day. Nikita Khrushchev was brought there after his famous shoe-pounding visit to the United Nations and he thought he was being taken to an American prison. Once inside, it is a magnificent mountain retreat. The sit-down interview was set up in the "Birch Cottage." The presidential residence is called Aspen. I had requested to do the interview in two parts, one with the president walking through Camp David. In the second part, he would sit for a one-on-one with Reasoner.

President Gerald Ford in the only exclusive interview ever granted at Camp David, 1974

Wildlife freely darts through the complex. The walkways and paths have been kept as natural as possible and there is a feeling of communing with nature. Camp David truly is a very special place for the presidents.

Harry Reasoner was given a Camp David jacket and President Ford came out of the president's house on a golf cart. Harry and senior producer Joan Richmond were as nervous as I have ever seen them. Reasoner kept asking me, "Are we sure we are asking him all the important questions?"

Before we knew it, President Ford was walking down toward us. White House still photographers, who seemed to record everything but bathroom visits on the trip, were snapping away so quickly it sounded like a horde of crickets. Harry said nervously, "We're right on time Mr. President, you're early." The tension quickly disappeared. There was no need to worry as I

Harry Reasoner, President Gerald Ford, Press Secretary, Ron Nessen and military escort at Camp David.

found Gerald Ford was just about the nicest man in the world, quickly calling me by my first name. He was sixty-one years old at the time but looked twenty years younger. He was a remarkably handsome man who looks much better in person than in photographs. It was hard to remember he was the president of the United States. He said, "Take as much time as you need, I'm not going anywhere." We quickly discovered Ford liked people and he enjoyed being president. He obviously knew he had to get off on the right foot with the media, having seen the public inquisition of Richard Nixon.

Halfway through the walking interview, Betty Ford appeared with "Liberty," a new golden retriever given to the first family by photographer David Kennerly. This was a real bonus for our coverage even though it was a perfect photo op. Seeing the First Lady looking well after her breast cancer operation made the Fords seem more normal. She was wearing a camel wrap-around coat with brown slacks. The First Lady, the president, and Harry talked on camera briefly. Then Betty Ford continued her walk with the dog, leaving her husband to talk about more serious matters with Reasoner.

Gerald Ford told us he would run for reelection in 1976 but said he expected a difficult time of it. His told us his philosophy was "prepare for the worst; the good will take care of itself." As it turned out, he was right about the election. He lost to Jimmy Carter, thanks in part to a New York *Daily News* headline that read, FORD TO CITY: DROP DEAD after he'd refused to give the city financial assistance.

Our visit provided the viewers with a unique look at the family behind the presidency. ABC loved what we'd brought back and actually preempted a prime-time program for our one-hour report, something rarely done for the news division.

At the time I had no idea how unusual our trip to Camp David was. Since our visit, no television news crew has ever been permitted to film inside the compound in that exclusive way.

But even with the Gerald Ford coup, I couldn't get ABC to bring the entire *Eyewitness News* format to the network. I decided to try another end run to my playbook. I wanted to start a system whereby the anchors of the ABC local stations would be used regularly on the network. This was met with apprehension, but wasn't completely discounted. I got only so far as using them occasionally on the weekend network newscast. I was able to get them to start going to each of the ABC-owned stations for wrap-up reaction to big stories from our anchors in the big cities. Av Westin quickly dubbed it the "wraparound" and took credit for the idea, a technique he had perfected over his long career in broadcasting.

Meanwhile, the life of a network news executive was pretty exciting with trips all over the world to visit news bureaus. It would have been very easy to get caught up in the status quo and just glide along with the rest of the pack and eventually float into retirement with a golden parachute. Resistance to change of any kind is embedded in the entire organization, but doing things differently was the reason I'd done so well. I couldn't simply sit back and collect a paycheck knowing I could help improve the product.

Elmer Lower was jetting all over the world attending conferences, and Bill Sheehan stepped right into the pattern even before he got the top job. Meanwhile, the news programs languished in last place. The ratings continued to be an embarrassment to all of ABC. Still, everyone was resistant to my ideas. They liked them for local, but not for the network. They had their cushy jobs and their kingdoms were safe so they saw no reason to rock the boat.

But ABC was sitting on a huge promotional opportunity. The network was finally starting to make headway in prime-time entertainment programming. And using hit shows to promote the news product was a no-brainer as I'd learned from *Marcus Welby*. So once the prime-time ratings began to go up, Elton Rule and the top executives finally began turning their attention to the network news division. I thought my time was coming. But Bill Sheehan, who had taken to flying Rule to Paris and London, beat out a tough Av Westin, a man who had his own campaign operating in full force. Westin had key supporters in every ABC bureau all over the world and a cadre of people at corporate headquarters.

When I joined the network, Sheehan had advised that I get close to Westin. In my first meeting, Av minced no words. He said out loud what everyone was thinking in the news division. It was a brutal attack on Sheehan. Av thought he should be running the show and really wasn't interested in anything but getting to be the president of ABC News.

He said, "I'll talk to you after I get the job." I thought it was a bad dream, but when I pressed him directly on the subject, he made certain I got his vicious message. It was an awakening to the shark tank network news was and really continues to be to this day.

When I told Sheehan about the problem, he simply smiled and said, "Oh, that's just Av." *What an idiot*, I thought. Sheehan kept Westin in charge of the evening news but went to San Francisco to meet with Steve Skinner, the original *Eyewitness News* producer whom I had appointed as news director of KGO-TV. He offered Skinner the job of senior producer. I was thrilled, thinking this might be the breakthrough to get some *Eyewitness News* concepts on the network.

Westin, who continued his assault on Sheehan even after he got the presidency, made the fatal mistake of telling a newspaper reporter some of the same things he told me in our fateful meeting. The reporter told Sheehan, who then fired Westin.

Skinner was made executive producer of the Evening News. The good old boys panicked and slowly but ever so surely undermined Skinner. It was a painful time for him and even more for me watching the news sharks circle and attack his every move. I felt I was twisting in the wind in my office in the ASCAP building watching higher-ups conduct their cold war while making no impact at all on the network. Skinner was fearful of even talking to me. I didn't press it.

Then we all came to work one morning to find that ABC had hired Barbara Walters away from NBC for a cool million dollars and announced she would be teamed with Reasoner. The pairing made oil and water look like a good mix and despite the talents of both, turned out to be one of television's most notable failures.

By this time, Sheehan had lost control of his own division. His reorganization plan was failing with executives turning down assignments. He wanted me to go to Washington to be vice president of News. My connection to *Eyewitness News* was starting to fade, as the glory days at WABC were getting farther back in the rear-view mirror. And since television news executives have a short memory, I thought if there was ever a time to start on my own, this was it.

Shortly after my fateful meeting with Sheehan, I swung into action. Success gives access. I decided to start my own consulting company. The Storer Broadcasting Incorporated, which owned stations in Atlanta, Cleveland, Detroit, San Diego, and Toledo, would be an excellent client. I called the president and he offered me a full-time job as vice president of News. Then more offers materialized from Dave Henderson, of Outlet Broadcasting, and Jim Connoly, of Meredith Broadcasting.

It was clear that many people still believed in me. But I realized that as a consultant I could work for all the companies. I was tired of corporate politics and really wanted to do something on my own. Connoly gave me New York office space, a video tape machine and a monitor, along with a one-year contract to work with his stations in Kansas City and Saginaw, Michigan. Henderson signed me up for a year to consult his stations in San Antonio, Providence, and Columbus. Storer became my biggest client with its five stations. Then I was hired to take care of two stations in Illinois, Champaign and Peoria.

With those stations alone, I more than tripled my ABC salary. But the money wasn't my only necessity. Consulting filled an even greater human prerequisite for me, the need to be needed. It was a natural transition from what I had been doing at ABC, spreading the *Eyewitness*

News format that made news more interesting and compelling viewing to a mass audience.

Even though it didn't work with ABC, I have learned that perseverance is the only approach that works. Just ask Dr. Joyce Brothers.

When I first saw her on *The $64,000 Question*, I was amazed, like most of the audience, with her encyclopedic knowledge of boxing. Dr. Joyce Brothers was an immediate superstar, one of television's very first. She was a producer's dream: soft-spoken, intellectual, and attractive. A lovely blonde psychologist who said she got all the boxing books she could find and memorized every name and statistic. The Marquis of Queensbury would have been proud of this petite woman, defeating all challengers on the game show while a nation sat mesmerized in front of their television sets. She commanded center stage for weeks and weeks. Even when scandal destroyed the quiz shows in the 1950s, Dr. Joyce Brothers escaped unscathed.

Years later she was being ushered into my dark office at WABC-TV, ironically by Don Dunphy Jr., my assistant and son of the most famous boxing announcer in the world Don Dunphy.

Dr. Brothers was wearing a business suit with a full skirt and a proper bow tie in her white blouse, appearing as she always did on television. Her golden spectacles blended into a face that held a faint smile. "Thank you for

Dr. Joyce Brothers

seeing me, Mr. Primo," she said. Being in my early thirties, I blushed like a kid. My face matched Dunphy's, who was always blushing except when he had something important to do. (Then his face glowed bright red.)

I didn't get a chance to say very much. Dr. Brothers told me she had seen *Eyewitness News*, liked the concept, and thought she could become a part of the team. I was amazed she wanted the work, but it soon became abundantly clear that work is her life.

She started pitching hard, pulling out tear sheets from newspapers and magazines for which she had written articles. She was in all the big ones—*Reader's Digest, Parade, Good Housekeeping*. She recited the weekly circulation numbers like a champ. Only Howard Cosell was better at self-promotion. He'd always carried around a couple of fan letters in his breast pocket to support his insecurity and never lost an opportunity to flash them to all his bosses, secretaries, and anyone else who would listen.

I was struck by her absolute determination. Her workload seemed unbearable. Public appearances at least twice a week, a daily radio feature, and a newspaper column. I asked if she had a large staff to prepare the material. "No, just a secretary and an assistant once or twice a week to help out. I work better alone," she added.

Now let's flash forward twenty or so years. I was working as an advisor to improve the new television version of *USA Today*. The executive producer was Steve Friedman, and we were having another meeting to jump-start the program. It was a joint effort of Gannett and Grant Tinker/GTG, which was finding it way in syndication but not fast enough for Al Neuhart who was working for Gannett. In the very first meeting with Neuhart, he told the staff, "Television programs fail because of two things: not enough money and not enough time to develop. We have neither of those problems."

Friedman and I had something in common. Tom Snyder. I gave Tom his first job as an anchorman and when Tom moved to Los Angeles at KNBC-TV, Steve was his producer. I always thought Friedman played a strong part in the successful evolution of local television news and we developed a mutual respect for each other, even though we were innovating three thousand miles apart on two different coasts. Steve parlayed his success to the network, eventually becoming the heart of *The Today Show*. It seems commonplace now, but Steve was the person who managed to return *Today* into the famous street studio in Rockefeller Center, a concept now imitated by *Good Morning America* on ABC and *The Early Show* on CBS. He left to join Tinker and was able to return to NBC after the fiasco that ensued when the network tried to reboot *The Today Show*. He would also create the original format for NBC's *Dateline*.

"Hey, we have a real treat today," said Friedman, as one of our meetings was about to begin. "Dr. Joyce Brothers is coming by to talk about coming on the show." Twenty years has passed, and another assistant was now escorting Joyce Brothers into another office. She was wearing an almost identical outfit. Dark blue skirt, pink top. She looked more substantial than she did two decades earlier, but the extra weight had actually improved her good looks.

She immediately launched into her pitch and the intensity was still there. Out came the articles, the magazine cover stories, and circulation figures and this time she had television ratings. She said she was doing special segments on KCBS-TV in Los Angeles, radio, articles for *TV Guide*, and so on.

Why was she in Washington? She said she was taking a vacation, visiting with her only child, Robin. She said her daughter has been a real comfort to her after the death of her husband the previous year.

"It's been a wonderful vacation," she said. She told us she was flying out that evening to make a speech in Detroit as she did Monday night in Baltimore. She had cleared the calendar and was taking this day to visit *USA Today*, the newspaper and the TV show, all while "on vacation."

She was talking in her quiet, determined manner and pitching very hard to appear on the show. It seemed nothing at all had changed. But she was not hired to be on the *USA Today* show, just as she wasn't hired to be part of the *Eyewitness News* team.

I learned two things from her: never quit, but don't spread yourself too thin. Too many irons in the fire can dilute your talent.

So one of the first rules made when starting Primo Newservice Incorporated was not to have so many station clients that I could not have time to develop new concepts and grow in the fast changing world of communications. I got lucky again with some very talented people. My first hire was John Kosinski, a young man just out of college and a fast learner. He quickly grasped the *Eyewitness News* concept. Better yet, he could articulate it to station news directors and was responsible for advancing stations to better serve their communities and consequently improve their ratings. He also had a good eye for talent. While working in upstate New York with Joe Coscia—who's work on our desk at Channel 7, Eyewitness News skyrocketed him to News Director of WRGB-TV, Schenectady—found a young woman slicing the cold cuts and making sandwiches behind a deli counter. They invited her to audition for a news segment, making a fast meal in 30 minutes, paying her only $50 a week and the rest is history. Her name: Rachael Ray.

Kenn Venit was working at WTNH-TV in New Haven when Capitol Cities Broadcasting asked me to consult that station. We were able to improve their news presentations against all odds largely through Kenn's ability to implement all of the recommendations. I convinced him to become a news consultant because of his natural ability to be a teacher and work well with newspeople. Together we extended the *Eyewitness News* concept all over America. Both of us got on an airplane each week for the next fifteen years to work with individual stations. Kenn is now training the next generation of journalists, teaching at Quinnipiac University in Hamden, Connecticut.

I instinctively knew it was important to own a business that could carry on without me. There was a wonderful weekly newspaper in Greenwich called the

Village Gazette. It was run for years by a gentleman named Wake Hartley and his wife. The minister of the First Congregational Church in Old Greenwich, which was incorporated before the United States, mentioned to my wife Rosina that Wake and Lois Hartley were looking to retire. We had a wonderful meeting with them and purchased the paper.

Rosina Primo, Co-Publisher, The Village Gazette, now VP Sales William Raveis Real Estate.

We hired Bob Samek as editor and began hiring some talented housewives who had left the big jobs in New York to raise their families. With their kids now in school, they began to write and report for our weekly which truly served the community. We won first prize from the New England Newspaper Association for our coverage of the Mianus Bridge collapse. Eight years later, we sold it to a newspaper chain.

At about the same time, we bought a radio station, WNVR, serving the greater Waterbury, Connecticut area. It was the eighth largest market in New England but unfortunately was located right between Hartford and New Haven. Advertisers could buy either of those two bigger markets and get coverage in our town. We still used all the talents of Kosinski, Venit, and myself to create a powerful radio station, 14 NVR. Our program manager was Joe McCoy, who was a master of the "oldies" format. He became program manager of WCBS Radio in New York. The sportscaster there was a kid out of college, Chris Berman, who has developed into a huge talent for ESPN. Each of our news directors were hired away by Associated Press radio. It's always about the people working with you that makes you a success.

One afternoon in Old Greenwich, Connecticut, my neighbor Robert Button, a retired teleprompter executive, asked if I was interested in helping secure a cable franchise for Fairfield County, one of the wealthiest parts of Connecticut. I thought he was crazy since everyone in the New York area could receive over-the-air television.

But after he explained the vast future for cable, I agreed. He said he was working to get Scripps-Howard newspapers and Charles Dolan of Cablevision to create a company with ten local limited partners to apply for the franchise.

I said I would only join the group if we made covering local news a key part of the application.

They agreed and I helped write the application that won the cable franchise for Cablevision. We set up one of the first regional news channels, News 12 Connecticut. It was a great success and Dolan hired our company to fully implement News 12 Long Island, the world's first twenty-four-hour regional news channel he started a year before.

Al Ittleson, Norman Fine, Melba Tolliver, and a number of other *Eyewitness News* alumni were brought in to create the next big news success. News 12 operations are the cable news leaders in Connecticut, Long Island, Brooklyn, the Bronx, Westchester, and New Jersey. They have won countless awards, competing against big-time broadcast news television stations with larger staffs. Charles Dolan recognized the value of community news service and has rewarded his investors with a company worth billions of dollars that is still controlled by his family. His son Pat Dolan is president of News 12 and Norman Fine works closely with him as vice president of News.

From there we helped set up *New England Cable News, NECN,* for the Hearst Corporation in Boston, under the direction of Philip Balboni. My constant advice to the cable companies was to set up a professional news organization to prevent incursion into their systems by direct-to-home satellite competitors. Many hired kids just out of journalism school and the product often looked like it. We urged them to find senior anchors and bring them back into the markets. In Boston, we got Balboni and News Director, Charles Kravetz, to hire *Tom* Ellis, the longtime anchor who worked at all of the broadcast stations in town and even did a stint at *Eyewitness News* in New York.he and other seasoned anchors from Boston, have brought them the highest ratings, especially Ellis on weekends where he is the prime-time anchor.

Foreign TV.com was the name we gave to an Internet start-up company in 1999. Wall Street was ablaze with interest in dot-com companies.

Jonathan Braun, an editor and reporter turned businessman who I have known for forty years, came to me with the proposal to start a public company. The idea was simple: bring news programs from China, Ireland, France, and other foreign countries and stream them on the Internet. We raised ten million dollars and set out to make the world

The Author on Foreign TV.com assignment with the late Prime Minister of Pakistan Benazir Butto in exile in London, 1995

a little smaller by helping viewers understand issues in foreign countries through their news programs. It worked! I hired Peter Arnett who had just been fired from CNN for narrating a flawed documentary. We positioned it to the press that Arnett was moving his skills and talent to the Internet. We rescued his career with assignments in the Middle East, Japan, (where most of the investors in the company lived), and London, interviewing top political leaders. Benazir Bhutto was living in exile there and granted us a rare interview. Her father was killed in Pakistan and she decided to follow in his footsteps. Twice, prime minister of Pakistan, she was ousted and escaped to England. I asked her why she was so intent on returning to her country and certain death, she replied, "I can not let terrorists stand in the way of my work for democracy. I just do not think about it and I will return one day." She did return and was on track to become the next prime minister when she was assassinated two days after Christmas 2007, throwing the country into turmoil. Then the Internet bubble burst, and no more money was available to small companies even though we became listed on the American Stock Exchange under the stock symbol IAO. The Japanese investors took over the company and still run it as a shell for Asian business. Peter Arnett was hired by NBC News and assigned to Iraq, just prior to the invasion. Tom Brokaw was introducing his reports on the *NBC Nightly News* with the caution to "stay safe, Peter." He was back on top of the journalistic heap.

One night, Arnett appeared on Baghdad television. He told the government-controlled interviewer that as far as he knows, Americans are not supporting the war in Iraq. By the time he returned to his apartment, NBC News had fired him, taken away his credentials, and banned him from ever working for the network. He hasn't been heard from since.

One of the most important things about working in television is to watch a lot of it. It occurred to me one day that the only time young people are seen on television is when there is a disaster, like the Columbine shootings or in stories about sex, drugs, and rock and roll. This is not reality, but I could not find a single positive television kids program on the air.

I wrote a treatment for a young person's news program called *Teen Kids News*. It's *Eyewitness News* with teenagers and stories about the issues they face daily. The networks, who keep wondering about the next generation of news viewers, loved the idea. For one reason or another, none of them could provide the time or money to develop the program. The reaction was so positive I decided to try and do it on my own. I went to Alan Weiss, an *Eyewitness News* producer who'd started his own production company, and we made a five-minute demo tape.

The next step was to set up an Internet site with the tape and program outline. It was done working with Robert Mertz, who owned Parrot

Media, a distribution company in Burbank. If we could get 50 to 75 stations to carry the program, we would go forward with it. We both got on the telephone and in the first week got 75 stations to agree to carry it. The next week the number had jumped to 150 stations and 200 stations eventually signed on to carry the program.

The first major broadcast company to sign up to telecast Teen Kids News was Hearst/ Argyle Television, which is the largest owner of ABC affiliated stations and the second largest operator of NBC affiliated stations. Its president, David Barrett and vice president of programming, Emerson Coleman, put us on 29 television stations, which covers 18% of the country. It is the only program carried on all of its stations.

I set up a limited liability company, *Eyewitness Kids News LLC* and began to go to family and friends to raise the capital to produce the program for one year. When I told Frank Gifford what I was doing, he reminded me that his son Cody was now a teenager. So we had our sportscaster. Paula Zahn's daughter Haley came on board as did Rosanna Scotto's daughter, Jenna, and Ron Perleman's daughter Samantha. In New York, the talent pool is enormous, and we selected Mwaanza Brown as anchor and Felipe Dieppa as the featured reporter. The press loved the idea of celebrity kids doing a news program and we got coverage in *People Magazine*, all the major newspapers, *TV Guide*, *Today*, and *The Daily Show* with Jon Stewart. We are in our fifth season, and in addition to the stations which cover 91 percent of the United States, we are seen in 1,000 locations in 177 countries via American Forces Networks on their prime-time channel and family channel plus all the navy ships at sea. Two years ago, we started sending the program to schools and are currently telecast in 10,000 schools each week.

Epilogue

Looking back on what we accomplished on *Eyewitness News,* you tend to focus on the high points. The Willowbrook story immediately comes to mind, along with dozens of others that made a difference and changed lives. What was the best story we ever did? Perhaps the perfect definition of a great story comes from Doug Johnson, who maintains that the best story is simply . . . New York. He'll tell you that nothing compares with it anywhere on this earth. That no place is more interesting, more exciting; that no place offers a more incredible variety of people who are, at the same time, tough as nails with hearts of gold. Often, our own *Eyewitness News* reporters wrote personal checks to those victims of tragedy they were covering.

Doug is absolutely right, and I could not have expressed it more perfectly.

I also look back and am amazed at the good fortune that followed me. In any successful venture, you need two things: a lot of luck and a lot of help. In my case, the two went hand in hand as I was lucky to have such great help. John Johnson tells the story which might just sum up the camaraderie of the team and its popularity in New York. On one occasion, several staff members, including Grimsby and Rose Ann Scamardella, had gone uptown for pizza. When it was time to return to the station, they decided to bypass the taxis and pile into Johnson's two-seater Triumph convertible. Grimsby ended up riding on the trunk. Then it started to rain. New Yorkers were treated to the city's number one-news team, piled into a convertible like college kids in a phone booth, rolling through midtown for forty blocks while soaking wet. At every stoplight people would yell and wave as John, Roger, Rose Ann, and other *Eyewtiness News* team members talked to people crossing the street. Johnson drove his little sports car with a few million dollars worth of talent in it like it happened every day.

One person alone cannot change the television news business. But one person with an idea and the perfect staff to make it work can. The stars truly aligned in my case, for without the ideas and hard work of so many people, *Eyewitness News* would have been just another newscast. The best baseball manager in the world can't win a pennant without good players. I was blessed with an all-star team working for my entire career. I could fill another chapter with names of people who helped me achieve my dream and who are still working in television continuing to develop the *Eyewitness News* concept all over the world.

The army of newspeople trained in the Eyewitness News Concept working in broadcasting are too numerous to mention but those wielding influence over large numbers of ABC, CBS, NBC, FOX and independent television station are:

Dennis Swanson, an ex Marine, was the Executive Producer of KABC-TV Eyewitness News in 1976 and was named Station Manager after taking the station to number one in the ratings. He became General Manager of WLS-TV, Chicago where he hired a young woman from Baltimore to become the host of the ABC stations morning program. Her name: Oprah Winfrey. The Oprah Winfrey Show was a significant factor in the success of ABC at the station level and on ABC News. Her lead in audience was the perfect transition to news viewing. That audience propelled Eyewitness News in the major markets to even greater ratings which in turn flowed into the ABC Evening News which has become America's most watched news network. From there, Swanson went to ABC Sports for 10 years. In a stunning move, he was named General Manager of WNBC, New York. He retired after a couple of years but became president of the CBS Television Stations. He was hired away by FOX to head up Operations of the entire FOX station group where News and Community coverage continue to drive the stations operations.

Before he left CBS, Swanson hired another Eyewitness News person, WABC-TV General Manager Tom Kane to run sales at CBS. Kane was named President of the CBS Television Station group and his news training and background are prevalent at those stations.

Peter Jacobus was a copyboy at KYW-TV, Philadelphia. I told him he could steal hubcaps for a living or go to college and study journalism while working at Eyewitness News. He rose through the ranks to become a great news director for ABC and now is chief consultant for Frank Magid Associates, the world's largest broadcast research and consulting company spreading our format at news stations all over the globe.

Joe Rovitto has the Eyewitness News concept in his blood. He is a major news consultant in America and a blood relative. He is my first cousin. For years he has measured the effect of news presentations whether they are called Eyewitness News or other titles. He still advises covering the human drama in news by reporters in the field and on set.

Television is a close-up medium. The most effective way to communicate with the audience is to drive the subject material through the TV set. This applies both to studio shots and reporting on the scene. As television news programs expand to the Internet, mobile phones, iPods, and other electronic devices, the close-up becomes critical because the television screens are so tiny. A grand wide shot in the movies sets the stage beautifully, but on today's delivery platforms it simply doesn't work. When your "television set" is a one inch screen on your cell phone, the last thing you need is to make things smaller.

The audience wants to clearly see the people who are reporting. They also want to see relationships between anchors and on-set reporters as well as the sports and weather talent.

Reporter involvement: Reporting from the scene of a news story should always include the reporter on camera, in a stand-up. I believe reporters have to establish their credibility for *every* story they cover in this way, and must include "reporter involvement" to show the audience they were actually there to cover the story and talk to the people involved.

Quick Tip: A walking stand-up always adds extra energy to the piece. The reporter should always take a few steps in the piece, moving slowly along the scene. It adds energy to the story and gives the audience a sense the reporter has command of the piece, while placing the reporter at the scene.

The Newscast: The ideal news program reports the major events of the day with some unique features presented by a team of professionals, in a unique electronic setting, that is comfortable to watch. The audience wants to see people who like their work and enjoy working together. There's no room for tension between the talents.

Years ago the six o'clock news was appointment television, but people are now working longer and have less free time . . . and there's the option to watch news "on demand" via the internet. And these days nobody watches a newscast five days a week; so long, multi-part series have gone the way of the television miniseries. The trick is to get the viewers to come back for one additional day. A two-part series can be helpful in this effort.

Know your community well enough to quickly grasp the event in which the audience is extraordinarily interested. Cover that story extensively in the newscasts—own it. The audience recognizes your effort and will reward the station with additional viewing.

A good way to more closely identify with a community is to use "Data Banks" leading into or between commercials. These can be used as "cluster busters" to break up long commercial breaks running two minutes or more. This is interesting information that makes viewing a socially rewarding experience for the audience and eases the commercial disruption.

DataBank: *"The area of Greenwich, Connecticut, is fifty square miles, the same as San Francisco."*

Teasing the next story before the commercial break is essential. Too often, it is the last element written and usually by the least experienced writer on staff. Many times it simply gives the story away rather than enticing the audience to resist changing the channel. Smart operations will appoint a single person to write all the teases for the newscast. A good tease must be just that . . . it must "tease" the audience into sticking around. But the story must deliver; viewers simply hate being led on only to see the story not measure up to the tease.

Fatal Error: Never start the next segment without using the exact story teased.

Kickers: The closing story should always be an interesting feature, but these days many stations have ditched the feature segment and replaced it with a final weather segment. (One reason is that this makes it easier for producers to time the newscast; weather anchors can talk as little or as much as needed.) But feature stories, or "kickers," are those light, fun moments that will keep your audience sticking around for the entire newscast instead of bailing after the weather segment. After thirty minutes of hard news, the audience deserves to be sent away uplifted or amused. Too often, a producer will select a heart-wrenching story to end the newscast. NBC News and its stations seem to do this more than others. My advice is to avoid this technique like the plague.

And when you're done with the content in your newscast, you're still not done. Beauty shots at the end of the newscast can add to that "warm and fuzzy" feeling, while close-ups of the talent with music underneath show the audience the news team in a unique and personal context while giving the viewer a quick look at the people when they're "off the clock." After thirty minutes of fast-paced serious reporting, a friendly, warm view presents the talent as real people who enjoy their work. This is a small but important element in creating a newscast that is comfortable to watch. And "comfortable to watch" is the key to a successful newscast.

People tell their own stories: I've worked with some of the best writers and reporters over the years, yet none have been able to tell people's stories better than the people themselves. A careful selection of sound bites within the story makes the best television. Reporters will often take the easy way out and get sound from officials on the scene rather than hunt down those truly affected and get the real information. My rule has always been that no story without real people in it gets on the air.

Quick Tip: "Writing to the video" is a must. Too often writers simply write the story with video playing over the copy. You must reference the video and match it to the copy. For instance, if the copy talks about high traffic, we need to *see* the traffic, not an exit sign on the interstate. Nothing looks sillier to the audience than an anchor or reporter talking about one thing and seeing video of something that has nothing to do with the copy.

Television makes its own stars: The people who present the news are the most important element to a newscast. You must build a team of presenters. If you take great care, you will never be at the mercy of a single talent the station has created with daily exposure and promotion. If that person departs, a replacement can step in without causing disruption to the organization. If the person is of equal or better talent, the audience will quickly adapt to the change.

In selecting talent, remember that all the great ones have a unique voice which cuts through and connects with the audience. The very best can read a teleprompter like they are talking directly to you . . . they "talk" rather than just "read." In screening tapes, when looking for potential hires, look away and just listen to the presentation and pick the person with the most distinctive voice.

You can accelerate the building of news anchors by getting them involved in the community. At least two or three times a week, station talent should make appearances before community groups. This should be coordinated by a single individual at the station. With so many places for the audience to get information, this grassroots form of personal promotion is the way to succeed in the twenty-first century.

The people in Iowa will tell you—they don't vote for a presidential candidate unless they've had an opportunity to meet him or her. TV news is the same as politics. There are choices. And the audience gets to vote each night—even minute-to-minute when you are on the air—with a remote control in a multichannel and multiplatform communications universe. Shake hands, kiss babies, be a solid citizen, and win over the community. Your job doesn't end when the red light goes off . . . it is just beginning.

Maximize exposure of news talent using other forms of communication. One of the most overlooked assets is radio. If the company owns or operates a radio station in town, have your news anchors read the drive time newscasts and promote the upcoming television news programs. Tease the big story of the day on radio, so that commuters will turn to your newscast when they get home, or watch it on demand. Many TV news programs air when the majority of the audience is driving home from work, so you must use the opportunity to remind the audience of your product.

Use every platform available to the news operation. The Internet is key to the future of broadcast journalism. The audience is moving rapidly in that direction. News anchors should have a blog on the station's website to communicate the inside story to the audience, but must be careful to be objective and leave personal opinions out of any commentary. The newscast of the future may have its genesis on the Internet, then find its way to the television screen.

The Internet also empowers the audience. Think of the most dramatic and compelling video and pictures you have seen from major news stories in the last few years. Close up views of tornadoes roaring through towns, near misses at airports, incredible rescues . . . they came from viewers—your audience—sending that information from their cell phones and digital cameras to your website. Your television station's website *today* makes the audience *the eyewitnesses of the future!* You have an entire staff of reporters and photographers out there (that aren't on your payroll) who *want* to be part of your newscast, so you must make it easy for them to interact and encourage them to participate. It is the same as the old "weather watcher" concept of the sixties, only taken to a new technological level.

Audience research is vital to the success of a news operation. Mistakes are often made in misinterpretation of the data. A properly conducted report will identify many elements of the program which can be adjusted without disrupting progress of news programming. Television stations go wrong when they take the research data as gospel. It becomes the guiding force for how the news is presented and promoted. Often, professional broadcasters and journalists forget to use their personal knowledge of the market as yet another tool to be coupled with the research findings. We are in the only business where art is measured by science (research and ratings.)

There are many techniques available to improve the perception of talent to the audience. Through the years, I have used a feature, "Wednesday's Child," to improve the perception of many talented newspeople that audience research shows are cold and aloof. Working with a local adoption agency, the anchor interviews a child, on camera, which needs a family. The interaction between the two brings out qualities that endear both to the audience. It has done a great deal of good in placing children with good families and saved many an anchor.

News Promotion: One of the most frequent mistakes made is in the area of news promotion. Very often, advertising people will want to create a big ad campaign with newspaper, radio, TV promos, and other gimmicks, leading up to the first day of a new initiative by the station. If they do their job right, the actual program will never be able to live up to the promise. My advice is to always get the newscasts on the air and let it establish itself before promoting it. Promising that your television station is "the worldwide leader in local news" is nothing more than promotion Viagra! You'll get the viewer's attention for a while—but it always fizzles away.

News promotion invariably takes the form of personalities, size of staff, helicopter coverage, and other elements with pounding music and an announcer, which simply says to the viewer, "Watch us because we want you to." We had our greatest impact at *Eyewitness News* with bold humor and guerilla promotion techniques. No one had ever used this kind of promotion in news. As writers know, humor is the most difficult and dangerous method to promote a credible newscast. Careful execution can bring it up to the line without crossing it and it will have great impact. It can still work well in today's environment.

One of the most successful ways to promote your news is to produce a thirty-minute prime-time special called, "The Anatomy of—News." This is a behind-the-scenes look at how a news program is assembled, showing producers, reporters, and anchors doing their jobs as real people. The audience has a great desire to see how the newscast is made—an inside look at broadcast journalism. Take the audience behind the curtain if you will. You are *vesting them* in how you do your job for them.

Building credibility for a newscast that has only a few viewers was a major challenge for WABC-TV as it was the last placed station in every market. One of the most effective building devices is to bring top newsmakers onto the news set for a live interview, especially during morning, noon and five o'clock newscasts. (The six o'clock and late newscasts are more traditional and faster paced and therefore not as conducive to live interviews.) The response is extremely positive. The audience soon begins to understand that if the governor, mayor, senator, or personality will come to your studio to be interviewed by your anchors on set, it is a program worth watching. Network morning shows will trample one another on a daily basis for a "get" that they can promote.

Technical errors during a newscast have a major negative effect on the audience. It signals a lack of planning which affects credibility. Producers must be excellent time managers and have the newscast ready at least thirty minutes before it hits the air. Too often the director and producer are running into the control room at the last moment. And when the director is not familiar with the script and has to wing it, bad things can happen.

Dressing for success advice is available from a number of sources, but Eyewitness Al's rule for television is dark suits and colorful ties for the men and a smart jacket and blouse outfit for the women. A young female anchor just out of college can add five years to her look by wearing a simple string of pearls.

The Set: Everybody likes the shiny new thing. Television news departments probably more than the rest of us. The news set has grown to almost epic proportions as evidenced by entire television studios being designed as on-air working newsrooms. (Something we did at KYW-TV, Philadelphia in 1965.)

We doubt that viewers have chosen a newscast because of the mahogany used on the anchor desk! But we do know that the audience wants to see the talent showcased in eye-appealing surroundings. After all, its television, and we have to use all the tools the industry gives us to present eye-appealing programming. The news and *American Idol* come out of the same box and as such, utilize some of the same basics of television: pleasing surroundings, music, visual pacing. And *American Idol* has borrowed from the news. Look at the racial/gender mix of the judges and host. The judges sit behind an "anchor" desk. A number of singers deliver different content the way reporters present the day's stories. We vote (TV news ratings). And those with the most compelling look and content win—on *Idol* and the local news.

Beat Reporting: This is one of the hallmarks of the Primo *Eyewitness News* concept. Reporters who have beats: city hall, police/crime, consumer, money. Sounds too easy, but most television stations have a roomful of generalists. As a result, reporters don't have a chance to develop stories, let alone as television personalities. And this is much more than merely creating "reporter/stars." Beat reporting is all about basic journalism: developing leads and contacts, digging for stories, becoming a specialist in a specific area. Think about it. You'll probably go to a specialist for an unusual medical problem rather than a general practitioner. Both practice medicine the same way reporters practice journalism in the broadest sense of that term. But, only one reporter—the beat reporter—has the greater probability of breaking the story first. Telling stories. Being first. Advancing the story. All essentials of a successful newscast.

Persistance And Luck Go Hand In Hand

There's an old saying that "luck occurs when preparation meets opportunity." And in the television news business, every successful person has had some good luck along the way.

The thing is, you never know when or how luck will present itself. A chance meeting, a network executive who just happens to see your story, a friend of a friend of a friend who passes your name on to someone with clout. Since you never know when stars will align, you have to be prepared and be persistent. Give your best every single day, because that might be the day when Lady Luck is in town and watching your station.

Few people know that before Peter Jennings became ABC's main anchor he was . . . ABC's main anchor. That's right, his first shot in the early 60's didn't exactly set the ratings on fire. Though he was talented, he really didn't have enough experience, so the network shipped him off to head its London Bureau. Jennings could have easily gotten discouraged and phoned it in, but didn't.

Peter Jennings - ABC News   Charles Gibson - Albert T. Primo

Years later the vacation schedule left me with single anchors for two straight weeks, as Roger Grimsby and Bill Beutel were taking weeks off back-to-back. I decided to see if we could "borrow" Jennings from the network, and asked him if he'd be interested in spending two weeks on the anchor desk in New York. He was, and ended up doing a terrific job with both Roger and Bill. I truly believe ABC's executives in New York saw his solid performance and soon chose Jennings to head the network newscast again. In that case, his luck arrived when two people thousands of miles away took some time off.

In June of 2008, Jennings' replacement Charles Gibson was presented with an award by Quinnipiac University. He later came over to introduce himself and told me the story of how he had once applied for a reporting position at *Eyewitness News*. One of my senior executives had interviewed him and said he "wasn't ready" for New York, so I had never met him. Then, in true Charles Gibson style, he said, "Your man was right, I wasn't ready." Gibson, of course, is now America's number one anchorman and has lifted ABC's fortunes because he didn't give up . . . and when luck came to him he was ready.

Getting That First Job

The broadcasting industry is unfortunately set up with a system that makes getting a job extremely difficult. We have evolved from the days at WDTV, Pittsburgh where people had to be convinced to work in television to a system that discourages people. Ninety percent of applicants take the "no" to heart and after a few attempts move on to other endeavors while the other 10 percent get the jobs. I have always said a no really means "no for today." Tomorrow is another day to get a yes. The same news director who said no today can be the same person who hires you if you get there at the right moment in time when the need is critical. Persistence pays off in broadcast journalism.

But these days technology and budgetary concerns have changed the playing field. The salaries of yesteryear are gone and will never come back, as cable and satellite have sliced up the advertising pie and left local news in a revenue pinch. New reporters need to be versatile, and in many cases, need to be their own photographers as well. The "one-man-band" concept, now known as the VJ (video journalist) is becoming more popular for two reasons. First, it cuts the salary of a field crew in half, and second, equipment has become very small and easy to use. Twenty-five years ago a camera, light, tripod, tape deck and battery belt weighed eighty six pounds. Now all of that combined weighs less than ten, which means anyone can act as a photographer.

However, being a VJ means more than just being able to operate the gear. While everyone can operate a camera, not everyone is a *photographer*. There is a very big difference.

Young people need to school themselves in the art of video journalism, as reporting is more than just gathering facts.

Quick Tip: Young reporters may be wondering how in the world they can shoot a stand-up if they are acting as a VJ. The answer is to take a light stand, extend it to your height, and place it in the location that you would use for your stand-up. Then get behind the camera, focus on the light stand and frame it up, hit the record button, and stand exactly on the spot you had placed the light stand. You will be framed up and in focus.

Writing for the web: Another talent that has been on the decline for years is now more essential than ever. Writing ability. As stations pour more and more resources into their websites, they are requiring reporters to "expand" on their assignments, taking their ninety second stories and turning them into newspaper stories for the website. It is essential that reporters be well versed in print journalism style as well as broadcast, as writing for the web is far different than anything used on television.

Quick Tips: Broadcasting is still a business that respects print journalism. Find a way to get published while in college and always include the article in your resume. It works wonders, as good writing skills can give you an edge over other applicants.

Connections are a familiar practice in our world. Spread the word to everyone you know that you want a job in TV. Nine times out of ten, someone in your family or circle of influence will know someone who can help.

LIVE Reporting: *Eyewitness News* started with film reports from the field. The reporters, seen on camera, were the "eyewitnesses" for the audience and reported events firsthand. The stories were shot earlier in the day, the film developed and edited, then presented on the air. Today, we do the same thing—instantly, often while the news is happening. Think 9/11. But not all stories presented live on television can be that life-changing.

How many times have you watched a reporter live from the field telling you about something that happened hours in the past? Have they been standing in the dark? You've seen that too many times on television, and the audience is wise to this tactic of being live for the sake of being live. Compelling live television, of course, has action. Something that is happening *now*. Live. On camera. When you don't have that action, the successful and compelling live report is an extension of the story. The "live on the scene" element is there for a reason: it's a part of the story. The reporter should tell the viewer where they are and why they are there. They should also show how their surroundings are a part of the story. Showing me how the surroundings fit in to the story suggests that the reporter move, walk, and talk on television. It's all about context and as basic as "show and tell." The live location means something. It's in context. And we should not just be standing "live" in the dark because we can do that.

Eyewitness Al's first rule of success:

There is no substitute for the news

Index

E

F

G

H

I

J